Life Courses of Young Convicts Transported to Van Diemen's Land

History of Crime, Deviance and Punishment

Series Editor: Anne-Marie Kilday, Professor of Criminal History, Oxford Brookes University, UK

Editorial Board:

Neil Davie, University of Lyon II, France
Johannes Dillinger, University of Maine, Germany
Wilbur Miller, State University of New York, USA
Marianna Muravyeva, University of Helsinki, Finland
David Nash, Oxford Brookes University, UK
Judith Rowbotham, Nottingham Trent University, UK

Academic interest in the history of crime and punishment has never been greater and the History of Crime, Deviance and Punishment series provides a home for the wealth of new research being produced. Individual volumes within the series cover topics related to the history of crime and punishment, from the later medieval to modern period and in both Europe and North America, and seek to demonstrate the importance of this subject in furthering understanding of the way in which various societies and cultures operate. When taken together, the works in the series will show the evolution of the nature of illegality and attitudes towards its perpetration over time and will offer their readers a rounded and coherent history of crime and punishment through the centuries. The series' broad chronological and geographical coverage encourages comparative historical analysis of crime history between countries and cultures.

Published:

Crime and Poverty in 19th-Century England, Adrian Ager

Print Culture, Crime and Justice in Eighteenth-Century London, Richard Ward

Rehabilitation and Probation in England and Wales, 1900–1950, Raymond Gard

The Policing of Belfast 1870–1914, Mark Radford

Crime, Regulation and Control during the Blitz, Peter Adey, David J. Cox and Barry Godfrey

Italian Prisons in the Age of Positivism, 1861–1914, Mary Gibson

Forthcoming:

Deviance, Disorder and Music in Modern Britain and America, Cliff Williamson

Fair and Unfair Trials in the British Isles, 1800–1940, eds. David Nash and Anne-Marie Kilday

Life Courses of Young Convicts Transported to Van Diemen's Land

Emma D. Watkins

BLOOMSBURY ACADEMIC
LONDON • NEW YORK • OXFORD • NEW DELHI • SYDNEY

BLOOMSBURY ACADEMIC
Bloomsbury Publishing Plc
50 Bedford Square, London, WC1B 3DP, UK
1385 Broadway, New York, NY 10018, USA
29 Earlsfort Terrace, Dublin 2, Ireland

BLOOMSBURY, BLOOMSBURY ACADEMIC and the Diana logo
are trademarks of Bloomsbury Publishing Plc

First published in Great Britain 2020
Paperback edition published 2021

Copyright © Emma D. Watkins, 2020

Emma D. Watkins has asserted her right under the Copyright, Designs and
Patents Act, 1988, to be identified as Author of this work.

For legal purposes the Acknowledgements on p. x constitute
an extension of this copyright page.

Cover design: Tjaša Krivec
Cover image: English convict ship in which criminals were kept awaiting
shipment to Australia. Wood engraving, English, early 19th century.
(© Granger Historical Picture Archive/Alamy Stock Photo)

All rights reserved. No part of this publication may be reproduced or transmitted
in any form or by any means, electronic or mechanical, including photocopying,
recording, or any information storage or retrieval system, without
prior permission in writing from the publishers.

Bloomsbury Publishing Plc does not have any control over, or responsibility for,
any third-party websites referred to or in this book. All internet addresses given
in this book were correct at the time of going to press. The author and publisher
regret any inconvenience caused if addresses have changed or sites have ceased
to exist, but can accept no responsibility for any such changes.

A catalogue record for this book is available from the British Library.

A catalog record for this book is available from the Library of Congress.

ISBN: HB: 978-1-3500-8126-0
PB: 978-1-3502-5458-9
ePDF: 978-1-3500-8127-7
eBook: 978-1-3500-8128-4

Series: History of Crime, Deviance and Punishment

Typeset by Integra Software Services Pvt. Ltd.

To find out more about our authors and books visit www.bloomsbury.com
and sign up for our newsletters.

Contents

List of tables		viii
List of case studies		ix
Acknowledgements and dedication		x
1	Introduction	1
2	Historiography	9
3	Crime	29
4	Punishment	49
5	Education, training and employment	81
6	Family life	123
7	Death	147
8	Conclusion	171
Notes		177
Bibliography		180
Index		193

Tables

1	Male juvenile convicts and their colonial offences	33
2	Female juvenile convicts and their colonial offences	34
3	Most common offences, per convict, grouped by sample (from convict record only)	35
4	Juvenile offences not in conduct record categorized by severity	37
5	Rate of juvenile offending at different life-course points	43
6	Male juvenile punishments	52
7	Male juveniles age-of-death	148
8	Male average age-of-death comparison data	148

Case studies

1	Mary Ann Oseman	3
2	George Pickering	38
3	John Patching	43
4	Charles Brewer	58
5	Robert Gardon (aka Gordon)	61
6	Lyon Levy	64
7	Robert Spencer	67
8	Ellen Miles (aka Smith/Jackson)	71
9	Susan Campbell	76
10	Richard Young	86
11	Matthew Cantlin (aka Cantlon)	99
12	Henry Hawthorn	103
13	Ellen Caley (aka Hunt)	113
14	Ellen Murphy	125
15	Jane Callahan (aka Callaghan)	139
16	John Press	142
17	James McAllister	151
18	John Burke	153
19	Anthony Barkwith	155
20	James Hudson	156
21	John Long	158
22	John Winford	158
23	Martin Gavan	161
24	Charles Henson	162
25	Eliza White	165
26	Elizabeth Jones (aka Walford)	166
27	Sarah Hodge	167

Acknowledgements and dedication

I would like to thank Prof Barry Godfrey for his supervision of the thesis that led to this book, not only through guidance, but also through going above and beyond in setting up opportunities which aided this study and my development as a researcher. One such opportunity was a fellowship at the University of Tasmania with Prof Hamish Maxwell-Stewart. I would like to thank Hamish for his assistance and guidance in that time.

I would like to thank my dissertation examiners Prof Heather Shore and Prof Barry Goldson for a positive *viva voce* experience and many excellent recommendations for improvement, which I hope are reflected in this monograph.

I thank my parents for their continuing and unquestioning support throughout.

This book is dedicated to Simon – *for everything.*

1

Introduction

In the nineteenth century many convicted juveniles were handed down a sentence of transportation to Australia. This book will explore the crimes and punishments of some of these individuals, as well as their pre- and post-transportation lives, including family life, occupational standing and mortality. These juvenile convicts will then be contextualized within the punishment system, economy and culture that they were thrust into by their forced movement to Van Diemen's Land (VDL) (now known as Tasmania). Were these juvenile convicts, who were convicted at the Old Bailey (the Central Criminal Court in London), able to form 'settled' colonial lives? This is not simple to determine. However, certain aspects surrounding the formation of relationships, employment and criminal desistance all point to a settled life. This may not mean climbing the social and economic spectrum of society, but rather the formation of a stable and normal working-class life free from crime. In essence, despite their early-life upheaval, were they able to form families and maintain employment? Or, were they plagued by unemployment, instability and criminal activity related to a lack of ties – be they social or economic? Marrying and having children, for example, did not necessarily result in a settled life but such factors supported one. Similarly, committing a crime in the colony after freedom does not conclude the life was unsettled. However, if a juvenile continued in crime up until his or her death, which resulted in repeated punishments and confinement thereby preventing any work and family life, this would be an unsettled life. As well as uncovering what a settled life was for these juveniles, the lasting impact of the experience of being transported to a penal colony *during youth* will be explored.

When convict transportation to Australia began in the late eighteenth century it was not a new concept. Not only had exile or banishment been a punishment for centuries, but also, by the seventeenth century, transportation was increasingly used for criminals. As early as 1607 criminals were transported to the Virginian plantations in Colonial America (Shaw 1966, 22–23). Britain was not alone or the first to use transportation; other European countries had already used criminals and vagrants to colonize imperial territories as has been demonstrated in Anderson's (2016) work on the Carceral Archipelago. The history of transportation has been widely studied (Shaw 1966; Hughes 2003; Brooke & Brandon 2005), with a focus on different aspects of convict lives, for example: on skills and employment (Nicholas 1988; Oxley 1996); family-life (Maxwell-Stewart et al. 2015); health (Kippen & McCalman 2015); and reoffending (Frost & Maxwell-Stewart 2001). Yet, there has been a concentration on adult convicts, and juvenile lives are only lightly touched on. That is not to say juveniles have been ignored. There has been significant work on juvenile offending, as Godfrey et al. (2017) have pointed out, including: administrative histories of judicial and penal reform for children (Bailey 1987; Radzinowicz & Hood 1990); more social- and cultural-based studies on juvenile delinquency (Pinchbeck & Hewitt 1973; Pearson 1983; King 1998, 2006; Shore 1999a, 2011; Ellis 2014); studies of juvenile institutions (Stack 1992; Cale 1993; Cox 2003); studies of the policing of juveniles (Jackson & Bartie 2014); and studies of juvenile court records (Bradley 2007, 2009). However, the study of the *whole* lives of offenders convicted as juveniles has been scarce. Thanks to the works of Shore (1999a), Slee (2003), Jackman (2001, 2009) and Nunn (2015, 2017) there has been an increasing focus on male juvenile convicts – but this focus has been largely from an institutional perspective. This is similarly the case for juvenile females. Research on female offenders has expanded but, excepting the work of Cox (2003) which concentrates on training and reform in Britain, the concentration has been on *adult* female convicts (Beddoe 1979; Oxley 1996; Smith 2008b; Williams 2014; Kavanagh & Snowden 2015) with only a passing notice of juveniles. Given the few female juveniles transported, it is not surprising that they were overlooked but this research has now focused on their young lives. As Nunn pointed out, it is difficult to form an adequate picture of the male juvenile lives beyond the institution (2017, 171). This is largely because research into convicts ends with the Conduct Records but this research goes beyond these records by combining them with non-criminal records including newspapers, and birth, marriage and death records, much in the manner of Godfrey et al. (2017). This will allow an understanding of both their lives under sentence and their life-outcomes.

Convicts were transported from England to VDL from 1803 until 1853. Approximately 10,000–13,000 juveniles, under eighteen years of age, were among the 73,000 convicts transported (Brooke & Brandon 2005, 221;

Humphrey 2008, 22). This subgroup is made up of *juveniles* and members of the *underclass* (Gatrell 1996, 448). Both characteristics made them of little importance, individually, to contemporary society. While middle-class children were idealized, contemporary descriptions of working-class juvenile offenders were immortalized as the Artful Dodger in *Oliver Twist* (Dickens 1838). Even before this, parliamentary committees, newspapers and penny dreadfuls all contributed to a stereotypical view of juvenile delinquents as a threat to society. Between 1800 and 1850, the English population doubled from 8.3 million to 16.8 million (Jefferies 2005, 3). By the 1830s half the population of England and Wales was aged below twenty, and nearly 40 per cent was aged fourteen and under (Kirby 2003, 26–27). As King (1998, 116) pointed out, the problematic relationship between youth and authority can be traced back to the sixteenth century, but the rapid population growth created significant new challenges for successive governments. 'Central among them was how the state should deal with its predominantly young, predominantly poor citizens' (Godfrey et al. 2017). This group may have been written about collectively, including the important historical works of Pearson (1983), and criminological works such as Pitts (2005), Hendrick (2006) and Goldson and Muncie (2006) which focused on the system as '"unjust" and that it perpetuated disadvantage' (Godfrey et al. 2017). However, here the *whole* lives of these juveniles will be explored in order to place the human at the centre of the administrative record. As such, case studies are an important aspect of this research.

Case Study No.1: Mary Ann Oseman

Born in Camden to Mary Ann Oseman and Thomas Oseman, a bricklayer in the Parish of St Pancras, Mary was described simply as a 'girl' under 'Trade' in her transportation record – implying that she had no employment at the time of her conviction. However, Mary previously claimed in court that she was paid one penny every morning to light the fire of her prosecutor, which her prosecutor denied.

Despite being transported by fourteen years of age, Mary had at least one previous conviction. Her first appearance in the courts was in September 1831, when she was just nine years old. This case was acquitted; however, she was again brought before the court in April 1834 under another charge of larceny, and this time she was given a one-week prison sentence.

Through exploring Mary's Description List, we find she was fourteen when transported. This matches her birth record which states she was born in late October 1822. Therefore, Mary was convicted aged twelve and reached VDL by age fourteen.

Mary was sentenced to seven years' transportation for stealing a watch to the value of one pound from a widow named Ann Moore. In fact, Mary had broken into her prosecutor's house while she was asleep, waking her up in the process. This gave rise to an alarm and the presence of police. According to John Fitzgerald, the police constable, Mary stated it was the first time she had ever stolen. Yet, she was indicted twice in the same session, which includes a guilty plea for stealing a shawl worth one pound from Elizabeth Naylor. It is very possible that it was because of these two successive prosecutions against Mary that she gained a place aboard a vessel bound for Australia. Especially coupled with the fact that she broke into a dwelling house at night. This was seen as a particularly serious crime because it was thought that the owners would be *put in fear*.

Just one of the 165 convicts transported on the *New Grove* in October 1834, Mary arrived at VDL in March 1835. The Conduct Record holds a wealth of information about offenders. While confirming Mary's two Old Bailey convictions, the record also reveals further information about Mary's contact with the criminal justice system. Namely, that she was in Newgate prison and that she also spent time in a refuge and/or at Mrs Fry's school. Elizabeth Fry established *The House of Discipline and School of Reform for Girls* in 1825, which later became known as the *School of Discipline* and took in girls for reformation. Mary's record states that she spent time in 'Mrs Fry's school' but it also mentions that she spent time in a refuge. It is unclear whether the refuge being referred to was Mrs Fry's school or another institution Mary spent time in. When the ship's surgeon superintendent refers to her character, he stated she was 'indifferent but young and thoughtless disposition', but he also added that she was not 'bad'. Indeed, Mary's behaviour while under supervision in the colony reflects this. Mary committed a series of non-serious offences resulting in several visits to a female factory for hard labour. Most offences were absenteeism. It was also noted that 'through extreme carelessness [Mary] let her master's baby fall to the ground by which its leg was broken'. This comment implies that there was nothing malicious in the incident: it was an accident.

Eventually Mary received her Free Certificate in 1841, a timely seven years after her sentence expired. If a settled life can be measured by such outcomes as marriage or steady employment, Mary did settle. Approved for marriage in May 1839 (before freedom), she married a free man named

George Clarke and they went on to have nine children. They migrated to Wallaroo, South Australia. George died in 1875 at Kadina, South Australia, but Mary lived for a further nineteen years. Mary remarried a Christopher Charlton who survived her (he died in 1903). Mary died at the old age of sixty-seven in January 1894 and was buried at the Wallaroo Cemetery in South Australia.

Mary is only one individual and we are not privy to – as with many studies of historical lives – her internal decision making. Yet, we can still assess collective life events and paths. It is not possible to ascertain if Mary was happy in marriage, but we do know she stayed with her husband until his death and formed a large family. Despite her arduous start to colonial life, Mary built a new life free from crime, but was Mary's life typical of these juveniles? By placing juvenile convicts like Mary in their colonial context and comparing and contrasting their life events, it is possible to explore these juveniles lives *collectively*.

Case studies like Mary Ann Oseman's were formed by nominally linking both criminal and non-criminal records.[1] The juvenile offenders traced were initially sampled from the *Old Bailey Proceedings* (2018). Those convicted under fourteen, who were sentenced to transportation in the early-nineteenth century, were selected.[2] Next, they were traced in the *British Transportation Records* to ascertain which juveniles undertook the journey.[3] The approach described here is one which closely follows the method employed by Godfrey et al. (2007, 2010, 2017). For example, in *Young Criminal Lives* the long-term impact of youth justice interventions was considered by incorporating the use of biographical data into life-course analysis. In this way, the information of individuals was retrospectively, sequentially ordered by life events, enabling analysis and examination of trends. This life-course method has become increasingly popular with historians (Turner 2009; Williams 2014; Maxwell-Stewart and Kippen 2015). After linking the lives of individuals, typical and atypical biographies were examined to interrogate those trends and humanize offenders. Criminologists have long emphasized the link between criminal behaviour and individual background, and have increasingly applied a longitudinal life-course perspective in their analysis (Vikstrom 2011, 861–862). This is demonstrated in the work of Elder (1974) and Giele and Elder (1998). When conducting life-course research, the encoding of historical events and social interaction outside the person is the key (Giele & Elder 1998, 22). Life-course, defined in terms of trajectories from birth to death, allows the uncovering of a line of development that includes phases from childhood to adulthood – including getting a job, having children, being transported, marrying or migrating (Vikstrom 2011, 863). This book uses this approach to explore the lives of juvenile convicts. While their criminal activity is important in understanding their whole lives, their criminality or desistance is not necessarily the most important factor under deliberation. As well as changing criminal legislation and the importance of structural factors, it is important to explore offenders' lives before, during and after any criminal activity (Sampson & Laub 2005; Vikstrom 2011, 862–863). Using a collective biographical approach, as described by Giele and Elder (1998, 19), it is possible to reveal the underlying features of these juveniles lives, which control mechanisms and structural changes fail to explain (Vikstrom 2011, 861–862). The wealth of records left behind in the form of criminal and social records allows this approach. And by historically contextualizing those individuals uncovered, including familial relationships and employment, as well as significant historical events, individual pathways can be understood.

The nature of historical evidence may not have changed, but our access to it and its presentation has (Cohen 2006, 391). The large-scale digitization of primary sources has allowed historians 'new insights' into working-class lives. Indeed, the 'elaborate bureaucracy of surveillance' established in VDL, which is now vastly digitized, is a prime example. These records contain numerous observations for the same individual allowing the piecing together of individual criminal lives and the carrying out of statistical analysis to varied research questions – at a scale unimaginable using non-digitized documentation (Shore & Johnston 2015, 3–4). Most criminal justice–generated documents have information not just on crime, but also on the criminal. When this is combined with detailed historical newspapers, thorough narratives can emerge (Godfrey 2014, 79). In research which depends largely upon documents generated by and for the state, every additional piece of information is welcome in confirming or altering interpretation (Frost 2011, 26). While significant interactions, events and decision-making will remain hidden in history, interpretation based on available evidence and knowledge of relevant social and economic histories will aid the construction of narratives. It was possible to uncover detailed information thanks to the rich sources used. From the criminal records created for surveillance to the newspapers created for public consumption, all provide different perspectives of the juveniles' life. The life events and narratives of these juveniles can never be understood if they are not contextualized. In order to do this, primary sources, including the Official Statistical Returns of VDL and correspondence of those in authority are vital. This allows aspects such as the economy, colonial offending, education, health, mortality and the population to be understood. In this way, a baseline by which to measure the life-outcomes of the juveniles could be produced to explore what life-outcome a juvenile convict, who had been transported to VDL in the nineteenth century, could reasonably expect. Only then is it possible to approach the question of whether they were able to settle into their post-transportation lives and which factors affected life-outcomes such as gender or criminality.

The difficulty of concentrating on the whole life of these juvenile offenders is that their context changed over time. While this does not make it impossible to assess the 'success' of their lives, it does make it difficult to point to the contributing factors. It is not possible to produce a hierarchy of causation, since the working factors which led to the life-outcomes of the juvenile's lives are the sum total of *all* the negative and positive conditions taken together. Meaning, no one main cause or turning point can be chosen. Yet, as Gorovitz (1965, 1969) pointed out, differentiated factors can still be chosen as the most important contributing factors. These are not arbitrary choices, but they are not objective choices either. While causation is ultimately objective, the working factors chosen here will be partial and pragmatic. However, they will be justified through a full outline of their context and explained in comparison with other competing contributing factors (Rigby 1995). Certainly the context of each individual changed over time, especially given that the period in question runs from 1816 to the turn of the century – when the last juvenile was known to have died. Consequently, factors acting on the lives of these juveniles will be difficult to uncover but this is where biographical narratives become important. It will only be possible to point to the major contributing factors with any certainty – through a thorough understanding of the whole lives of these juveniles combined with their acting background factors.

Book outline

By using the method outlined here, it is possible to uncover the lives of historical actors which have been overlooked. To explore these individual lives, the following themes were assessed, including: crime; punishment; education, training and occupation; family life; and death.

In order to address questions of recidivism and desistance, the crimes committed by these juvenile convicts will be explored in Chapter 3. The severity, number and timing of offences committed by these young offenders will be considered. Next, the punishments they endured will be investigated to further understand their experience under servitude in Chapter 4. From hard labour and flogging, to confinement in the cells and extended sentences – what did these juvenile convicts endure? And, did this effect their life-outcomes? One of the measures of their life-outcomes will be their employment, and important in assessing this will be not only their education and training, but also the changing economy. This will be explored in Chapter 5 by turning to the Official Statistical Returns – taking particular notice of the economy, the average wage rates and changing populations (referring to migration and transportation). Allowing the following questions to be approached: Were the juvenile convicts (dis)advantaged in the labour market? Were they able to gain employment, and what was that employment? To gain a rounded understanding of their whole lives it is important to assess if they married or formed relationships. From the behaviour of the juvenile convicts themselves to the decisions of the administrators and the conditions of the penal colony into which they were thrust, were these female and male juvenile convicts able to form 'settled' familial lives and which factors inhibited or facilitated this process? This will be explored in Chapter 6. The conclusion of juveniles' lives is just as important as their experiences. Chapter 7 will explore whether their mortality was affected by being transported as convicts to VDL. This question will be addressed by comparing the mortality rate of this sample with the rates for the whole population, including convicts. Did the juveniles in the sample die young? Also to be considered are causes of death – were they victims of disease or were they dying in old age? Was there a correlation between repeated punishment and early death, for instance? Finally, the concluding chapter will bring together the compartmentalized parts of these young offenders lives. In doing so we will understand whether these juveniles were able to have 'settled' colonial lives and which factors affected their life-outcomes.

2

Historiography

Our views and understanding of crime and criminals have changed over time. Moreover, the way in which society views criminality does not necessarily reflect reality. This has always been the case but understanding these changes and continuities in attitudes is important because they influence how offenders are dealt with (Emsley 2010, 291). This is as true for adults as is for juveniles, and it has fed into ideas about juvenile delinquency. Important to the understanding of the concept of the 'juvenile delinquent' have been the changing views of childhood, the position of the urban working-class child and the emergence of the juvenile justice system. These aspects will be explored before turning to the practice of transportation and the changing management of convicts, which will be important in understanding the experiences of the juveniles whose lives have been uncovered.

The criminal class

The existence of a dark figure of crime has long been acknowledged (Phillips 1977; Godfrey et al. 2007; Emsley 2010). Simply defined, crime is the behaviour which violates the criminal law, which if detected would lead to prosecution (Emsley 2010, 2). As such, official crime is produced by a process of interaction between those who make and enforce the laws, and those who break them (Phillips 1977, 45). Whether a crime is prosecuted depends on the attitudes of authorities and the public (Phillips 1977, 42). Although historians have taken up the idea of social construction to differing extents, early revisionist's extreme views have been largely dismissed. While stimulating debate into criminal research, such ideas were also constricting. Foucault (1975), Ignatieff (1978) and Garland (1985) all pointed to the deep structures of power (Wiener 1990, 7). These revisionists inverted the Whiggish internalists and pragmatists argument into 'an onward march of surveillance and control'. The Whig humanitarian reform argument, and the revisionist's argument of social control, is too simplistic. Both the complexity and variety of human motives, as well as the discourse of power relations, need to be combined to begin to understand the history of crime and offenders (Wiener 1990, 8). Much misunderstandings of crime have resulted from national histories which have uncritically relied on unreliable statistics and contemporary commentary (e.g. Tobias 1967; Chesney 1970). However, regional investigation has allowed for a more nuanced understanding of criminals and crime (e.g. Phillips 1977; Conley 1991). Until the 1970s the history of crime in Britain was told as one of reform and modernization (Wiener 1990, 1). Yet, to understand crime and criminals we need to take into account the values, interests and context of society, and avoid a positivistic approach. Essentially, crime is not an 'objective fact which constitutes a problem' (Wiener 1990, 4–6). Whig historian Tobias took nineteenth-century contemporary views of offenders and presented them as the 'criminal class', a separate group that could be 'distinguished by their clothing and habits and lived wholly or largely on the proceeds of crime' (1967, 14). Historians have since dismissed the idea that his assertions 'may be regarded as an acceptable explanation of the phenomena of the time' (Tobias 1967, 70; Phillips 1977, 16–17). Even Tobias himself noted: 'Even if contemporaries are agreed on something, we cannot be sure that they were right' (1967, 13). Ultimately, if crime is viewed as inevitable in the 'criminal class', crime and its perpetrators can never be understood. Many non-offending working-class poor lived in housing among those who relied on theft to live. Moreover, there were those in full-time work who stole, just as there were those occasional workers who did not (Godfrey 2014, 9). Phillips (1977), for example, found that only 10 per cent of crimes committed in the Black Country were committed by 'professional criminals'. Most had normal jobs, stealing only to supplement income or due to opportunity (Conley 1991, 137). As Emsley stated, both statistics and court records suggest that the overwhelming majority of theft was opportunistic and petty – rather than being major, planned and carried out by professional criminals (2010, 181).

Conley argued that the idea of a criminal class was really bound up in the idea of respectability, where respectability was a 'social category posing as a moral category'. Meaning that the middle classes were born respectable, while the poor had to earn it (Conley 1991, 4). Indeed, the notion of a criminal class was a convenient way of shifting the blame of criminal actions onto an alien group (Emsley 2010, 181). Notwithstanding some individuals who did live off criminal earnings, the term 'criminal class' implies a large homogenous group, which did not exist (Emsley 2010, 88). Historians have now further debated the existence of the criminal class (Phillips 1977; Conley 1991; Shore 1999a; Godfrey et al. 2007; Emsley 2010). While they have found that most defendants were not professional criminals, judicial authorities and the general public believed criminals to be a threatening breed apart (Conley 1991, 136–137). It was a popular belief in its existence that fuelled debate (Godfrey et al. 2007, 73). Therefore, nineteenth-century attitudes towards, and ideas about, crime and criminals are important but need to be understood critically and cautiously (Phillips 1977, 18).

The historiography of childhood

Along with nineteenth-century concern that the criminal class was marching against societal mores was a special concern with juveniles and their delinquency (Shore 1999a, 1). In order to understand the centrality of the juvenile delinquent in the nineteenth century, we must consider the changing ideas of childhood. As Pinchbeck and Hewitt highlight, a 'remarkable feature' of our time is the considerable social and statutory concern centred on children's welfare (1969, 1). By the twentieth century childhood was recognized as a universal condition (Munchie 2009, 50), and historians have shown a burgeoning interest in childhood but they have been rarely in agreement. The 1970s saw a consensus where the history of childhood was viewed as one of progress. Yet, just a decade later, with all historical genres moving away from modernization theory, the accepted orthodoxy became continuity (Cunningham 2005, 4). Although this historiography begun with an overarching history of sentimentalization by those including Aries (1962), Mause (1874), Shorter (1976) and Stone (1977), the works of Pollock (1983), Wrightson (1982) and Macfarlane (1986) have produced more nuanced histories (Cunningham 2005, 3–16). This new historiography moved towards the role of political and social structures, particularly that of demographic philanthropy and the state.

Partly owing to Middle Age languages not distinguishing juveniles from adults, Aries radically proposed that prior to the seventeenth century there was no conception of childhood (Munchie 2009, 48). Pollock, on the other hand, had already pointed out that there was no evidence of parental indifference predominating at any time. Instead, she argued that parents had always held an emotional attachment to their children and, therefore, some conception of childhood must have always existed (Munchie 2009, 48). Moreover, Pinchbeck and Hewitt demonstrated that children were considered in the paternalistic legislation from the sixteenth century (1969, 1). Notwithstanding differing ideas of harshness from today, early-modern children and their proper place in society *were* a national concern (Pinchbeck & Hewitt 1969, 2). However, Pinchbeck and Hewitt also found a 'conspicuous lack of concern for the welfare of children' in the eighteenth and early-nineteenth centuries. Until a 'public re-awakening' of the importance of child welfare in the late nineteenth century, they suggested that 'childhood was but a brief introduction to the heavy responsibilities of the adult world' (1969, 1; 299). Stemming from the reformers' reactions to the changing context of social and family life, in a country with increasing population and urbanization, both poverty and delinquency were re-problematized (Pinchbeck & Hewitt 1969, 2). Similarly, Cunningham (2005, 2), while allowing for differences in social class, country and gender, argued that the patterns of childhood experiences eventually encompassed all. Indeed, childhood cannot be studied in isolation from societal, economic, demographic and political changes. For example economic development allowed the shift of importance from employment to education in childhood, influencing the idea that childhood should be a time of dependency, leading childhood to become increasingly separate from adulthood (Cunningham 2005, 3). Certainly, the idea that society was 'wasteful and heedless' with its children was replaced by Pinchbeck and Hewitt's stance which focused on continuity. Yet, this does not mean that the nineteenth century did not undergo significant alterations (1969, 1). Along with, and largely due to, conflict over the history of childhood came similar disagreements over the historical origins of the concept of the 'juvenile delinquent' (Shore 2011, 4).

Juvenile delinquency

[Juvenile] Delinquents were differentiated not only by their offence, but by their life-styles, by their impatience of restraint, their dislike of discipline and aversion to settled employment. (May 1981, 106)

During the 1970s and 1980s there was an 'academic renaissance' in terms of understanding the concept of juvenile delinquency (Shore 2011, 1). This new orthodoxy challenged previous historiographical assumptions that juvenile justice developed as a humanitarian response to a real and dramatic increase in juvenile offending (Munchie 2009, 62). Following the new history from below wave, marginal juvenile offenders were brought to the forefront of historical analysis (Shore 2011, 4). Despite the term 'juvenile delinquency' being coined in 1776, revisionist histories largely placed its origins as a creation of the late-eighteenth to nineteenth centuries due to processes of industrialization, urbanization and criminalization (Munchie 2009, 62). These revisions came with numerous explanations of the discovery or invention of the concept, along with various chronologies.

While being subsequently challenged, the key works from Magarey (1978) and May (1981), and later Springhall (1986) and Bailey (1987) introduced the idea of the Victorian invention of delinquency, which they argued led to the Victorian and Edwardian development of the juvenile justice system (Shore 2011, 2). Magarey explored the interplay between changes in some juvenile behaviour and changes in the criminal law and its enforcement in Britain between 1820 and the 1850s (1978, 12). Magarey demonstrated that there was some justification for increasing nineteenth-century fears by pointing to prison statistics. The number of offenders under seventeen years of age imprisoned increased from 9,500, in 1838, to 14,000, in 1848. This was not attributed to increased lawlessness but instead to the criminalization of juvenile behaviour: behaviour which previously warranted no official response (Munchie 2009, 54). This argument was supported by pointing to contemporaries, for example William Crawford and Whitworth Russell (who were newly appointed inspectors of prisons for the Home District in 1836), who ascribed the 'striking increase' of juvenile male committals to 'other causes than the positive advance of crime' (cited in Magarey 1978, 17). Magarey argued this was initiated by the presumption of *doli incapax* for those under fourteen falling into disuse, and the 1820s Acts (including: Vagrancy Act 1824, Malicious Trespass Act 1827 and Metropolitan Police Act 1829), which she believed were partly designed to control delinquent juveniles. Together, by broadening legal definitions of criminal activity the apprehension of all 'loose, idle and disorderly persons not giving good account of themselves' was enabled, and street children became increasingly liable for arrest (Munchie 2009, 54). Thus, Magarey argued that juvenile delinquency was legislated into existence due to a decreasing willingness to overlook juvenile crime, and declining acquittal verdicts (Shore 2003, 110; Munchie 2009, 54).

Another pioneer in the field, Margaret May, described the ideology and legislative forces which clarified the conceptual idea of the juvenile offender as taking place between the 1830s and 1840s (Shore 2002, 82). May pointed out that juvenile delinquents were identified by a process which distinguished them from both other children and adults; this was partly a function of the investigators' approach, and the reliance on area and behavioural studies.

In surveying the 'moral topography' of cities, the juveniles under question became associated with the 'deteriorating and squalid neighbourhoods' they lived in, which resulted in the transfer of the characteristics of the area onto the juveniles in question (1981, 98). May's seminal thesis explored the social process underlying the identification of juvenile delinquency, the pressures leading to policy innovation, and the implementation of a new treatment philosophy in the form of the reformatory and industrial School movement. May argues that 'consciousness of delinquency stemmed from a disruption of traditional social controls consequent on industrialisation'. It also reflected new sensitivities to childhood and the demands of the casual child labour market (May 1981). May (1981, 74) achieved this by specifically looking at the subjective factors, tracing the growth and changing focus of investigations, and the analytical process which isolated delinquency as a specific social problem. May critically outlined the relationship between the changes to the criminal justice system, the new police establishment and changing attitudes to juvenile criminal responsibility. In doing so, she concluded that Platt (1969) had over stated his argument. Platt argued that current delinquency controlling programmes could be traced to enterprising 'child savers', who in the late-nineteenth century helped create special judicial and correctional institutions for the labelling and management of troublesome juveniles. Platt concluded that these reformers brought attention to, and in doing so invented, new categories of misbehaviour (Platt 1969, 3). This, May argued, was overstating the reformers' role in a complex process of change. More empirically detailed explanations of the apparent growth in juvenile crime soon entered the debate (Shore 2011, 9).

Empirically rooted research soon developed, which allowed for a meaningful measure of the growth of nineteenth-century juvenile delinquency. King (1998) provided detailed statistical analysis of juvenile offenders at selected courts throughout Britain, including the Old Bailey. In doing so, he found that the rise in juvenile prosecutions pre-dated the Victorian 'invention' of delinquency by two decades.[1] King's (1998) findings point to the issue of urban growth as central to the increasing willingness to prosecute juvenile offenders. Stressing the complexity of the situation, he highlighted the shifting cultural, social and political landscape. Concluding that the existence of a growing number of vulnerable, poor and urban juveniles, and of a general increase in post-war anxieties about rising crime rates, resulted in the conditions for an increase in juvenile prosecutions in the 1810s (Shore 2011, 10). Rush (1992, 6), who utilized social construction, argued that juveniles emerged as a distinct problem in the nineteenth century. Conceding that both social control and the term 'juvenile delinquency' existed before the nineteenth century, Rush nevertheless asserted that the concept emerged with the increased administration of juveniles. He argued that reformers invented the problem of juvenile delinquency in answer to urbanization and industrialization, which brought new societal needs and problems (Rush 1992, 6; 12). He further demonstrated the progress of this 'social imperative' by highlighting the increasing significance of the juvenile's age in trial and punishment. The extension of summary jurisdiction brought a corresponding emphasis on the sentence and mode of punishment. Because of concern over the risks of juvenile contamination through association with hardened adult criminals, swift justice was implemented under the 1821 Bill[2]; this allowed juveniles to be processed quickly under summary powers. This resulted in the age of the offender taking on a new significance but it had no 'practical relevance to the guilt and responsibility of the offender'. Still, the chronological age of the offender became important at the stage of sentencing and punishment (Rush 1992, 16). Similarly, Shore highlighted that juvenile offenders were increasingly viewed separately in the nineteenth century through stressing the importance of the 'large-scale criminalization of children' (1999a, 29). This is not to dismiss other factors, including the changing form of the household in the early-modern period (Shore 1999a, 149) – specifically, the repeal of the Statute of Artificers (1814) and the decline in apprenticeships which predated this (Shore 1999a, 18), and the influence of the long wartime period which provided the government with experience of penal detention through prison-of-war camps (Shore 1999a, 23). Essentially, with the changing definitions of criminality and legal demarcations, juveniles who would previously have been informally dealt with were undergoing a more formal and punitive process (Shore 1999a, 149). This is evidenced by an increased tendency to use custodial punishment for juveniles after the cessation of war in 1815 (Shore 1999a, 23). A decreasing willingness to overlook juvenile crime was combined with decreasing acquittal verdicts and the growth of secondary punishments. This suggests 'that to some extent the problem of juveniles was exacerbated, though not created, by the policy-makers of the time' (Shore 1999, 150).

The edited collective essays of Cox and Shore (2003) further challenge the invention of the nineteenth-century juvenile delinquent through exploring different European cultures. Significantly, they locate the continuities between the early-modern and modern periods in terms of perceptions and treatment of delinquent juveniles. The idea of the invention of juvenile delinquency, as Griffiths suggests, is problematically tied to modernization theory. Indeed, Griffiths demonstrates that confinement of the young, concerns over rough youths in domestic service and apprenticeships, forms of policing disorderly youth and attempts at reformation all preceded the nineteenth century (Shore 2011, 12). Age-specific offences, penalties and policing measures were prevalent in the houses of correction, in transportation and in the discourse of youth reformation long before the 'semantic twist' of juvenile delinquency (Munchie 2009, 64). By turning to linguistic reconfigurations, however, Griffiths demonstrates that sharp nineteenth-century shifts were partly introduced by the regulatory language of juvenile delinquency into the penal lexicon (Shore 2011, 12). He argued that changing vocabulary promoted a separate discourse and engendered this judicial separation, adding that the emergence of new terminologies is key to understanding both continuities and discontinuities. Thus, it is likely that powerful class-based dichotomies increasingly shaped how juvenile offenders were managed. Consequently, the difference between hardened and corrupt working-class children, and the innocent middle-class children fed into penal language. These discourses increasingly focused upon the 'hardened', 'incorrigible', 'dangerous', juvenile offender, and persistent juvenile offenders became an 'emblem for social breakdown and domestic instability' (Shore 2003, 114). The combination of juvenile-specific legislation and institutions in the early-nineteenth century continues to signify the nineteenth century as important in the definition and management of disorder. 'Juvenile delinquency' may not have been invented but it underwent a 'dramatic reconfiguration' at this time (Munchie 2009, 64).

The correlation between the emergence of a separate juvenile justice system and the increasingly visible categorization of juvenile offenders in the nineteenth century has been repeatedly highlighted (Rush 1992; King 1998; Shore 1999a, 17; Shore 2003, 116). Also pointed to has been its slow progress and significant continuities from the early-modern period (Shore 2003, 113). In addition, Shore points to the consequences of the shift to the separate treatment of juvenile offenders. Specifically, as soon as juveniles were considered separately they were the first to be viewed as having some hope of redemption and reformation (1999, 131). However, the separation of juveniles from adults was 'double-edged'. They were categorized and consequently problematized in their own right (Shore 1999a, 135). Notwithstanding early-modern continuations, the systems of juvenile justice which developed in the twentieth century were rooted in this separate categorization of juvenile criminals, which evolved in the early-nineteenth century (Shore 1999a, 148; Shore 2003, 110). Much of this increased nineteenth-century focus on criminality was directed at juvenile offenders. This was partly fuelled by the belief that these delinquents could be saved and reincorporated back into respectful society before they were lost as hardened criminals (Shore 1999a, 1). Yet, as Shore points out, this paradigm of explanation is not neat (1999a, 14). There were various explanations of causation – from societal explanations centred on parents and popular entertainments, to the underworld of crime and the justice system itself (Shore 1999a, 34). Juvenile delinquents were even subject to their own classification system: the 'perishing class' and 'dangerous class'. Members of the perishing class were merely in danger of falling into crimes, while the dangerous were actual offenders (Radzinowicz & Hood 1986, 167). This perception of crime was driven by the prevailing stereotypes. Consequently, when the ideas of the criminal class reached its height, poverty-stricken juveniles were seen as being 'cradled in iniquity' (Shore 1999a, 35). Contemporaries also thought that other children, specifically older juvenile gangs, were bad examples, including the swell-mob who they believed 'epitomized the rewards of the life of crime' (Shore 1999a, 45). Contemporary commentators believed there were numerous child thief-managers, who both trained juveniles and fenced their goods (Duckworth 2002, 29). While pickpocketing was seen as a progressive step into the criminal career (leading it to be a capital offence until 1808), in reality the average juvenile offender did not resemble these professional groups (Shore 1999, 55–59). Nevertheless, contemporary fear of juvenile offenders maturing into adult burglars was embedded in many arguments for penal reform and 'colonial retraining' (Shore 1999, 61), and much of this debate centred on the city of London.

Moving into the nineteenth century, increasingly crime was seen as something inherent, and external factors took on less importance. Then, during the 1820s and 1830s, juvenile crime was linked to the much narrower explanation of the criminal class, as already discussed (Shore 1999a, 19). Importantly, this increased contemporary focus on juvenile criminals, Shore argues, could have subsided if it had not been for its coincidence with metropolitan life pressures, along with institutional creations for the poor and criminals (1999a, 23). As the early-nineteenth century progressed, it was no longer only the dark alleys which held danger for potential robberies, but also the 'crowded thoroughfares of the developing metropolis' (Shore 2015, 70). There was an acceleration in the industrialization process that had begun in the previous century. A falling death rate also ensured a steady population growth and internal migrants moved into towns and cities from all over the UK, and in particular they moved to London. Britain's population doubled between 1801 and 1851, from approximately 9 to 18 million (Gray 2010, 56). It is clear from the social commentary circulating in the second decade of the nineteenth century that there was a widespread belief in the rise of crime. Contemporaries, in London especially, were increasingly concerned about the perceived increase in population, and the 'rising tide of iniquity and poverty' (Shore 1999a, 19). The awareness of increasing juvenile committals, which 'dramatically and unexpectedly' emerged during the inquiry into metropolitan policing of 1811–1816, also first centred on London (May 1981, 76). Consequently, working-class London youths, just like the ones sampled in this research, were seen as being particularly problematic.

The separate treatment of juvenile offenders

The 1816 *Report of the Committee for Investigating the Cause of the Alarming Increase in Juvenile Delinquency in the Metropolis* was one of the first reports to deal solely with crime committed by juvenile offenders. Specifically, it was concerned with the growth of juvenile crime following the end of the Napoleonic Wars (Johnston 2015, 136). Despite not always explicitly categorizing juveniles as distinct from adults within the justice system, they were often treated differently in practice. Then, from imprisonment and transportation to reformatory schools, juveniles were increasingly distinguished as having different needs to adult offenders. Still, this change was piecemeal. And it would be wrong to suggest that because there was no explicit differentiation in the early-nineteenth century that, in practice, juveniles were not treated differently. While the prison system was not organized on a national basis until 1877, the government had involved itself increasingly from the turn of the century (Shore 1999a, 100). In the early-nineteenth century, imprisonment (gaols/bridewells) simply meant confinement. In these privately run establishments juveniles would be confined with adults. Largely due to philanthropic drive, there was growing awareness that this 'association' should stop (Radzinowicz & Hood 1990, 138). Yet, a Select Committee in 1818 found free association between prisoners in most gaols (Duckworth 2002, 54–55). In 1816 separate accommodation for juveniles on the hulks was called for, but it was not until 1822 that juveniles were transferred to a juvenile-only hulk – the *Bellerophon* (Radzinowicz & Hood 1990, 142). Juveniles did not leave the hulks for labour; conditions were poor; reformation was lacking; and reports of vice and bullying were rife. Despite being seen as a failure, the *Euryalus* juvenile hulk continued until 1843 (Radzinowicz & Hood 1990, 144). The hulks were not the only cause for concern; prisons too came under the scrutiny of reformers.

Despite the aims of the 1823 and 1824 Gaol Acts, brought by Robert Peel, they were not enforceable until prison inspectors were appointed in 1835 (Radzinowicz & Hood 1990, 145). They also only stipulated classification based on offences and gender, not age (Johnston 2015, 140). Because of concern over contamination through association with hardened *adult* criminals, swift justice was called for under the 1821 Bill.[3] While allowing juvenile offenders to be processed quickly under Summary Powers and resulting in *less* association during pre-trial imprisonment, it did not eliminate association completely (Rush 1992, 16). Many juveniles were still sent to local prisons, both awaiting trial and for petty offences. Separate accommodation existed in some prisons in England but at the discretion of the prison governor. For example in Lancaster and Gloucester all offenders were 'associated', but at Worcester the young prisoners were not only separated but also given reading and writing instruction. Meanwhile other prisons were arguably early versions of the industrial training establishments which came later in the century, including Warwick Gaol which saw boys manufacture pinheads (Radzinowicz & Hood 1990, 145). The number of young offenders in English prisons fell throughout the century, from approximately 10,000 boys in 1840, to almost 900 juveniles under twelve years of age, and 5655 male juveniles aged between twelve and sixteen in 1879–1880 (Radzinowicz & Hood 1990, 124). Numbers fell due to the Juvenile Offenders Act (1847) which instructed that all those under fourteen be tried at the petty session court in cases of simple larceny (up to the value of five shillings). This not only gave a maximum sentence of three months' imprisonment, but it also allowed for whipping to be used without imprisonment. The age was later increased to sixteen (Johnston 2015, 139). While sentences were short, they still resulted in the confinement of juveniles in inappropriate prisons, often with hard labour. The opening of reformatories also diverted many children and juveniles from the prison system. However, first developing alongside prisons, and influencing the perception of how to deal with juveniles at this time, were aftercare institutions.

Aftercare institutions were, at this point, not officially part of the criminal justice system. Yet, their ideas and practices fed into the discourse surrounding juvenile offenders and criminal justice, and influenced the concept of *diversion*. For example the Marine Society, founded in 1756, catered for *non*-criminal twelve- to sixteen-year-old boys (Radzinowicz & Hood 1990, 134). Similarly, the Philanthropic Society sought to reform and re-integrate juveniles. Formed in 1788 by Robert Young, it sought to create a 'superior class of mechanics'. It was not until 1816 that Young's ideas were revisited, and Sir Eardley-Wilmot collected funds to establish an 'aftercare asylum'. These institutions were not established to replace prisons but they were progressive establishments which influenced how juvenile offenders were treated. Emerging was the idea that juveniles needed different care from adult offenders, and some saw these new prospects as lying in the colonies. Captain Brenton established the 'Children's Friends Society'. Concerned for impoverished juveniles, Brenton housed and trained them for up to six months and then indentured them as apprentices in the colonies (Radzinowicz & Hood 1990, 135–137). While criminal juveniles were not included and transportation of juveniles predated Benton's venture, what was new was the explicit idea of prior training. Partly due to these schemes, there was a growing awareness of children as deserving of separate treatment within the justice system itself.

Juveniles were transported throughout the nineteenth century. However, it was only in 1835, in the Duke of Richmond Committee, that different management (not just separation) was officially discussed. The evidence compiled pointed to the greater benefits of reformation in transporting juvenile offenders after prior training in English penitentiaries. Despite a complete reversal two years later by the Molesworth Committee, which was steadfastly against transportation because it was 'costly and futile', transportation continued. The Molesworth Committee pointed to a lack of reformation, sexual abuse and savage punishments which should not be ignored. However, others believed that these juveniles would be able to gain employment in the colony and re-enter society away from criminal connections (Radzinowicz & Hood 1990, 139–140). England was not alone in wishing to rid its mother country of convicts. Spain, Denmark, Italy, Portugal and Holland, at some point, used a form of transportation (Radzinowicz & Hood 1990, 485). However, none of these European schemes matched the transportation activities of Britain (except Russia). Inevitably, how convicts were disciplined in the English colony changed over this long period.

Shortly after the establishment of Point Puer in the colonies, reforming zeal led to the establishment of a juvenile-only prison in England in 1838 as recommended by the 1835 Select Committee on Gaols and Houses of Correction. The Isle of Wight was the chosen site to instruct juveniles 'in a manner best calculated to render them efficient labourers in the colonies' (Radzinowicz & Hood 1990, 148). Despite aiming to educate, Parkhurst was also penal in character to ensure criminal desistance. Parkhurst did not close until 1864, but the experiment began cautiously by only accepting 'hopeful' cases. Still, they were treated harshly even by contemporary standards; an iron manacle was worn on one leg continuously. This was ordered to be discontinued after two years, but 'uninterrupted surveillance' and the silent system persisted. Although criticized by Horne, instruction in the way of reading, writing and trade training was provided. Others, including Elizabeth Fry, praised the system (Radzinowicz & Hood 1990, 150–151). A change of the system coincided with the move, in 1847, to reserve Parkhurst for juveniles over fourteen. Younger and 'more hopeful' cases were sent to the Philanthropic Society at Red Hill. In this final phase Parkhurst simply became a prison for young convicts – mirroring itself on the adult system. There was no longer emigration or aftercare (Radzinowicz & Hood 1990, 153–154). Just as Parkhurst became more penal in nature towards the end of its life, similar institutions in Europe also became increasingly penal. For example Nederlandsch Mettray, under Meeter in the 1870s, increasingly took on prison barracks and punishment features, and by the end of the century education became less important (Weijers 1999, 77–78). However, in England the 1852 *Select Committee on Criminal and Destitute Children* rejected Parkhurst as a model for future reformatories (Radzinowicz & Hood 1990, 154). Parkhurst may have been considered a failure by contemporaries, but it did establish a president for the separate treatment of juvenile offenders. By its closure there had been significant moves to accommodate juvenile offenders within the reformatory and industrial schools (Johnston 2015, 144). This move to accommodate juvenile offenders in *special* institutions was not specific to England and its colonies.

The French agricultural reform school Mettray was held up by those including Rev Sydney Turner (founder of the Philanthropic Society) and reformer Matthew Davenport Hill, as an example to emulate (Trepanier 1999, 304). It was thanks to a visit there in the 1840s that Turner recommended 'with the support and sanction of the government' receiving conditionally pardoned juveniles at Red Hill. Therefore, *some* juvenile offenders under thirteen were diverted to Red Hill (Duckworth 2002, 147). For the first time the criminal justice system was explicitly linked with reformatories. The first of the juvenile institutions in Europe were: Seville, Spain, as early as 1725 (Tikoff 2002); Rotterdam, Netherlands (1833); Parisian La Petite-Roquette, France (1838); and Saint-Hubert, Belgium (1844). Nonetheless, it was the establishment of Mettray, in 1839, which pulled in travelling philanthropists from the Netherlands, Germany and England. As well as Red Hill, these visits led to the formation of similar establishments, including the Netherlands' Nederlandsch Mettray, Belgium's Ruysselede and Beerem. Mettray became an icon of reformatory education, but so too was Germany's Rauhes Haus (Trepanier 1999, 304; Dekker 2005, 321–322). Rauhes Haus was the first to adopt a 'family' organization and recruit religiously motivated staff; it was a leader in the farm school movement. However, Mettray, by the 1850s, had become the 'highest example of all the more recent efforts of the same kind'. The boys lived in huts in family units and responded to 'moral influences' and elaborate reward systems, instead of severe punishment (Radzinowicz & Hood 1990, 155–157). Moves towards the segregation of male convicts according to age in VDL coincided with general calls for prison reform to have a moral and not economic focus. Experiments in age, segregation, training, religious instruction and secular reformist principles were beginning during the 1820s (Jackson 2001, 7).

Such changes were *ad hoc* and not without fault. For example from 1832 juvenile convicts began to be transported separately. However, the *Lord Goderich*, a juvenile transport sailing as late as 1841, contained eleven male convicts aged twenty-four and above. They may have been overseers or there may have been spare berths. Either way, it evidences that separation did not mean that juvenile convicts would not be associated with adult convicts – and so the abuse, be it physical, sexual or emotional, was still possible (Jordan 1985, 1094). This is not to mention the differences, both mentally and physically, between an eighteen- and an eleven-year-old. But what of the management of those taken from London and transported to Australia?

The practice of punishment and transportation

Major professional research into Australian history was pioneered by the likes of Clark (1956), Shaw (1966) and Robson (1976). They used new data and techniques, and in doing so overturned Wood's (1922) argument that transported convicts were victims of British colonial cruelty. Like Wood, Shaw (1966) used a traditional qualitative methodology but he utilized the results of other researchers including Clark (1956), and later Robson (1976), for support. These two researchers had innovatively employed what were then neglected sources, the Conduct Records, in a quantitative manner. Payne (1961) also utilized similar methods but he presented, through a study of Tasmanian female convicts, a picture which tallied with Wood's. Yet, it was the works of Clark, Robson and Shaw, due to their comprehensive nature, which have underpinned the subsequent interpretation of Australian history. As Oxley explains, Clark (1956) did employ empirical methodology but he was heavily influenced by 'subjective assessments formulated by impressionistic readings of qualitative sources' (Oxley 1996, 5). Robson (1976), on the other hand, was rigorously quantitative and systematic. He studied 7000 convicts sent to the eastern colonies. Nevertheless, he presented descriptive statistics located within a qualitative framework. Fundamentally, the notion of a criminal class *determined* his statistical analysis. Criminal offences were concentrated on, and trades and skills were largely ignored. Nicholas and Shergold (1988, 5) argue that when statistical results and their hypothesis did not correlate, they were overlooked. For example although Clark found that convict literacy levels were surprisingly high, he characterized convicts as having 'low cunning and ignorance' (Nicholas & Shergold 1988, 5). Consequently, these publications resulted in a picture of male convicts as professional criminals, with female convicts as professional prostitutes (Oxley 1996, 5).

By looking closer at the experience of different categories of convicts and their contributions to the colony, historians have presented a more nuanced picture (Smith 2008b, 10). For example *Convict Workers: Reinterpreting Australia's Past* saw economic historians ask new questions about the early economic and social development of NSW. Using empirical and comparative methodologies, they explored 'human capital' and demonstrated the beneficial effect of the convicts, and the convict system, on the colony. By assessing the occupational skills, education and physical fitness they overturned the pervading convict stereotype (Nicholas 1988). In this vein, this book will explore the whole lives of juvenile convicts, not simply their crimes and punishments. First, both individual and group experiences cannot be understood without knowledge of the history of transportation as a whole.

The punishment of transportation allowed the practice of banishment to be combined with the idea that the offender could also repay the common good through colonization (Shaw 1966, 22–23). Undeniably, this punishment was makeshift and informal. It was not until the Habeas Corpus Act (1679) that transportation without trial was prevented. It was the 1655 Act which allowed the practice of mitigating criminals awaiting execution with transportation, and transportation became increasingly systematic. The Transportation Act (1718) outlined that the purpose of transportation was to deter criminals and supply the colonies with labour. Because of the need for servants at the American plantations, all clergiable offences were commuted to seven years' transportation. By the eighteenth century, transportation became 'a major ingredient of English criminal law' (Shaw 1966, 24–25). This left Britain in a predicament when the American colonies revolted, and they would no longer accept Britain's convicts. While awaiting a decision on a new penal colony, decommissioned war ships were used to house prisoners, which were known as prison hulks. Parliament authorized the use of these hulks for two years: they lasted eighty-two (Shaw 1966, 42–43).

Eventually Botany Bay in Sydney (NSW) was chosen to be the new penal colony (Shaw 1966, 43). Accordingly, the First Fleet departed there in 1787. By 1868, 132,308 men and 24,960 women were transported to the Australian colonies from Britain and Ireland (Quinlan 2014, 220). The majority were sent to NSW and VDL. Others were sent to Moreton Bay (Brisbane), Queensland, Norfolk Island, and, after 1850, Western Australia (WA). There were also a negligible number of 'offenders' exiled to Victoria (Brooke & Brandon 2005, 221). Transportation to NSW ended in 1841, to Tasmania in 1853 and to WA in 1868 (Smith 2008a, 35). The juveniles explored in this book were transported to VDL. In 1642, some 128 years before Captain James Cook visited Australia, an island was named by explorer Abel Tasman. He called the island Van Diemen's Land (VDL) after the governor of Batavia in the Dutch East Indies. This small island was about 160 miles long by 80 miles wide (Fleming 2012, 33). It received 73,000 convicts over fifty years, beginning in 1803. It became a separate colony from NSW only in 1825 (Brooke & Brandon 2005, 221). VDL became self-governing in 1856, when it gained its own fully elected legislature, which was after transportation had ended (Fleming 2012, 48). The British government advocated transportation because it was seen as a cheap, deterrent punishment. While the American colonies were substituted for the Australian colonies, the economic reasons for transportation remained the same as stated in the first Transportation Act (1717), which was labour supply (Meredith 1988, 14). Practically speaking, those who it failed to deter would be removed from the country, and would be unlikely to return. It was also initially believed that removal from criminal connections, in a new environment, with 'ready' employment would result in reformation (Shaw 1966, 17).

How convicts were disciplined in the colony changed over time. This was partly because it was believed that the once-primitive colony of the late-eighteenth century had become ordered and civilized by the mid-nineteenth century. Accordingly, transportation became increasingly seen as not severe enough. This was largely fuelled by the perception of rising crime rates in Britain, and so it followed in the minds of contemporaries that transportation was not a sufficient deterrent. The governors were ordered to increase the severity of the punishment by the mother country (Shaw 1966, 17). Consequently, the supposed lottery of the assignment system was replaced by the probation system, which was quickly accepted as a failure. The experience of transportation for individual convicts varied not only due to age, sex, behaviour and skill, which resulted in differing punishments and rewards, but also due to these large shifts in the management of convicts. The changing circumstances will be explored in order to contextualize the lives of the juveniles uncovered in this book.

When a convict arrived in the formative days of the colony they would usually be assigned to a free colonist for the purpose of carrying out labour (Shaw 1966, 211). Assignment dated back to the first settlers but it was formally established by Governor King in 1804 (assignment was made legal only under the Transportation Act of 1824). Convict assignment was handled by the assignment board which comprised three persons, including a Chief Police Magistrate and the Principal Superintendent of Convicts (Brand 1990, 5). From the perspective of convicts, the benefits of the assignment system were the increased freedoms it offered. Predicated on good behaviour and provided the Lieutenant Governor gave approval, it was possible to earn a ticket of leave (ToL). This allowed convicts to work for an employer for wages or to hold a government post, and own property (Brand 1990, 6). However, ticket of leave regulations were tightened by 1823, and prisoners had to serve a fixed period before they were eligible to earn one. Then the 1832 Act forbade early tickets altogether, which had been locally granted in special circumstances (e.g. for capturing bushrangers). On top of this, legal protection was taken away from ticket of leave holders with regard to their property (Shaw 1966, 229–231). Nevertheless, tickets were still sought after. While their Certificate of Freedom was given at the end of their sentence (introduced in 1810), a revocable, conditional or absolute, pardon could also be granted by the crown under governor recommendation (Brand 1990 6; Brooke & Brandon 2005, 80). The merits of assignment for the governor of VDL, free settlers and the British government were largely financial (Shaw 1966, 211). Even so, assignment did not come without criticism even early on. This is alluded to in Bigge's 1825 report which suggested the continuation of assignment but recommended the dispersal of convicts into the countryside to avoid the 'evils' of association. Convicts would also no longer be granted land upon freedom. These changes, it was hoped, would result in a perceived increase of severity (Brooke & Brandon 2005, 245–246). Moreover, with the continuation of assignment, employers would continue to be responsible for the food, clothing, medical care and accommodation of their assigned servants. As such, the government would only pay administration costs, and for those in public gangs, gaols and penal settlements. Simultaneously, colonists benefited from a low-cost labour force which required no wages. Moreover, it was at least initially believed that assignment encouraged convicts to reform through rewarding good conduct (Brand 1990, 6).

Despite restrictions to ensure well-behaved masters, assignment was increasingly seen as a lottery. Excepting special approval, those such as ex-convicts and relatives were not permitted assigned convicts (Shaw 1966, 219). However, while one convict might get a tolerant and lenient master who indulged his servant with tea, sugar and tobacco, another might be overworked and abused (Brand 1990, 6). Assignments could be revoked upon complaint but many unsuitable masters remained and their actions went unnoticed (Shaw 1966, 219). A master could not punish their own servant; complaints had to be taken to the magistrate. However, although magistrates were arbitrators, Shaw argues that they had an interest in the subordination of convicts because they had their own assigned servants (1966, 224). Simultaneously some magistrates, like other masters, indulged their servants (Shaw 1966, 219–220). Material rewards including extra rations and wages (even after government opposition to the practice in 1823) were given to *some* convicts (Meredith 1988, 15). These inconsistencies in punishment led to doubts about the systems reformatory capabilities, as did the connotations of slave labour (Brand 1990, 6).

Lieutenant Governor Arthur, like many colonists, thought the assignment system was a good punishment. However, many back home and in Australia disagreed. While its detractors thought it a lottery, those who defended the system argued it was a severe, economical and reformatory punishment (Shaw 1966, 216). The British government was convinced that more severe discipline was needed as a deterrent to increasing crime rates at home (Shaw 1966, 250). The Select Committee (1837), known as the Molesworth Committee, criticized the lack of distinction made between the sentence, age, character or nature of offence in the treatment of convicts, finding instead that their fate was determined by skill (Meredith 1988, 15). The committee concluded that transportation was an 'ineffective instrument of reform'. Not only did it recommend the abolition of assignment, but it also recommended the establishment of penitentiaries at home and abroad. Yet, until these prisons were built, transportation would continue under an altered system (Brand 1990, 11), which they demanded should be less vague and arbitrary (Shaw 1966, 298). In 1837 the British government finally stopped assignment (Shaw 1966, 268). From this point convicts would work in gangs for a fixed period upon arrival, and subsequently obtain private employment for wages. Under the comptroller of convicts, the probation gang would be put to hard labour of differing degrees of severity according to conduct. Good behaviour would allow convicts to progress to the next stage, in which they could earn a probation pass enabling them to work for wages. If a convict lost their pass through bad behaviour, all wages earned were forfeited to the Queen. If the pass holder was unemployed, it was possible to resort to the public works in exchange for food and clothing. The penultimate stage was the ticket of leave, which was valid only in the colony it was granted. Only when they earned their ticket of leave could unpaid wages be accessed, and it could be earned only after completion of half of their sentence (Brand 1990, 19–20). The final stage was a pardon, conditional or absolute (Shaw 1966; 272–274). In this way the probation system was introduced, as an experiment, in 1839.

The end of transportation to NSW led to VDL receiving more convicts than anticipated. This, along with the abandonment of assignment, meant the probation gangs were bigger than intended (Shaw 1966, 275–277). This increased costs and many of the overseers and superintendents were unqualified due to low salaries (Brand 1990, 16). Stanley (Secretary of State for the Colonies) dispatched instructions for the *new* probation system in late 1842. Sir Eardley-Wilmot was chosen as Franklin's replacement as governor but he had no administrative experience (Shaw 1966, 297). Wilmot arrived (in 1843) into a colony which had been under economic depression since 1841 (Brand 1990, 24). From the outset there were issues with the system. There had not been enough time to erect appropriate buildings, making classification impossible (Shaw 1966, 298). On top of all this, there was also a labour shortage in 1840–1841. This was due to the end of assignment, the suspension of assisted migration into VDL and many mechanics migrating to the mainland. To meet these labour shortages Franklin had promoted free immigration to VDL. Unfortunately, this meant that when convicts emerged from the probation gangs looking for waged work, there was none (Shaw 1966, 279–281). (*For more information on the Van Diemonian depression, see* Chapter 5.) Whoever was to blame for the failure of the probation system, the result was a perceived British indifference which increased anti-transportation sentiment (Brand 1990, 103). Moreover, Charles La Trobe's report, published as a British Parliamentary paper in 1848, condemned the system (Brand 1990, 2). The probation system lasted for fourteen years, from the formation of Franklin's gangs to the cessation of transportation (Brand 1990, 97). Several of the probation establishments, however, remained open after 1853 until the last convicts served out their sentences (Brand 1990, 2).

Eighty per cent of transported convicts were male (Nicholas & Shergold 1988, 4). Consequently, the experience of female convicts was initially overlooked; however, their importance has been increasingly acknowledged. Robinson's (1988) work on the first forty years of settlement showed that female convicts were petty, first-time offenders who had suffered harsh conditions in Britain. Beddoe (1979) looked at the demographics and occupational circumstance of Welsh female convicts, thereby uncovering their convict experience. Subsequently, Oxley (1996) explored female convicts transported to NSW in aggregate, finding that they arrived with much needed skills and trade experience. Other important works on female convicts include: Robinson 1985; Perrott 1983; Weatherburn 1979; Salt 1984; Lake 2003; Smith 2008b; and Fleming 2012. Building on the work of these historians, this book will explore the lives of the *juvenile* female convicts, who have often been amalgamated with the adult females. On arrival in VDL female convicts were kept in factories until they could be assigned (Shaw 1966, 240). They were also confined there when they offended. (*For further information on female factories, the institutions in which females were kept, see* Chapter 4.) It is noteworthy that, while *some* juvenile males were in theory at least, separated from adult males, females underwent no such separation. Even during voyages after 1837, no such arrangements applied to female convicts; at least 25 per cent of whom were juveniles. Yet, it is difficult to believe that there was not the potential for abuse under these circumstances. This is not to say females were completely neglected. Juvenile females who were transported were generally slightly older than the male juveniles and they were also far less of them. This is partly because they were often diverted into other institutions such as the Philanthropic Society, the Refuge of the Destitute and the Bridewell House of Correction in Britain (Brooke & Brandon 2005, 118). Still, the lack of separation of female juveniles in the colonies has hitherto not been explored.

In 1852 the Secretary of State for the Colonies Sir John Pakington advised Governor Denison that transportation to VDL would cease. No further convicts arrived after the landing of the *St. Vincent* in 1853, and Denison received the order for the end of transportation in 1854. Certain penal institutions and settlements, for example Cascades and Impression Bay, continued to hold prisoners until all probationers had passed through into freedom (Brand 1990, 95–96).

3

Crime

Did these female and male juveniles go on to have, what has been termed, criminal careers? This chapter will explore the number, severity and rate of their offences. Their offending under sentence and whether they were able to turn away from crime after they had served their transportation sentence will be uncovered. Were they persistent offenders? An evaluation of their continued offending, or desistance, must be taken in light of offending before they were transported. Prior to their transportation sentence, 77 per cent of these juveniles had previous convictions for which they were imprisoned. These juveniles were imprisoned for periods of between five days and six months. Imprisonment was often the first step before transportation. The next stage in the punishment process for these juveniles, if they re-offended, was often a sentence of transportation. Even so, not all of those who were sentenced were transported. Thirty-eight per cent of those sentenced had their sentence commuted from transportation; 32 per cent of female juveniles were actually transported, compared with 64 per cent of males. Despite there being fewer females sentenced to transportation in the first place, a lower proportion of females were transported compared with males. If females were not transported they were generally sent to Millbank Prison for approximately two years. Similarly, some males spent time on the hulks and were then released back into Britain.

Of all the juveniles who arrived in Australia, 99 per cent were convicted of theft. There were only two violent offenders, one of whom was Francis MacDonald. Francis was charged with highway robbery. Convicted in 1817, during the course of the offence he struck his victim on the chest and put him 'in fear'. This happened in Somerset Street where he stole a watch, its chain and a key, worth just under five pounds. There was reportedly a mob involved but only Francis was convicted. While Francis was only convicted of stealing from the person, this offence was considered serious and he was sentenced to transportation for life. More common offences were pickpocketing and larceny.

While these offences were certainly considered serious at the time, more serious offences which involved breaking into the dwelling house or physically confronting the victim were less common in this sample: only five juveniles were convicted of burglary. Among other factors, the place in which the crime occurred influenced how serious contemporaries perceived the crime. In the majority of cases the items were stolen from public spaces. That is, anywhere outside including shops. Shops are included here because juveniles were welcome to enter them without direct invitation from the owner. This suggests that both male and females, as a general rule, did not enter unknown spaces to commit their crimes. Spaces chosen were ones which juveniles were familiar with. A typical example is that of Samuel Linton who was found guilty of stealing a dead goose worth seventy-two pence from a shop. The average value of the stolen item for all juveniles was 332 pence, which was not a small sum. However, the mode is thirty-six pence. This is because the data is not normally distributed. The mean value of the stolen item has been pushed up by those few offenders who stole expensive items. This is not to ignore those few juveniles who did steal items worth a considerable value, but it is to put them in context. For example James Alder was indicted of stealing to the value of twenty-two pounds. This was the highest value stolen in the sample and was made up of the following items: one writing desk, five watches, twenty-three spoons, one pair of sugar tongs, four broaches, six seals and two rings. These items were all stolen from the dwelling house and resulted in fourteen years' transportation. This was a serious, but not typical, offence. While some juveniles did steal expensive items such as jewellery, more often (in over 50 per cent of cases) juveniles stole clothes, fabric or handkerchiefs. However, at least 36 per cent of juveniles did not steal items which were of immediate use to them such as food, money or tools to work with. This means that it is likely that what they did steal was stolen in order to exchange, pawn or sell. While some of these cases may have been unplanned, others would have been stolen with a purpose. This is to some extent organized because these juveniles planned how to fence their goods, whether that was giving it to their neighbour or pawning it in a shop. Despite some exceptions, these juveniles generally stole relatively inexpensive items from public spaces but they also stole items which they could later fence. Many juveniles would have stolen due to opportunity, but it would be wrong to suggest that some juveniles did not steal in response to external demand. Notwithstanding the probable fluidity and informality of these exchanges, a market of goods cannot be ignored and neither can juvenile agency (Shore 1999b, 12). While there was some organization, given the circumstances and value of the items, these crimes *were* petty. However, the majority of these juveniles were not first-time offenders prior to transportation.

As research into nineteenth-century crime history has increasingly shown, these juvenile crimes were not always perpetrated due to poverty and distress. However, they were not hardened or dangerous criminals either. As pointed out by Shore (1999a, 47), juvenile offending was relatively mundane, but the causes were wide and varied. Opportunity, need, desperation, peer pressure and excitement all played a role in juvenile offending. Importantly, need through disease, abuse and neglect did not necessarily cause offending, since offenders with relatively stable and 'respectable' backgrounds existed (Shore 1999a, 47). This is demonstrated by juvenile offenders whose parents arranged Criminal Petitions on their behalf.[1] These parents often point to their own stable employment. Nevertheless, there was a contemporary prevailing stereotype of criminals and the idea of a 'criminal class' which was at its height in the nineteenth century, and juvenile offenders were a key subject in the debate (Shore 1999a, 35; Muncie 2009, 54). For example pickpocketing, a common juvenile offence, was viewed as a progressive step into the criminal career leading it to be a capital offence until 1808. In reality, the average juvenile offender did not resemble these professional groups (Shore 1999a, 55–59). Still, contemporaries feared that juvenile offenders would mature into burglars, and this was embedded in many arguments for penal reform and 'colonial retraining' (Shore 1999a, 61). Therefore, while they were not viewed as 'serious' offenders, they were associated by contemporaries with criminal *professionalism* and as being a breed apart (Wiener 1990, 31–33). Added to this was the belief that juveniles *could* be saved and reincorporated back into respectful society before they became hardened adult criminals (Shore 1999a, 1). This all fed into the belief that transportation was necessary to deal with this group of offenders.

The Magistrate Francis Const. Esq. wrote in 1818 that those who were actually transported were 'seldom [sent] for the first or second offence' (Evans & Nicholls 1984, 142). This magistrate also grouped 'pickpockets' with 'atrocious' and 'violent' criminals, thus highlighting the contemporary view of pickpockets as particularly problematic. He also added:

> Though the specific offence may be petty larceny, you sometimes on account of badness of character, sentence them to transportation – yes it is not so much the crime, as being well known to be dangerous characters. (cited in Evans & Nicholls 1984, 142)

This magistrate went on to equate 'badness of character' with previous offences. Certainly the majority of juveniles had previous offences and many were pickpockets. However, it was by no means certain that a pickpocket would be sentenced to transportation, or indeed be sent: 66 per cent of pickpockets were sentenced to transportation, and of those only 69 per cent were sent. It is in fact unclear why some were sent, while others were not. Nunn argues that bad behaviour and production on the hulk were factors linked with being chosen for transportation. When awaiting transportation, juveniles sewed prison garments; and based on the figures presented by the superintendent, John Capper, 'production levels on the juvenile hulks appear to have been quite substantial'. Nunn argues that while the work was unskilled, there was a vested interest in maintaining the most reliable workers on the *Euryalus*. Adding it was 'normal practice' to transport male juveniles above fourteen years of age (2015, 61). This research sampled juveniles who were fourteen and under, but it was found that of those who arrived in VDL, the majority were at the upper end of the age range: 80 per cent of the males (and 77 per cent of the females) were aged between thirteen and fourteen. Having said this, some were younger. Nunn argues that for those under fourteen who were transported, it was because it was noted on their indent that they were 'bad' or 'very bad', stating that: 'Placing certain juveniles on transports was an effective strategy of getting rid of the most disruptive inmates' (Nunn 2015, 61–62). Of the male juveniles under fourteen who were transported (there were eighteen), there was one juvenile who was referred to as 'bad' and another as 'indifferent and artful'. All others were described in positive terms: 'orderly', 'good', 'remarkably well' and 'very good'. Therefore, there were at least some exceptions.

While most of those transported had previous convictions, many were pickpockets, and they tended to be at the upper end of the age range, this was by no means necessary to be transported. The question remains: did their offending continue in the colony and how did this effect their lives?

Offending under sentence

To explore the colonial offences of the juvenile convicts they were categorized into severity levels. Here we are only concerned with offences recorded in the Conduct Records, offences committed later in their sentence and recorded elsewhere will be explored subsequently.[2]

Table 1 shows the breakdown of offences which is based on contemporary views of crime. What they reveal, unsurprisingly, is that these juveniles were more likely to commit 'minor' and 'medium' offences, than 'serious'

Table 1 Male juvenile convicts and their colonial offences

Severity	Examples	Average No. of Offences
Very Serious	burglary; bushranging; (attempted) murder; manslaughter	0.8
Serious	property offences; violent offences (excluding violence against prisoners which would make it a 'medium' offence); unnatural acts; non-consensual sexual offences	3
Medium	escaping; neglecting work; violent offences, which are either only threatened or attempted; consensual sexual offences; vagrancy; drunken behaviour	8
Minor	obscene language; quarrelling; communicating without authorization	4
	Total	16

offences – and that they were even less likely to commit 'very serious' offences. This was markedly less than their adult counterparts who were also transported to VDL, and less than other juveniles transported to VDL from the rest of Britain.[3] While the juveniles, traced from London, committed many offences, there are some provisos. They were initially sampled systematically from the *Old Bailey Proceedings*. However, those who could not be traced into freedom were excluded. There is likely to be an over-representation of offending caused by this sampling process. While tracing was sometimes assisted because of something as innocuous as an uncommon name, other times it was due to an extraordinary life. For example James Hudson was locally admired for his religious work which led to a very detailed obituary in the newspaper (*Case Study No.20*). Perhaps more challenging, it could also be because of a greater number of offences or more serious offending, and therefore more documentation. As in the case of Charles Brewer (*Case Study No.4*) who was repeatedly in the newspapers due to his high-profile offending career. These cases are exceptional. Nevertheless, it is inevitable that those with more offences will be more readily identified and, therefore, more readily traced. Consequently, the male juvenile sample may over-represent the offending of juvenile convicts transported to VDL.

While sampling bias maybe at play, accepting that the male juveniles had a high number of offences recorded against them allows the exploration of what is different about *this* group. What characteristics do these male juveniles have in common which contributed to their increased offending? And if it is accepted that this group consists of some of the most persistent offenders while under VDL colonial oversight, were they able to desist from crime afterwards and settle into colonial life despite it? There is the possibility that, as modern criminologists have theorized, the more severe the punishment for juvenile offenders the more likely they were to go on to repeat offending (McAra & McVie 2007). The impact of being transported away from family, friends and familiarity may have been greater on juveniles than their adult counterparts. The juveniles were all from London, and rural offenders transported in particular have been shown to go on to less offending in the colony in comparison with London convicts (Godfrey & Maxwell-Stewart 2016). Lastly, juveniles also inevitably spent a long period in the colony since they were sent at younger ages. It is reasonable to assume they potentially had a long time to offend in the colony. Consequently, the rate of offending is important and will be explored later in this chapter.

The females, unlike their male counterparts, did not go through a second sampling stage. All females fitting the criteria were traced.[4] As can be seen in Table 2, they committed no 'very serious' offences and relatively few 'serious offences'. The most commonly committed offences were of 'medium' severity.

Female juveniles committed fewer offences overall than the males in all but one severity level. They, on average, committed slightly more 'medium' offences than their male counterparts but they committed more offences than both adults and juvenile convicts of both sexes. The arrival of the female juveniles into the colony straddled the two convict management periods: the assignment and probationary period. However, this shift in management structure is of lesser concern for the females because while the management of female convicts did undergo modifications over time, the shift from assignment to probationary management was less dramatic for females than males (see Chapter 2 for more information). Still, they committed a high number of offences. As with

Table 2 Female juvenile convicts and their colonial offences

Severity Level	Average No. of Offences per Convict
Minor	3
Medium	8.7
Serious	1.5
Very Serious	0
Total	13.2

This table includes offences in Conduct Record only.

the males, an important factor is their geographical origin: being transported from London. Historians, including Godfrey and Maxwell-Stewart (2016), have argued that convicts sent from certain areas, especially London, were 'worse' with regard to behaviour and skills. Was this the case for these juveniles or are there other explanations such as the differing management of these convicts and different expectations placed on them? How did their youth factor into their offending; did the fact that they came from London and had a generally younger profile mean that they were less skilled and therefore struggled more in assignment, leading to more offences being recorded against them? The types of offences these juveniles were committing under sentence are just as important as the number.

Common offences

Being temporarily absent was the most common offence. This included being absent for the day but coming back of their own accord, and missing muster (not escaping or attempting to permanently abscond). While it is the most common offence, it is more common for female juveniles than males. This may reflect the fact that males at Point Puer would have found it more difficult to abscond than females in free-settler service.

The offences committed by female juveniles were less varied than for the males, and they were centred on not being where they should. This is demonstrated in the case of Susan Campbell (*Case Study No.*9). Female juveniles' most common offences were behavioural, as can be seen in Table 3. There were also female-specific offences, which by their nature only female convicts were punished for, for example having an illegitimate child and prostitution. However, they were relatively uncommon among this sample. Only two were known to have an illegitimate child and be punished for it through imprisonment in the female factory. And

Table 3 Most common offences, per convict, grouped by sample (from convict record only)

	Increasing in Number from Left to Right				
Female	drunk	misconduct	absconding	impertinence/ insolence	temporarily absent
Male	storage of contraband	disobedience of orders	impertinence/ insolence	misconduct	temporarily absent

there were only four incidences of females being in a brothel or being a prostitute. All other offences were not female-specific. However, there are some nuances. A female could also be brought before the courts by her husband. For example in the case of Caroline Watson, who struck her husband in the presence of another man. As a result, this offence was included in her Conduct Record and she was punished. As highlighted by Kavanagh and Snowden, what was private for the general population was subject to scrutiny for female convicts (2015, 201). Since none of the males were assigned to wives, no similar offences were committed by males while under sentence. But George Pickering (*Case Study No.2*) did go on to be punished for domestic violence after freedom. Like the females, common male offences were usually not felonies, for example storing contraband. This involved having possessions, such as clothing, food or tobacco without authorization. In fact, a common theme of these offences is that they were mainly status offences.

The national statistics of VDL shows a rise in minor offences, such as those common offences described above, and contemporaries, as shown by the statistical returns, attributed them to convicts (Anon 1836). Certainly, these juveniles did commit many non-serious offences. However, the same statistical returns also posited that this was due to an increase in the detection and punishment of minor offences, largely attributed to the introduction of the new police in 1827–1828. The increase in all minor offences, particularly from 1827, was also attributed to the implementation of police magistrates (Anon 1836). The suggestion here is that minor crime did not increase, it was simply more efficiently detected. Given the minor nature of much of the juveniles' offending, it may be that many of these offences were recorded due to similar administrative reasons. Juveniles were more likely to be in an institution and, therefore, be subject to easier detecting and processing of offences. It is also possible that masters were more prone to seek punishment of juveniles than adults reflecting societal norms. The chastisement of children was accepted in nineteenth-century society (Rowbotham 2017). Moreover, there may have been a relationship between the skills of convicts and the likelihood of punishment. The more skill and experience a convict had, the more valuable they were to an employer, and therefore the more likely the master would be to overlook less serious offending. When the annual maintenance bill for convicts increased in VDL, the number of convicts sentenced to hard labour in road and chain gangs by magistrates' benches increased: 'The effect was to shift the costs of maintaining convicts from the private to the public sector at the points when it became most advantageous to disinvest in unfree workers.' As Maxwell-Stewart points out, this trend exposes an important issue. Conduct Records are not the complete list of all indiscretions but are instead the product of a complex set of factors culminating in a decision to prosecute. That decision could be affected by many things including the convict's worth. Thus, convicts with skills that were not in demand in the colonial economy were at a greater risk of punishment. This is why the number of charges brought against serving prisoners was inversely correlated with colonial wage rates (2016, 426). Juveniles arrived with fewer skills and less work experience than their adult counterparts, thus increasing the chances that masters would be willing to seek their punishment in order to gain a replacement servant. This would lead to more offences being reported and processed for juvenile convicts.

Because juveniles were managed differently under sentence than their adult counterparts, which may have led to an increased chance of their offences being reported, offences committed outside the Conduct Record were explored. This allows for a fuller picture of their offending when removed from the VDL colonial conduct recording.

Offences not recorded in conduct record

The offending patterns so far discussed were extracted only from the Conduct Records and are therefore not all the offences committed. If juveniles migrated or had long periods of time before they reoffended, their Conduct Records were not updated. However, such information can be traced through newspapers and official records of other colonial territories. As can be seen in Table 4, there are 104 offences which were found in this way and they were committed by twenty-four juveniles (three were females). These are not the only offences committed after freedom; these are the offences which were committed that are not included in the Conduct Record.

Taking away those male juveniles who died under their initial servitude (a total of twelve), on average there were 1.03 offences per male. However, only twenty-one males went on to have offences recorded against them outside of their Conduct Record. The majority of these offences were of 'medium' and 'serious' severity. This is because 'minor' offences were less likely to reach the newspapers

Table 4 Juvenile offences not in conduct record categorized by severity

	Minor	Medium	Serious	Very Serious
Males	5	39	43	4
Females	5	6	2	0

The offences are taken from newspaper reports and other records *not* including VDL Conduct Records.

due to their less sensational nature. Moreover, as the severity of the offences increased, the details included in the articles increased, and consequently the more readily identifiable the offender becomes. Therefore, despite every effort, it is impossible to assert that all offences outside of the Conduct Record were either contemporaneously recorded or subsequently found. However, it is reasonable to assert that it becomes less likely an offence is missed as the severity of the offence increases. It follows then that the four 'very serious' offences, which were only committed by males, are likely to be the only 'very serious' offences. These include burglary, bushranging, piracy and murder. The latter was committed by James McAllister (*Case Study No.17*), and the former three offences were committed by one offender, Charles Brewer (*Case Study No.4*). Therefore, while there are four 'very serious' offences, there are only two 'very serious' offenders. There are forty-three 'serious' offences committed by the males outside of their Conduct Records. These include: theft (fifteen incidences); absconding (nine incidences); presenting a weapon (one incident); assaulting an authority figure (six incidences), e.g. a member of the watch, police or overseer; violence towards another person (seven incidences), i.e. a free person, not their master or another convict or member of authority; robbery (two incidences); uttering, forging and defrauding (one incident); wounding (one incident); riot or mutinous conduct (one incident). While many of these offences are serious, it is clear that offending outside of the Conduct Record was carried out by a small number of these juveniles. Moreover, repeated offending under the VDL administrative gaze was not necessarily indicative of offending when removed from said gaze or vice versa. This is exemplified in the case of George Pickering who had few offences in his Conduct Record, but went on to commit many offences after migration.

Case Study No.2: George Pickering

Aged thirteen, George was convicted in 1840 of simple larceny. He stole a pair of shoes worth one shilling and nine pence while he was living in Whitechapel. George pleaded guilty and was given seven years' transportation. It was not his first offence. George had been previously convicted and punished with six days' imprisonment, as well as a previous acquittal. He was no stranger to the authorities. His father, Thomas, petitioned on his behalf through stressing his youth, good character, and blaming bad and designing associates. The Criminal Petition also pointed out Thomas's own good character and how he had done everything to put his family on an honest path. Further pleading that George was suffering from remorse and wished to retrieve his character and become a useful member of society. Moreover, he stated that he had heard in some cases that mercy was shown on the grounds of age and hoped this would be extended to George by sending him to Parkhurst Prison and not transporting him to Australia. This would allow for George to be restored to the 'bosom of his family' upon release. The petition had several signatories – including the prosecutor. Nevertheless, the petition failed and George was separated from his family. He would never see his mother Jane and his father, who was a wine cooper, or his siblings again. In September 1841 the *Lord Goderich* set sail from Portsmouth on a four-month voyage to Hobart, with George in the hold.

When George arrived, he could neither read nor write; he was a Protestant and was described as 'orderly' and 'indifferent' by the hulk and ship authorities, respectively. His first offence in the colony was not until April 1847, when he 'wilfully' assaulted George Moore. For this offence he received one month's imprisonment with hard labour. Later that year he was recorded as fighting in a public street and representing himself as free, for which he was given six days' solitary confinement. Both of these offences were after he had received a ticket of leave (received in September 1846). George was free-by-servitude in 1847 but despite this initial low offending rate, he went on to repeat offending.

Domestic violence was a repeat offence by George and took varied forms. George was brought up on a warrant for wife desertion and destroying the clothes of his children while intoxicated. He was required to find sureties of fifty pounds for each and to keep the peace for twelve months (*The Age* 17 April 1854, 3). George was also brought up on a warrant charged with using threatening language to his wife and was remanded, but his wife did not appear to prosecute (*The Age* 22 January 1855, 5; *The Age* 23 January 1855, 5). He was only recently out of gaol for beating his wife, and charged with threatening her again, he was let off after a promise never to insult her again (*The Argus* 23 January 1855, 5). On another occasion, described in *The Age* as 'a violent character, who had the appearance of a digger', George was charged with threatening to stab his wife and assaulting a constable. Again she did not appear against him and he was discharged with a caution from the Bench. His Worship observing that if George came again before them he would most likely be sent to gaol for six months (4 September 1855, 5).

George was repeatedly in trouble for violent behaviour. *The Age* reported that on hearing he was going to be arrested he declared he would not go without a fight and gave a violent blow to the officer's chest. In 'self-defence' George wielded himself vigorously with the help of his friends, who were described as pickpockets and oyster men. Eventually he was hauled off. His wife, at whose instance he was arrested, appeared against him. George had just been released from the gaol and went directly to where his wife resided and brutally ill-treated her. His wife, who supported herself by washing, had her hard work thrown into the streets by George. They had two children, one of whom had their leg broken by George in a fit of drunkenness on a previous occasion. George was sentenced to three months' hard labour, and at the conclusion of the term was ordered to pay sureties of twenty-five pounds and to keep the peace towards his wife for twelve months (*The Age* April 1856, 3). *The Argus* simultaneously reported that he was a wife beater and 'a violent vagabond'. Adding that it took five constables to take him to the watch house (24 July 1856, 5).

In 1857 he was charged with stealing fourteen shillings from the Manchester hotel bar, where he had been employed as a barman. Because of insufficient evidence the case was dismissed but in 1859 he was recorded as being 'idle and disorderly' and given twelve months' imprisonment with hard labour. In October 1857 George was described in the newspapers as 'a savage' and was charged by Mr Hogan with violently ill-using his wife.[5] She was beaten and driven out of her house. She fled for refuge to the Russell Street Barracks. George then proceeded to tear up her dresses and break her crockery. On being taken into custody he assaulted a constable. George is described as being 'no stranger to the police court'. Mr Stuart stated that the court was at a loss as to know what to do with George, or how to 'devise the means of saving his wife and family from further brutality'. It was finally decided to bind the prisoner over for six months in two sureties of fifty pounds. George stated he could not procure the sureties. Mr Stuart said, 'It would be a matter of surprise to him if he could', such 'conduct as his deserved that he should meet with imprisonment as the alternative' (*The Age* 24 October 1857, 6).

In the early 1860s George was still being convicted of domestic violence. He was convicted of an aggravated case of assault and simultaneously described as 'a rough looking middle aged man', and was charged by his wife of deserting her and her child for two years, and providing no kind of subsistence for them. Giving him another chance, his wife brought her husband to her residence in the hope he would remain and support his family. Instead 'he got mad drunk and beat his wife fearfully about the head and shoulders and kicked her in the abdomen.' His wife's cries fortunately brought help, one or more of whom attempted to separate George from his wife. The constable arrived but a man named Christopher Collis then saved Pickering from another young man named George Ward. Ward had been holding Pickering for the constables' arrival. Collis attacked Ward ferociously and ultimately Pickering got away. Ward ran to get more police when he was again brutally attacked by friends of Pickering and Collis. Both were shortly afterwards taken into custody. Pickering was fined forty shillings and ordered to find sureties of twenty pounds to keep the peace towards his wife for six months. He 'stoutly intimated to the bench that he was unable to do this', and was informed the alternative was six months' imprisonment (*The Age* 3 August 1860, 7). The following year George was again charged with being drunk and threatening the life of his wife and ordered to find sureties of twenty-five pounds to keep peace for six months (*The Age* 7 February 1861, 6; *The Argus* 7 February 1861, 6). He was, on top of these domestic incidences, time and time again fined for drunkenness.

In June 1864 he was convicted of malicious wounding, for which he was given two years' imprisonment. He had stabbed James Miller with an oyster knife. Both the accused and the victim claimed they were not involved in the incident. Instead two witnesses stated they saw the struggle. Consequently, George was committed for trial and Miller was detained for stealing boots which instigated the altercation (*The Cornwall Chronicle* May 1862, 3). The newspapers described this as a 'serious case of stabbing'. A gathering mob attracted the attention of a sergeant. Miller was lying on the ground with a deep wound on his head and was covered in blood. When Pickering was searched, an oyster knife was found. Miller was sent to the hospital where it was ascertained he had also been stabbed in the back of his right shoulder. Although serious, they were not dangerous injuries, and he recovered (*The Age* May 1862, 5). George had only been recently discharged from prison, and the prosecutor himself was a ticket of leave man. When in court Miller had forgotten the circumstances of the assault. The constable who had arrested Pickering stated that he knew the details very well at the time and so Miller was held in contempt of court to sharpen his memory (*The Age* March 1862, 6).

Changing tact, in 1865 he was convicted of stealing money from the person at the Melbourne General Sessions and given five years on the roads. In 1871 he was convicted of stealing a blanket and given three months' imprisonment. Later that year he was convicted of 'intent to commit a felony' which resulted in twelve months' hard labour. This was followed by a 'robbery in company' in 1875 for which he was given seven years on the public works. Subsequently, he was convicted of the less serious offence of being 'drunk and disorderly' for which he was given only three days' imprisonment.

George was a prolific offender after his migration to Melbourne; he did have a family but he abused them, but he does seem to have held down employment. George was described as a fisherman, seaman and oysterman at different points.[6] While being only 4 foot when he was transported, he grew to 5.4 feet by adulthood. His ill-treated wife Jane (formerly Askeet) married him in 1852. This marriage took place only a few years before his offending began on the mainland. They had at least two children, but George died alone in the Benevolent Society in 1884 of progressive paralysis, aged sixty.

Only one female did not survive until freedom and, therefore, did not have the opportunity to commit offences and have them recorded outside of her Conduct Record. The majority of females did not offend outside of their Conduct Record. The majority of these offences were 'medium' level offences, and only two offences were 'serious' (theft and violence towards another person, i.e. a free person). The details of these female and male offences tell us that 23 per cent of juveniles carried on offending – not simply after freedom but also outside of the ties of their convict life. Of those males who did have offences recorded outside of their Conduct Record, 52 per cent had migrated and one had headed for the bush. Of the females who had offences recorded outside of their Conduct Record, two out of three had migrated. Despite many of these juveniles migrating, they were unable to achieve the fresh start they sought. However, these offences were concentrated among a few juveniles suggesting that most, when removed by time and space, were able to achieve a 'fresh start'. It can be argued that the offences not included in their Conduct Record cannot be identified in their entirety, which is indeed likely to be the case. Nevertheless, it is fair to assert that the majority (at least) did stop offending. Moreover, for those juveniles whose offences were located outside of their Conduct Record, it is unlikely that any but the very minor offences, which would be less likely to be recorded, were not evidenced in the newspapers. There is no reason to suggest that some offences could not be found for otherwise identifiable individuals. Still, the number of offences located outside of the Conduct Record may be under-represented, despite the great care taken. Simultaneously, since the male juveniles were only traced if information after freedom was found, the amount of offending by this group is likely to over-represent male juvenile offending after freedom. Therefore, on balance, the wider picture of offending after freedom for the male juveniles is one of desistance in adulthood when removed from VDL colonial oversight.

Rate of offending

Since the total number of offences committed by an offender is affected by the length of time they had to commit offences, this chapter will now turn to the *rate* of offending. Table 5 shows the rate of offending calculated at different points, including the rate of offending within their Conduct Record when they were under VDL colonial oversight (pre- and post-freedom); the rate of offending for their colonial offending period (up until their last known offence); and the rate of offending for their whole life (from birth to death).

Table 5 Rate of juvenile offending at different life-course points

	Rate of Offending – in Conduct Record					Rate of Offending – in Offending Period					Rate of Offending – Based on Whole Life
	Minor	Medium	Serious	Very Serious	All	Minor	Medium	Serious	Very Serious	All	
Male	0.87	1.45	0.6	0.01	2.91	0.86	1.46	0.62	0.01	2.94	1.64
Female	0.42	1.26	0.29	0	1.92	0.44	1.27	0.23	0	1.94	0.27

As can be seen in Table 5, the rate of offending of male juveniles was higher during the time that their Conduct Records were updated as compared with their rate of offending over their whole lives. While this was not true of all offenders, such as George Pickering (*Case Study No.2*), this was the general trend. The rate of offending of those who had offences recorded outside of their Conduct Records (looking at only that offending) was 0.15. This shows that those who did carry on offending, when removed from the time and/or space of their conduct recorders, offended at a lower rate. This suggests that when the offenders were removed, either through time and/or space from VDLs penal authority, not only did the majority (79 per cent) stop offending, but also even if they carried on offending the rate slowed down. The rate of offending over their whole lives is also lower. This highlights that these juveniles rarely offended up until their deaths and when they did the rate slowed markedly. When comparing the offending within the Conduct Record with the offending of adult convicts generally, it is clear that the greater number of offences committed by male juveniles is not simply due to a longer period spent in VDL – as their offending rate is high. While the rate of offending within the Conduct Record is revealing, the offending rate over the offender's whole life is more informative. This can be seen in the following case study:

Case Study No.3: John Patching

Born in approximately 1816, John Patching was thirteen when he was convicted of pickpocketing a handkerchief worth three shillings, in Regent Street, from an attorney named Nathaniel George. For this offence he was given a sentence of fourteen years' transportation. There were two accomplices who were not caught. There are no previous offences known to be committed by John. While kept on the hulk he was described as: 'bad twice'. He was transported aboard the *Gilmore* after a thirty-six-month wait, in 1832. He was described as being sixteen on arrival. Unfortunately, we do not know whether he was able to read and write before he was transported. However, he did go on to be able to sign the marriage register.

John's first offence in the colony was for disobedience of orders and insolence while on assignment. For this he was punished with six weeks on the treadmill. Within the first year he was moved to a road party after a series of absences. Following this, he had his original sentence extended by two years for absconding. Later, due to 'refusing to work until he received some clothing' he was imprisoned with labour in Richmond, and it was further recommended that he be put in a chain gang. Again he absconded and he had his original term extended by three years. It was still only 1834 by this point. After breaking out of Richmond Gaol to abscond, he was sent to Port Arthur for two years. Now in Port Arthur, he was ordered to be placed in irons. After a series of offences involving the damaging and losing of government property, he was then insolent to his overseer, was idle, had stolen property in his possession, and then he was under 'strong suspicion of [a] felony'. This latter charge was dismissed, and he was placed back in the assignable party in 1838. Unfortunately, by October, he was brought before the court on a charge of theft for which he was found guilty and sent to Port Arthur for three years in irons. His last offence was in 1840, again for absenteeism for which he was given two days' solitary confinement.

Finally, John was free-by-servitude in 1847, after 144 months in the colony. After just four months of freedom, John made his way from Launceston to Port Fairy via the *Essington* ship. He did not go alone. Before his freedom he was married in 1842 to Mary Ann Miley. Also a convict, Mary was seventeen when they married at Launceston. While they may have had children, none were recorded. Unusually for convict marriages Mary Ann and John's marriage made the papers. The couple were the first to be wed in their church. John died in Great Western, Victoria, in 1882 aged sixty-seven. During his years of freedom there were no offences recorded against him. As a result, his offending rate dropped from 5 in his Conduct Record to 0.5 when including his whole life.

The rate of female juvenile offending was lower than the males but the pattern was the same. When female juveniles were removed from time and/or space in which the Conduct Records were updated, their offending decreased (when looking at those offences only). Yet, overall their offending rate was high, and there is no sampling bias which would account for the increased offending rate. This means other aspects need to be turned to. The youngest probationary juvenile (taken from a 1 in 25 sample of all females transported to VDL) was sixteen, where as the juveniles were, in 50 per cent of the cases, under sixteen. This reflects the practice of transporting London juvenile offenders at younger ages. This may have affected their ability to cope in assignment. If they lacked the skills and experience of being a domestic servant or nurse maid, their masters may have been more prone to report non-serious offences. Certainly the female juveniles were recorded as committing many 'minor' and 'medium' offences which led to them being returned by their masters – who rarely took them back after their punishment.

Desistance?

Assessing whether these juveniles stopped offending is important to understand the lives of these juveniles. However, given regulatory conditions in which bad language and falling asleep in church were recorded as offences and punished, it is perhaps surprising that 10 per cent of these juveniles managed to avoid committing any offence at all. By focusing on summary offences heard by the police and superintendents of convicts during 1848, it is immediately clear that convicts under sentence committed more offences than free persons. This reflects the added surveillance and restrictions placed on convicts. As such the base line to which these juveniles reoffending is measured needs to be considered. Consequently, desistance here will be measured as follows: did these juveniles carry on committing offences up until their death and, if so, did they slow down in their offending? Meaning, did they commit fewer offences over time and did the severity of those offences decrease? The opening of convict institutions, such as Hobart Barracks in the 1820s, marked the beginning of the end of certain freedoms convicts had enjoyed, including having their own houses and domestic arrangements. This was a 'direct assault' on the convict private sphere. From this point, convicts found out of institutions or away from the property of their assigned masters were more likely to be regarded with suspicion (Reid 2007, 131). When looking at the summary offences for VDL as a whole, the following six offences markedly decreased from 1838: absconding, absence without leave, disobedience of orders, drunkenness, insolence and neglect of duty. Whereas the remaining offences increased: insubordination, idleness and misdemeanours (Ewing 1843, XV). These changes reflect the change in management of convicts whereby there was increased surveillance and decreased freedoms. Governor Arthur addressed the inability to punish convicts further by systematically expanding the police and judiciary, and splitting the colony into districts. With the formal separation of VDL from NSW and the establishment of the Courts of Quarter Sessions and Supreme Court in 1824, the Governor's authority was more secure. This coincided with the creation of a number of criminal offences, some of which were exclusively aimed at convicts and the institution of summary jurisdiction over convict servants. All led to an increased difficulty for masters to overlook their servants' offences (Reid 2007, 129). From 1820 onwards, the punitive resources of the state expanded with gaols, watch houses, convict barracks and houses of correction, for both female and male convicts, as well as penal settlements for males (Reid 2007, 130). This demonstrates the increased ability of the state to control and punish convicts.

The 10 per cent of juveniles with no reoffending equate to only nine individuals, five of whom died under sixteen, none of whom had the chance to offend due to dying either on the voyage or soon after arrival. This leaves only four individuals who did not offend in the colony. There is no doubt that the added surveillance of the penal colony increased offending. Therefore, a more important question than the number of offences is: did they carry on offending up until their death? Excluding the female who died en route, no female offended up until death. However, 29 per cent of males continued offending until death. Of those who offended throughout the whole of their lives, all apart from ten individuals slowed down in their offending. Therefore, 10 per cent of male juveniles carried on offending up until their death and they did *not* slow down. One of these juveniles was Charles Brewer (*Case Study No.4*). The majority of juveniles did not continue offending in adulthood. This is reflected in the findings of Godfrey et al. (2017) who found that nineteenth-century English juvenile crime history was 'a "crime history" dominated by desistance' when examining the lives of juveniles back home in the late nineteenth century. This is in contrast to adult experiences of desistence detailed in cognate historical studies (Godfrey et al. 2007, 2010) and more contemporary studies (Maruna 2001).

Conclusion

Male juveniles were more likely to commit 'minor' and 'medium' offences than 'serious' and 'very serious' offences. It is acknowledged that there is bias in favour of over-representing high offending in this group. However, while they committed many offences, they did not commit a high number of 'very serious' offences. Moreover, the fast rate of offending suggests that their high number of offences were not simply due to a longer period in the colony. Nonetheless, when removed from the Vandemonian colonial gaze, the majority did not offend. And, of those who did, the majority were 'serious' offenders and there were two offenders who went on to become 'very serious' offenders. Not only did the majority of the juveniles not have offences recorded outside of their Conduct Record, but also the offending rate slowed down for those who did. Despite some exceptions, the offending rate of their whole lives was also lower. Therefore, male juveniles were generally frequent petty offenders while under sentence, but most of them stopped offending after freedom and removal from their colonial servitude. The female juveniles present a different offending picture and they offended less than their male counterparts. They committed no 'very serious' offences, but similarly to the male juveniles, they were more likely to commit 'medium' and 'minor' level offences. The majority did not go on to offend after removal from the colonial gaze, and of those who did only two committed 'serious' offences. None of the female juveniles carried on offending throughout their lives. Despite the higher number of offences and the quick offending rate, female juveniles both slowed down and ultimately stopped offending before death. Maxwell-Stewart (2016, 427) found that female expirees were less likely to be rearrested than males. This is significant since, when looking at all female convicts, females confessed to worse offending prior to transportation. Maxwell-Stewart argues that transportation was effective at breaking cycles of female offending (2016, 427). While it is true that all female juveniles eventually stopped offending, it would be wrong to suggest that transportation broke *their* offending cycle. Both female and male juveniles offended repeatedly, and in quick succession, during servitude. However, despite this, after freedom most turned away from crime.

It is likely that the high number of 'minor' and 'medium' offences in both male and female juveniles while under sentence was affected by the assignment masters and the increased time sent in institutionalized settings (in female factories and Point Puer particularly). Both situations led to the reporting of relatively non-serious offending in juveniles more likely. This increased tendency to report juveniles is likely to be due to a mixture of increased surveillance of the group and a decreased willingness to overlook the offences observed. This decreased likelihood to overlook offences is likely to be due to the normalization of reprimanding children for poor behaviour and performance, as well as the decreased likelihood that these juveniles would possess the skills, experience and competencies that were wanted. As already noted, the less skill a convict had the greater the likelihood that a convict would be reported for offending. This reasoning is further enforced by the finding that most juveniles did not go on to offend outside of their Conduct Record, and even of those who did most desisted from crime before death.

4

Punishment

Where a master in England finds fault, the master in Australia threatens the lash; where the master here grows angry, the master there swears, and invokes the lash; where here he talks of turning away, there he procures the infliction of the lash; for idleness, the lash; for carelessness, the lash; for insolence, the lash; for drunkenness, the lash; for disobedience, the lash; wherever there is reason, and wherever there is not reason, the lash. Ever on the master's tongue, and ever in the prisoner's ear, just as he himself urges his drowsy bullocks, sounds the lash, the lash! – the lash!

(Bishop Ullathorne cited in Wolter 2014, 202)

The punishments these juveniles endured will be investigated to further understand their experience under servitude. From hard labour and flogging to confinement in the cells and extended sentences – what did these juveniles experience? Governor Arthur's scale of punishment was, as he explained in 1830, as follows:

> On the one hand [it descends] from the least severe species of punishment, in the service of the settlers, by regular steps, through the usual public service, road-gangs, chain-gangs, the penal settlements of Port Arthur and Macquarie Harbour (a last alteration, next to capital punishment), and ascending on the other, by encouraging to reform, through the links of probationary service in the field, and other descriptions of duty in the public service, distinguished by some mark of conferring different degrees of liberty by conditional, and lastly by absolute pardons. (cited in Reid 2007, 130)

Alternatively, the hierarchy of punishment at Point Puer, from the point of view of the authorities, was as follows: first, confinement to the muster ground or to a particular separate part of the jail, depriving them of their usual hours of play; second, sleeping in a silent apartment which included confinement to the cell except during the hours of labour; third, confinement to the 'Old Jail' which prevented them from mixing with the general class at trades or at school, and restricted play. They were then taught for one hour in the morning, employed during the day in breaking up new ground or in working on the land, and during their spare time they were confined to the yards. They were expected to labour for two hours a day longer than the general class, and had no dumpling at dinner, but an equal weight of bread was given instead; fourth, confinement to the crime jail which may have included chains. They were then employed during the day in breaking stones; fifth, solitary confinement on bread and water for any period not exceeding fourteen days; sixth, corporal punishment to the extent of thirty-six lashes; seventh, in 'very bad cases' they were transferred to Port Arthur (Horne 1843, 5).

Views about the harshness or otherwise of punishment were always contested and changed over time. The House of Lords Select Committee on prison discipline in 1863 concluded that solitary confinement should be used as a substitute for hard labour where possible, stating that a term of three to seven days' solitary confinement could be substituted for twenty-one days with hard labour (House of Lords 1863, vi). This is partially due to the difficulty of making hard labour a uniform punishment in prisons. They urged in their report that hard labour should only include the crank and tread mill, and where necessary the shot-drill. Industrial occupation was seen as so varied in amount and character that it was less penal and fatiguing to the offender (House of Lords 1863, vii). They also suggested that corporal punishment should be reserved for hardened criminals who repeated offences, thereby implying that solitary confinement was a lesser punishment than corporal punishment (House of Lords 1863, viii). However, views expressed in the report varied greatly. Major General Sir Joshua Jebb stated that he felt solitary confinement alone was not as severe a punishment as alternated with hard labour, whereas W Merry Esq stated that:

> I believe it is the most terrible punishment to a man, but every hour that he is taken out of that cell is a relief, a man would jump mast high to get upon the treadwheel rather than be confined in a solitary cell.

W. A. Guy Esq of Millbank prison, on the other hand, argued that solitary confinement may lead someone on the 'verge of unsoundness of mind' to develop it, but that is the risk of imprisonment and not the fault or concern of the prison or its staff (House of Lords 1863, 370). Despite differing opinions, this report concluded that solitary confinement was the way forward. This may partly have been due to the greater ability to standardize the punishment. Yet, it was found not to be standardized in the colonies. Hence it is very unlikely that other punishments such as hard labour were standardized in VDL. While this parliamentary report is based on anecdotal evidence of those working within the prison system, it does reveal the *ad hoc* nature of punishments. Hard labour, for instance, was varied in the British prison system in the 1860s and so was likely to have been even more varied in VDL. It is therefore difficult to find the effects of hard labour on mortality when that hard labour would have been very different from person to person. Some forms of hard labour may have affected the life expectancy of convicts but it is difficult, if not impossible, to uncover which forms of hard labour these would have been. Such details are generally not noted in the Conduct Records. Solitary confinement too would have depended on who the punishment was enforced by. While solitary confinement generally meant no communication, this was not necessarily the case as chaplains and warders were able to converse with these offenders, and where cells were not fit for purpose it was even possible for offenders to converse with each other. Therefore, the experience of punishment was so varied per juvenile; it would need a far larger sample to uncover any connections with mortality. What will be demonstrated in this chapter is that this sample of juveniles did receive a great deal of punishment.

Knowing how the authorities ranked punishment informs us which punishments *they* thought were the most severe, but since none of the juveniles left behind diaries or written testimony we cannot know how individual experience differed. Helen Johnston (2008, 78) argues that prison policy and practice were 'ambiguous, contradictory and paradoxical' in Britain, and that this is exemplified by prison officers working in these institutions. The same can be said of overseers and masters in VDL. Johnston points out that, while the magistrates and policy makers may sentence offenders, it was the officers who had most contact with them (Johnston 2008, 78). It is inevitable that, whether a warder or overseer, as individuals they were different and so punishment for the offenders under these individuals will have differed and, therefore, so did the experience of punishment. For example, at Birmingham Gaol the governor, surgeon and visiting justices were severely admonished for the cruel regime which had resulted in the death of a fifteen-year-old prisoner. As a result of this incident some of the subordinate officers were dismissed. Whereas one warder was praised for the 'great sympathy' he exhibited towards the prisoners (Johnston 2008, 89). This demonstrates how in one institution, at one time, there were varying practices. Such a phenomenon would be amplified at an earlier period in the colonies. Moreover, as found by Ginneken and Hayes (2017), in their study of contemporary offenders, 'there is no agreement among offenders in their interpretation of punishment', and 'the experienced severity of a punishment is contingent on the interpretation of punishment' as well as individual circumstance. Punishment in practice is the interaction between offender and the punishment itself and as such differs between offenders (2017, 74). If their perception of the punishment is different presumably so too will the effects of the punishment, in both the short and long term. Still, it is possible to build up a picture of the punishment for these juveniles.

Male juveniles

Building up a picture of the punishments convicts endured is important. This is because any punishment would have affected the convict lives and possibly their life-outcomes from their recidivism or desistance, to marriage and migration. Table 6 shows the punishments endured by male juveniles. Broadly speaking, the most common type of punishment for males was hard labour, flogging and confinement to the cells, whereas the punishment of the treadmill and fines was relatively uncommon.

As Maxwell-Stewart points out, it is hard to 'comprehend the savagery of such a punishment' as flogging. The convict would be stripped to the waist, legs splayed and arms secured above the head, and fixed to a frame. The lash was made of nine whipcord strands with knots that had been stiffened with wax or wire (2008, 79). Often for juvenile males stationed at Point Puer, the punishment differed slightly. This involved being struck on the breech with a bundle of sticks forming a 'birch rod'. Boys were strapped to a birching pony, where they were bent over and stripped naked from the waist downwards. This of course 'heightened the humiliation' (Nunn 2017, 163). This sample would have endured both scenarios. Despite Booth's declaration that he 'never resorts to the lash except as a measure of dernier resort', corporal punishment was frequently used at Point

Table 6 Male juvenile punishments

	No. of Lashes	Cells (Days)	Fine (Shillings)	Sentence Extended (Days)	Tread Wheel (Days)	Hard Labour (Days)
Average per Convict	62	31	2	107	4	445

Information gathered from Conduct Records only.

Puer. In 1839, 2709 offences were committed at Point Puer, of which 374 were punished with corporal punishment (Nunn 2017, 163). While the punishments for juveniles were not carried out all at one time (the fewest number of lashes given at one time was twelve) the most common number given at one time was twenty-five. This would have inflicted severe physical pain and caused bruising and bleeding. After examining a seven-year-old boy who had received only four strokes of the 'lesser' punishment of the birch, Sir Walter Foster, a medical doctor, described the effects:

> I saw the boy two or three days after the infliction of this punishment, and his little back was covered with wounds which extended right through the skin to the muscles, and not only was his back a mass of rawness, but the wounds had come round to the front of the abdomen, and they had cut down to the muscle on the front of his frame. (cited in Radzinowicz & Hood 1990, 717)

While flogging is seen as abhorrent in today's society and was contested by some contemporaries, it was a common punishment. The arguments for flogging were that it allowed for: the infliction of immediate physical pain (although this was seen as the remnants of medieval torture by its opponents); humiliation (though it was seen as brutalizing by its opponents) – what Bentham termed a 'characteristic punishment' which was a punishment appropriate to the perceived nature of the offender as a distinct criminal type; the punishment was quick and cheap (an aspect humanitarians preferred to the alternative in which offenders lingered in gaols); 'active public revulsion'; and lastly, its deterrent role for those witnessing the spectacle (Radzinowicz & Hood 1990, 699–702). Only from 1862 was flogging in public abolished (Radzinowicz & Hood 1990, 689). However, it had ended for females in 1817 (after being in decline since the 1770s) and had declined for adult males from the 1830s (Old Bailey Online, 2017). Yet, even as late as 1874, it was believed by some that flogging exercised 'perhaps stronger moral influence than any other power in the world ... the lessons which are taught by discomfort and suffering are wonderfully valuable' as written by barrister Fitzjames Stephen (Radzinowicz & Hood 1990, 702). Indeed, it was not until 1920 that a Home Office Report concluded that corporal punishment of juveniles was largely ineffective as a means of deterring youths from re-offending. Although it remained in widespread use for boys, it rose significantly during the two world wars until the passage of the Criminal Justice Act in 1948 (Gard 2009, 115–123). Still, despite its advocates, over the course of the nineteenth century attitudes were changing. Referring to juveniles in particular, Horne pointed out:

> Corporal punishment has the same effect here [Point Puer] as elsewhere. It tends to degrade and harden, and after having been twice or thrice inflicted is evidently useless. Some boys take a pride in enduring all that can be given them, and consider flogging a manly sort of punishment as it is generally inflicted upon grown up Convicts. When anyone seems to feel its severity he loses caste in the eyes of his companions who jeeringly tell him that they could take as much upon their faces. (Horne 1843, 6)

Alexander Maconochie, a penal reformer, asserted that settlers had developed a taste for flogging and hard labour, and that such punishments were ordered lightly for non-serious offences. Flogging, in particular, was preferred because it resulted in less work interruption (Reid 2007, 170). 'The "effect of the lash is not confined to the marks" on a man's "back" but rather "enters his soul"', stated former colonist Charles Rowcroft (Reid 2007, 171). Flogging was deemed to have powerful debilitating effects. It was said to defy natural masculine independence. It also violated the corporeal integrity of the convict: 'the wiry cords struck and eat their fill of the flesh and gore of the wretched man' remarked Ullathorne – 'the scourge drinks the blood of their flesh' and 'devours the spirit of their manhood' (Reid 2007, 229). Flogging, declared the exiled Chartist leader John Frost, was a contest between flogger, a man who 'felt a gratification in inflicting and witnessing human misery', and the man who still retained his natural feelings of pride and self-respect (Reid 2007, 230). Conversely, according to Shergold, the lash was used judiciously in colonial Australia and he asserts that there is little evidence of a society terrorized by corporal punishment (1988, 11). Selecting 1835 as a starting point, the peak year of floggings, the probability of being beaten every year during a five-year sentence was 0.001; and roughly two-thirds of all convicts received one or no floggings during servitude. The official statistics on corporal punishment disprove the popular picture of convictism as a society where workers were demoralized physically and psychologically by the whip. Physical violence in Australia was no greater than in the British army or navy, and less than for American slaves (Shergold 1988, 11). Compared with the convict system, drunkenness, absence without leave and violence towards officers earned the death sentence in the army (Nicholas 1988, 181). Physical violence against child workers and apprentices was a daily occurrence in early-nineteenth-century Britain (Shergold 1988, 11). In an official report to the Molesworth committee, it stated that fifty lashes with the regulation cat were equal to one hundred lashes using a military cat (Evans & Nicholls 1984, 56). Yet, even if flogging was uncommon for the general convict population, it was *not* uncommon for these juveniles under study. On average the male juveniles received sixty-two lashes each during the period their Conduct Records were updated. However, the spread of the punishment was not equal. Thomas Mihan received 425 lashes, compared with another who received only 12. This highlights the marked difference in experience for these juveniles. While the majority of these juveniles (65 per cent) were flogged, and the majority of those who were flogged (69 per cent) had under one-hundred lashes, twenty male juveniles were flogged over one-hundred times.

The juveniles certainly underwent more lashes on average than their adult counterparts. Similarly, at Point Puer, one-third of the boys were flogged in 1835 and 1836, and half in 1837 and 1838. They were subject to severe corporal punishment (Shaw 1966, 244). Therefore, it was not just the juveniles in this sample but also juveniles at Point Puer generally who were flogged relatively frequently. While it cannot be ignored that juveniles did commit a high number of offences, there is a suggestion that it was seen as acceptable to flog juveniles to discipline them. Despite opposition to flogging of adults, often those same individuals did not oppose flogging the young. Unlike Horne, many in authority did not feel the degrading effect flogging had on adults extended to juveniles. This was largely because 'the chastisement of the young was, by tradition, a well-established method of child discipline'. Flogging for adult men was seen as a last resort, but for juveniles it was placed at the other end of the scale. The idea being that a 'short, sharp punishment' was better than periods of imprisonment for the young (Radzinowicz & Hood 1990, 712). A number of leading commentators on juveniles, including Matthew Hill, were doubtful that lower class juvenile delinquents could count as children – their depravity had aged them and the only way to redeem them was to reduce them to childhood once again, 'by force if necessary' (Rowbotham 2017, 101). Many studies of Victorian and Edwardian childhood agree that corporal punishment was a significant factor in child-rearing strategies (Rowbotham 2017, 102). It was held that a parent was behaving lovingly by chastising the young, to discipline them through infliction of physical pain so that they would become useful members of society (Rowbotham 2017, 105). Such normalization of punishment against juveniles in the home was also reflected in the courts where the ordering of judicial corporal punishment was frequently handed out to those up to fourteen but was more rarely used for adults (Rowbotham 2017, 105).

Solitary confinement was a punishment in which offenders were confined in the cells alone, and communication was prohibited. Seen as the 'penal panacea', by the late 1830s there was serious consideration to set up a separate system of confinement throughout Britain as an alternative to transportation (Radzinowicz & Hood 1990, 490–491). As early as 1842 there were 'voices of dissent', including Charles Dickens, who was unconvinced by the 'miracles' brought by isolation.

Dickens noted the consecutive phases of 'initial shock, through depression, over-sensibility, detachment from reality, placid adjustment, down to helpless mental state of dissolved responsibility' by the time individuals were released from solitary confinement (Radzinowicz & Hood 1990, 492). Henry Mayhew and John Binny argued that separate confinement eventually produced 'long suffering and deep mental affliction'. Indeed, the Pentonville Chaplain, Joseph Kingsmill, admitted the number of converted was over-rated (Radzinowicz & Hood 1990, 503). However, not only could solitary confinement (in the early days especially) be enforced to different degrees, but also Conduct Records did not always specify 'solitary' when recording the sentencing of convicts sent to the cells. Another issue was the availability of appropriate buildings. For example there was no means of solitary confinement at Port Arthur until 1835 (Shaw 1966, 211). Horne, in referring to Point Puer, stated that 'solitary confinement is a punishment which seems more severely felt when of any duration, as the diet is merely bread and water and communication with their companions is as much as possible prevented' (Horne 1843, 6). Yet, he stated, when referring to solitary confinement at Point Puer:

> I can only say that two boys are sometimes found in one of the separate cells in the morning, and that I have heard the boys in the solitary cells keep up a conversation at the full pitch of their voices during the middle of the day. They sometimes break out of them and abscond, and at other times remove boards so that provisions may be conveyed to them from without. In short the whole is a mockery of separate or solitary confinement. (Horne 1843, 2–3)

It would be wrong to suggest that all incidences of 'to the cells 24 hours' or even 'one month in separate working cells' were *true* solitary confinement. When speaking of prisons in Britain, Johnston (2008) pointed out that although these prisons claimed to operate a silent regime it is difficult to see how the prisoners would have been prevented from communicating at all times, especially in larger prisons with low staff levels. This suggests that 'despite growing ideas of the use of different regimes, to ensure the conformity and possible reform of prisoners, practice varied considerably'. While the prisons of Coldbath Fields and Pentonville embraced the silent and separate punishment regimes, many rural prisons, observed John Howard, 'still suffered problems of poor management, dilapidated buildings and were ill constructed for the new philosophies of punishment'. The opposing system of separation could be imposed with fewer staff, but the required architectural alterations cost money. While Johnston is considering Britain, the same can be said of VDL: there was considerable difference in the experience of punishment (Johnston 2008, 81). Some prisoners did live a solitary existence for the duration of their punishment, but the practice of keeping convicts in solitary was not uniform through different institutions. That is not to say that confinement in the cells for long periods was not arduous on the body and mind. It was still a punishment. Nevertheless, the degree of rigour would have depended on the time and place of the punishment. While Conduct Records clearly record the date of such punishments, they often do not clarify where the confinement, solitary or not, took place. Therefore, for the purposes of exploring punishments here, all incidences of confinement to the cells, whether specified as solitary, separate or neither, were grouped as being 'confined to the cells'. While true solitary confinement is attributed to mental breakdown in both contemporary and secondary sources, we cannot say which convicts endured true solitary confinement. Nevertheless, the punishment of being confined to the cells, even for a convict under servitude, was a further deprivation of liberty. There were on average thirty-one days of confinement for each male juvenile, and 72 per cent actually received a sentence of confinement to the cells. Nonetheless, the majority of those (75 per cent) only spent between one and fifty days in the cells. Only seven spent over one hundred days confined to the cells.

Hard labour was also a very common punishment in VDL but the experience of such labour would have varied widely. In parliament the work carried out in Portland was described as insufficiently laborious and the convicts 'pampered'. Meanwhile, convicts labouring to excavate the new naval dockyard at Chatham were simultaneously described as of an 'arduous character' and a 'waste, misapplication and indolence' (Radzinowicz & Hood 1990, 505). Hence, hard labour varied within the British Isles and so it is reasonable to assert that hard labour in VDL would also have varied. Some offenders would have endured more severe working conditions than others sentenced to the same period of hard labour. The majority (82 per cent) of male juveniles did undergo hard labour. While sixty-two of these juveniles underwent under one-thousand days of hard labour, eighteen underwent *over* one-thousand days – approximately three-years' hard labour. Moreover, thirty male juveniles underwent at least one-year of hard labour. As well as punishment, most of this labour would have been for the betterment of the colony. Treadmills, on the other hand, were not very common in the colonies, but were a popular punishment in early-nineteenth-century Britain. It is likely that it was seen as more desirable to put these convicts to useful labour for the development of the colony. Whereas in Britain by 1842, over half of the two hundred gaols and houses of correction had treadmills. While initially such machines were used to generate power in the use of, for example grinding grain, it quickly became a machine for generating 'useless' toil. The punishment of 'grinding rogues honest', as Bentham termed it, could be carried out only in areas where a treadmill was available (Maxwell-Stewart 2008, 142–143). This accounts, partly, for the scarcity of colonial punishments involving treadmills. However, it is likely that the want of labour for the benefits of the colony weighed in on the decision also. Certainly, the increasing popularity of the treadmill in England up to the 1840s was not reflected in the punishments experienced by these juveniles. There were only twelve male juveniles who were sentenced, to between ten and seventy days, on the treadmill. While six spent at least a month on the treadmill, it was not a common punishment for this sample.

The majority of male juveniles (82 per cent), despite their many offences, did not have their sentences extended. However, this still leaves 20 per cent who did. Indeed, 17 per cent of male juveniles were re-transported. Meaning they had at least two sentences of transportation. Such convicts would not be transported to another colony but they were usually sent to a penal station for at least the beginning of their new sentence. Approximately one-fifth were re-transported. On top of their existing sentences: five juveniles were sentenced to another seven years' transportation; two were sentenced to an additional ten years; one was sentenced to two additional seven-year sentences; another juvenile was sentenced to seven and fourteen years respectively; two were sentenced to an additional seven years and an extra life sentence; four were sentenced to life; another was sentenced to death but it was commuted to life; and lastly one juvenile was sentenced to a life of transportation (again on top of their original sentence) and after this he was sentenced to death but the sentence was subsequently commuted to life. Therefore, five were re-transported twice within the colony. Meaning in total they had three sentences of transportation. Moreover, two convicts were sentenced to death. Fortunately for them, their sentences were both commuted to transportation for life. Nevertheless, as many as 2 per cent of these juveniles were sentenced to death within the confines of the Conduct Record. One of these juveniles was Charles Brewer.

Case Study No.4: Charles Brewer

Charles committed many offences over the course of his life. Born in 1821, Charles was convicted in 1835, aged fourteen, of pickpocketing a handkerchief worth six pence. Charles received seven years' transportation. Previously he had been convicted of a similar offence and was imprisoned for three months. Charles's father petitioned on his behalf: Thomas Brewer argued that he was led to believe his son would serve out his sentence in England on the hulks. Unfortunately, this was not the case. Thomas had visited Charles aboard the *Euryalus* several times and strongly believed that 'the discipline on the ship has taught him a lesson'. The authorities disagreed and Charles was sent aboard the *Lord Lyndoch,* in 1836, to Hobart. The journey took four months, during which time Charles spent two weeks in the hospital with catarrh, but was discharged cured. Charles was fifteen when he first set foot in Australia.

He was recorded as 'good' and 'orderly' aboard the hulk and ship respectively. However, within just one month Charles committed his first offence: gambling while on assignment. The following offences were minor: making a noise, bathing without permission, idleness on the works and insolence to a constable. He was at Point Puer at this time, having been taken out of assignment due to bad behaviour. Insolence to authorities and general misconduct continued. He was also in possession of restricted items, and was recorded as throwing stones and destroying government property entrusted to him. Charles was then under strong suspicion of attempting to kill a goat, and in 1838 was recorded as 'aiding and assisting Edward Gares in using violence to an overseer'. By this point it appears that Charles was in Port Arthur. Charles was repeatedly caught working privately and continued to threaten and be insolent to overseers. He did not reserve his ill-treatment for overseers – he was recorded as ill using a fellow boy in 1839. After numerous offences, largely disorderly conduct, Charles was convicted of larceny under the value of five pounds and had his term of transportation extended by two years (which was recommended to take place at Port Arthur). Then, while already illegally at large, Charles was convicted of attempting to commit a felony by use of force in 1843. For this he was re-transported for seven years. During this incident Charles, along with another absconder Michael Conway, stole the property of Mr Bryant. They tied the hands of Robert Baker and took possession of a musket, but they were both apprehended and sent to New Norfolk Gaol. Before passing sentence his honour stated that the police books showed no less than between sixty and seventy charges against Charles. He further commented that 'men such as he should be kept from settled districts' and recommended that he be sent to Port Arthur for the whole term of his sentence (*The Courier* 28 April 1843, 2). Later, Brewer and a James Smith were charged with assaulting John Forster, with intent to rob. On his way home Mr Forster and his son were stopped by two men who demanded his money or his life. In the struggle one of the men was wounded. Both men escaped and neither victim could describe the assailants. However, two prisoners who had absconded had been seen in the vicinity. The prisoners were apprehended in Bothwell; they both claimed to be free men and one had a stab wound. They were found guilty and sentenced to be transported for life (*Colonial Times* 18 January 1850, 2). By 1845 Charles was in chains for two months for having a pipe in his possession, this was then extended by one month for stealing wood. In total, Charles committed eighty-four separate offences in his Conduct Record. This was by far the highest number of offences. It is not surprising that Charles was unable to earn either a ticket of leave or conditional pardon. The last offence recorded in his Conduct Record was in 1846. However, this was not his last brush with the law.

In 1853 *The Courier* described him as a 31-year-old labourer sentenced to death. In a capital trial, Charles Brewer, Quinn, Bridget Stokes and John Twitty were accused by William Jones. Both Quinn and Brewer cross examined the witness at length. Quinn, in particular, stressed the civility he had displayed throughout the incident. However, Gardiner, a victim, pointed out that he was under the impression that they would have injured him if he did not comply – but did confess they were 'very kind'. For example in being asked to light their pipes Quinn replied: 'with pleasure' and 'good night, friend'. Lacking counsel, Charles referred chiefly to 'some apparent improbabilities in the evidence', but stated, 'nothing material against general tenor'. His honour pointed out the evidence was incontrovertible in respect to the male prisoners but slight in respect to the female (22 October 1853, 3). *The Courier* had described the 'celebrated' Quinn and Charles as bushrangers. They were captured thanks to an officer who discovered them using a house in Murray Street. Armed police were put on standby and then burst open the door with an axe and charged at the prisoners with a bayonet. Both prisoners were apprehended in 'respectable clothing and armed with two pistols capped and loaded to the muzzle' (26 September 1853, 3). They were capitally convicted. Fortunately for them, this punishment was mitigated to a life of transportation at Norfolk Island. However, in 1854 when Charles and twenty other prisoners were being conveyed to the island aboard the *Lady Franklin*, they took over the ship.

The party of convicts, reportedly headed by Quinn, Brewer and Twitty, seized the ship. Captain Willett was suddenly awakened and overpowered by prisoners. Three of the crew were employed in working the ship, while the master and mate were confined. Days later they ordered the crew to launch the long boat and cutter which were laden with provisions. The 'desperadoes' left, having cut the sails and part of the rigging thus disabling the ship. The prisoners were able to take the ship because after breaking from the prison into the hold they got possession of some old firearms which the crew were not aware were useless. All the crew and soldiers, except two sergeants, proceeded to run below deck, and the prisoners therefore got 'peaceable possession of the vessel'. They also tried to take a *Sydney schooner* but failed (*The Courier* 28 January 1854, 2; *The Courier* 2 February 1854, 2; *The Argus* 1 February 1854, 4). The *Lady Franklin* and her prisoners were never recovered. The newspapers reported that it was likely that they perished in a storm en route to Fiji. Charles had had his sentence extended by two years twice, by seven years once, was given a life sentence and had a death sentence commuted to a life sentence. Charles was approximately thirty-three when the pirate ship was reported lost at sea.

Evidently, Charles had an eventful and extraordinary life. As can be clearly seen in this life-narrative, Charles's offending increased in severity and he offended up until his death. Charles committed serious offences and was given severe punishments – even so he had his sentence of death commuted.

Whereas none of the female juveniles were sentenced to death, there were four death sentences handed down to the male juveniles and two of these sentences were *not* commuted. Robert Gardon (*Case Study No.5*) was executed in VDL, in 1832, and therefore had the event recorded in his Conduct Record.[1] James McAllister (*Case Study No.17*), on the other hand, had migrated to Melbourne and was executed there in 1855. While only one of the death sentences described here was carried out in VDL, it was after the number of death sentences had declined on the island. There was a decrease in executions, from 1 1/3 in 1000 of the population from the last six months of 1824 to 3/30 per 1000 for the year of 1835 (Anon 1836, 6). This declining trend in capital sentences continued (Ewing 1843, xiv). Notwithstanding the high number of offences, there was little wish to execute these juveniles. However, it must be remembered that they committed very few 'very serious' offences.

Case Study No.5: Robert Gardon (aka Gordon)

Born in 1807, Robert was thirteen when he was indicted for pickpocketing. He stole a purse valued at one pence, which contained a half crown and a one-pound bank note. He was found guilty of 'stealing but not of the person'. In his defence he stated: 'My master told me to call and ask whether they sold eggs. I saw the purse on the ground, and picked it up'. He was transported for seven years. Robert had been previously imprisoned but the details are unknown. He was transported aboard the *Albion* in 1823. Robert was originally from Lambeth, where he worked as a labourer and punter waterman.

Robert's first offence in the colony was in April 1825; it was noted that he had neglected his duty and disobeyed orders. For this offence he was given twenty-five lashes. This was when he was still on assignment. His next offence was 'neglect of duty and insolence to Green his overseer' in June; he was again flogged twenty-five times. He was again disobedient of his overseer in July. This time he was only reprimanded. When he aided and assisted an absconding prisoner, he was demoted to the Crime Class. In August he was accused of throwing a blanket over the head of Edward Broxholm, a prisoner, and robbing him in the prisoner's barracks. This offence was discharged, but the very next day it was recorded that he did the same to William Smith. This time he was punished with twenty-five lashes and demotion to (or to remain in) the third class. In November, Robert was insolent to his overseer, which resulted in him being returned to the public works of Black Snake Road Party. In February 1826, he returned to the prisoners' barracks drunk and tried to break back into the cell he was supposed to be confined in. For this offence he was given fifty lashes and was sent to Maria Island. Disobedience of orders and neglect of duty resulted in twenty-five lashes in July, and he was put (or was already in) a chain gang. In August he absconded from his chain gang and remained 'at large' until he was apprehended in the woods at Brickes Bay. He broke out of the prisoner's barracks and remained at large until apprehended, and was consequently given one-hundred lashes and was put in the chain gang for six months.

Next he was convicted of highway robbery. This offence seems not to have been proven but in August he was out of his lodgings for an hour in the evening and was reprimanded. In September 1830, when free-by-servitude, he violently assaulted Andrew Berry and was fined two pounds. In 1831 he was found guilty of burglary and stealing nine promissory notes and other articles worth one pound each. Consequently, Robert and two others were executed in Hobart with a large crowd assembled 'to witness the humiliating spectacle'. Two others were involved in the burglary, James Sheady and Sarah Davis; they were sentenced to fourteen years' transportation. They both visited Robert on the eve of his execution, and Robert entreated Sarah Davis 'to forsake [her] evil course' and 'sincerely to amend her life'. He also accused her of 'being a hypocrite' and having 'prevented himself from turning to a virtuous course'. It seemed he blamed her for his death sentence. Robert 'died almost without a struggle' (*The Hobart Town Courier* 5 May 1832, 4). Robert was executed in 1832 aged only twenty-six. Robert had never married but he had a relationship with co-offender Sarah Davis.

When convicts were re-transported they were often sent to penal settlements to serve (at least) the beginning of that sentence, and this was no different for juveniles. However, a sentence of re-transportation was not required to be sent to a penal settlement. It was also possible to be placed there after offending under an initial sentence of transportation.

Penal settlements

The first penal settlement was Macquarie Harbour, established in 1822 by Governor Sorrell. It was considered a place of severe punishment by contemporaries (Porter 2003, 32). At first, half of the prisoners were flogged every year, although this diminished after Governor Arthur sent a Wesleyan missionary there. This missionary also introduced a school there to teach reading and writing, and generally improved conditions (Shaw 1966, 210). Macquarie Harbour was a remote spot 'beyond the pale of colonial society' where 1136 males and 16 females were sent until 1833 (Maxwell-Stewart 2008, 2). It was at the height of its use in 1828 when it held 386 prisoners. This spot was advantageous because of its natural resources, and its remoteness made it ideal for dangerous prisoners (Maxwell-Stewart 2008, 5). As Governor Macquarie proclaimed, 'escape from thence would be next to impossible' (Maxwell-Stewart 2008, 2). As pointed out by Maxwell-Stewart (2008, 43), the convicts transported to Macquarie Harbour had not necessarily committed crimes of the 'deepest-dye'. In fact, 'only three per cent of convicts transported to Macquarie Harbour were sent for crimes that explicitly involved violence' and a similar number were banished there for mutiny and insubordination. Only one convict had committed murder (Maxwell-Stewart 2008, 44). Some were sent for more 'trifling reasons' such as stealing a loaf of bread worth five pence, absconding, misbehaving on the voyage over or because it was their second sentence of transportation (Maxwell-Stewart 2008, 48–55). Indeed, the Lieutenant Governor could decide to send any convict in VDL to any penal station for any reason without a court ruling (Maxwell-Stewart 2008, 57). The point of Macquarie Harbour, according to Maxwell-Stewart (2008, 58), was deterrence from offending. Indeed 'power at Macquarie Harbour was given immediate effect by the score of the lash' (Maxwell-Stewart 2008, 77). There were times when the 'flagellator was excessively busy' such as in July 1823 when over six days he administered 1700 lashes to just fifteen prisoners. Such occasions would have involved the observance of all convicts (Maxwell-Stewart 2008, 79). Therefore, while

Macquarie Harbour was not filled with the most dangerous offenders, it was a place of brutal punishment in comparison to those assigned in VDL. Because of difficulties in controlling Macquarie Harbour (there were a number of mutinies) it was replaced by Port Arthur (Brooke & Bandon 2005, 229–230). Port Arthur was established on the South East coast in 1829 and became a thriving station. In 1835, for example, there were approximately 800 convicts working in chain gangs at this station (Brooke & Bandon 2005, 229–230). Up to 1835, 15 per cent of convicts sent to VDL spent time at Port Arthur (Shaw 1966, 211–212). Port Arthur's convict population grew rapidly peaking at 1218 in 1846 (Jackman 2009, 102). The 'success' of Port Arthur allowed the breaking up of the penal stations in Macquarie Harbour by 1833 and Maria Island by 1832 (Shaw 1966, 211). Approximately from 10,000 to 12,000 sentences were served at Port Arthur during the forty-seven years it operated (Jackman 2009, 102). Port Arthur could be easily reached from Hobart by boat across Storm Bay but it was both secured and easily controlled (Shaw 1966, 211). A number of male juveniles spent time in penal settlements. Unfortunately, it is possible to find their location only when it is written alongside their offences. It is also not always possible to find out how long the offender spent at given penal stations. For some convicts, after committing an offence, it noted next to their name that they were recommended to be sent to a specific penal settlement. However, it is not always possible to determine whether they were sent or for how long, but it is clear that between the juveniles sampled they spent time in most convict establishments. Many of them, such as Lyon Levy, were also moved between establishments.

Case Study No.6: Lyon Levy

During the course of his time in VDL, Lyon was assigned to a free settler, sent to Macquarie Harbour and Port Arthur, worked on different public works, spent time in Hobart Gaol and was placed in an invalid party and in New Town Pauper Establishment. Lyon was one of the first juveniles in this sample to be transported. He was born in 1805 and tried for Grand Larceny when he was thirteen. Lyon had stolen one hat and a pair of gloves valued at ten shillings and six pence from a shop. During his trial he stated: 'I beg for mercy'. Unfortunately, he was found guilty and Mr Common Sergeant sentenced him to seven years' transportation. This was not his first court appearance. He had been in custody six months earlier, for a period of three months, for stealing a coat worth twenty shillings. He was transported in 1821 after a thirty-nine-month wait on the hulks. He had been received at the *Bellerophon* hulk from Newgate in October 1818, and then he was discharged to the *Richmond* ship to set sail in November 1821. The gaol authorities stated he had 'bad character in custody before', and the hulk authorities reported that 'his general conduct has been good until lately he has been put to learn different trades but does not appear to have any capacity'.

He was approximately sixteen on arrival. It was not until 1823, when out on assignment, that Lyon committed his first offence in the colony. He stole five brooches from a dwelling house. This resulted in fifty lashes and being sent to the public works. He was not heard from again until 1825 when 'insolence to his master on Saturday his master does not prosecute and it appears that he is not regularly employed by his master'. Consequently, Lyon was put in the third class of the penitentiary. In 1826 it was reported in his Conduct Record: 'stealing 338 yards of printed cotton from a window of Merrers Murray & Burns store in Elizabeth-street, on the 15th feb last. He most daringly threw a sack over the goods, whilst he kept Ms Murray in sight, inside the window – Levy had lately returned from three years' transportation at Macquarie'. There is no reference of Levy being sent to Macquarie Harbour. The punishment of being placed in a penitentiary may have referred to the penal settlement but it is unclear. Therefore, it is only possible to discover he was sent there because of the added information in a later offence. For this offence of stealing cotton, Lyon was re-transported for seven years. However, he broke 'the walls of the H M Gaol Hobart Town on the night of sat past with intent to escape from the Gaol' in 1826 and was subsequently given fifty lashes. It was in this period he was sent to Norfolk Island.

In June 1827, he disobeyed orders and refused to work resulting in eighteen lashes. However, after indecently exposing himself, in November, he was sentenced to one-hundred lashes and one month in irons. This was followed by neglect of duty for which he was given eighteen lashes. In 1828, he again refused to work and was given another eighteen lashes. This was followed by three more offences of neglecting duty in quick succession, which resulted in twenty-five lashes and two sentences of thirty-six lashes respectively. Then after leaving work contrary to orders, in 1832, he was given '3 weeks on bread and water – 9 days remitted'.

Lyon's offending in the colony began relatively seriously (with theft offences) but they were followed by repeated status offences. Then, in 1840 when Lyon was free-by-servitude, he was sentenced to death for sodomy. This was later commuted to ten years' transportation at Port Arthur. From this point his regulatory offending resumed. Because he was not performing his work in late 1840, Lyon was given five days' solitary confinement. This was followed by gross neglect of duty in 1841, which resulted in three days' solitary confinement, and misconduct which resulted in six weeks' hard labour in chains. Lyon did not offend again until 1864 when he stole items valued under five pounds, for which he was sentenced to four years at Port Arthur. In 1865 he was reprimanded for misconduct and offended no more. It would appear he was again free-by-servitude in August 1868. However, before this, Lyon had been placed in the invalid gang in 1866, and was put in hospital in 1867 and 1869. There is limited detail on the circumstances of these hospital stays and the reason he was put in the invalid party, but it does state he suffered from Ophthalmia (inflammation of the eye).

Lyon was free-by-servitude in 1825. Lyon had earned his first ticket of leave in 1848, which was followed by a conditional pardon in 1851 but his ticket of leave (and presumably conditional pardon) were both revoked. He again earned his ticket of leave in 1861 and was again free-by-servitude in 1868. At the time of his death, in 1883, Lyon was a hawker, he was unmarried, and lived his last days at the pauper establishment at New Town, Hobart. Lyon's cause of death, at seventy-eight, was senility.

As Lyon Levy's case demonstrates, it is not always possible to know exactly where a given convict is at a given time, but it is possible to *roughly* track them during the course of their sentence. Many of the male juveniles spent time in secondary penal settlements. Short of execution, the most dreaded sentence was secondary transportation to one of these stations (Shaw 1966, 203). One of the most infamous of penal settlements was Norfolk Island. As Causer points out, much of the historiography of Norfolk Island is dominated by its legend (2011, 1). This legend includes assumptions that the convicts sent there were 'universally brutalized and had no hope', that 'commandants and their subordinates were sadists' and that sexual violence and unnatural crimes were widespread. This all culminated in a view that those sent to Norfolk Island were the 'worst of the worst' (Causer 2011, 3). In challenging this orthodoxy, Causer points out that only 48 per cent of those at the station had previous convictions before their original sentence of transportation (2011, 14). They were also not a 'particularly dangerous sub-stratum of convicts' – their original crimes show that there were few explicitly violent crimes, and nearly 70 per cent were non-violent crimes against property such as pickpocketing and burglary. Many others were court-martialled soldiers (Causer 2011, 16). Essentially, Causer found that convicts transported to Norfolk Island were representative of convicts transported more generally (2011, 17). As in the case of Macquarie Harbour (Maxwell-Stewart, 2008), the punishment of being sent to Norfolk Island was 'frequently arbitrary and unequal' (Causer 2011, 18). Of those colonially convicted males sent to Norfolk Island, the majority committed violent property offences, including burglary, housebreaking, highway robbery and stock theft. But there were many who were simply transferred there from other stations for no obvious reason (Causer 2011, 20). Nevertheless, for those who were sent there: 'Norfolk Island had a far more arduous labour and punishment regime than Port Macquarie' (Causer 2011, 33). One such unfortunate individual was Robert Spencer.

Case Study No.7: Robert Spencer

Robert was baptized at Finsbury in 1824. Aged thirteen, Robert was convicted of pickpocketing a handkerchief worth one shilling at Greenwich fair. For this offence he was sentenced to seven years' transportation. This was not his first offence; Robert had previously been imprisoned for a similar offence on two occasions. At least one of his punishments took place at Tothill Fields prison. His father, also named Robert, was a bookbinder, and his mother was Ann Sarah. Originally from Fleet Street in London, Robert junior could read; he was a Roman Catholic and was described as 'good' during his time on the *Euryalus*, and 'indifferent' by the surgeon superintendent on the voyage over. Robert was transported on the *Frances Charlotte* in 1837.

Since the *Frances Charlotte* is known to have transported its juvenile-only passengers straight to Point Puer, we know Robert was sent there. However, there is no indication on his Conduct Record that he was. Instead, his first offence, in 1838, lists Robert as being at Port Arthur. Since Point Puer was attached to, and reliant on, Port Arthur, it is likely that the conduct recorder saw Point Puer as part of Port Arthur – and saw no reason to specify. His first offence was 'insolence' for which he was given twelve lashes. Shortly after, for the same offence he was given four days' solitary confinement on bread and water. Then he had thread in his possession, was absent from the underground when confined there, was disorderly in church, was insolent and misconducting himself, had part of a shoe improperly in his possession, was on the rocks contrary to orders, was insolent and had a cape improperly in his possession, and was grossly disobedient by being in the School room without authority. All of which respectively earned him three or four days' solitary confinement on bread and water. When he was absent from the establishment he was given fifteen lashes. All of these offences took place in the first year of his arrival. This offending continued as follows: having his blanket torn, absenting himself from the establishment, having a cap, insolence, obscene language and having a penknife improperly in his possession. These offences led to varying lengths of solitary confinement. Only three months after freedom, in 1842, the *Colonial Times* reported:

> *Quarter sessions* – Robert Spencer in appearance a mere boy, was indicted for stealing on the 24th of July last a pair of trousers of the value 7s Mr. Lake of Liverpool-street's property. A witness saw him in coming out of the shop with trousers and followed him, finding he had gone in to the tailor's shop and concealed himself under some forms in a passage behind the house, on being desired to come out he ran away up Harrington-street where he was apprehended. While Mr. Lake proved the loss of the trousers they were not found. But witnesses proved the identity of the prisoner. The prisoner who was in the employ of Mr. Reeves said that he had never been away from his master's house five minutes during the day. The jury found the prisoner guilty, but recommended him to mercy on account of his youth. The learned Chairman expressed his commendation of the recommendation of the jury, but stated that they could not be aware of the character of the prisoner who was 22 years of age and have been already transported to this colony, where he arrived in 1837, he since became free-by-servitude but in addition to having been convicted several times of picking pockets in England, he had conducted himself in a very bad manner since his arrival in this colony. His honor deemed it necessary to mention these circumstances in order that the jury might not think the Court had acted unkindly with respect to their recommendation. The prisoner was sentenced to be transported for 7 years and he left the bar laughing! (23 August 1842, 3) (Also reported in *The Courier* 26 August 1842, 3)

While at Port Arthur his offending continued in a similar vein but the punishments were harsher. In 1842, he misconducted himself 'in fighting and [unknown] Disorder' and was given eighteen lashes. For refusing to work he was given twenty-five lashes; for using obscene language he was given three weeks' hard labour in chains; for having something illicitly in his possession he was given three months' hard labour in chains; for being absent without leave he was given six months' hard labour in chains; and for disobedience of orders he was given seven days' solitary confinement. When he was again absent without leave, in 1844, Robert had his existing sentence of hard labour in chains extended by six months and was placed in the third class. Two separate offences of misconduct that same month led to seven days' solitary confinement, followed by twenty-five lashes for the repeated offence. Because Robert misconducted himself again, he was given thirty-six lashes in November, but at the end of the month, due to insubordination, he was given one-hundred lashes. Two offences of misconduct in 1845 led to two sentences of solitary confinement. Since being sent to Port Arthur in 1842, he seems to have spent all of his time there. However, when he was convicted of disobedience in 1846, for which he was given three months' hard labour, Robert was at Oats depot. Robert does not appear in the records again until November 1849, when he was transported for life for 'breaking and entering a dwelling house and stealing a pair of pistols and other utensils'. It is not clear at what point he was sent to Norfolk Island; however, he seems to have been sent there corresponding with this last offence. The *Colonial Times* recounted this story as follows:

> William Morgan, John Williams and Robert Spencer were charged with burglary. On the night of the 18th October last, Mr. Gellie heard a noise in his house, when he could not account for, but on the following morning he discovered that the kitchen window was open, although it has been closed on the previous night. He missed a pair of pistols and ammunition. On the 10th, the prisoners were taken at the Cocked Hat Hill, and the missed property found upon them. A verdict of Guilty was returned. (30 November 1849, 2) (Also reported in: *The Cornwall Chronicle* 24 November 1849, 1034; *Hobarton Guardian* 1 December 1849, 3; *Colonial Times* 4 December 1849, 2; *The Courier* 5 December 1849, 3)

> Hobart Town – At the Quarter Sessions of peace ... [they] were severally sentenced to transportation for life. Mr. Home said there could be no question they had intended to commit highway robbery and perhaps murder at or near Launceston. (*Launceston Examiner* 8 December 1849, 5)

In 1850 Robert was given two months' hard labour for fighting. After disorderly behaviour in the following months, Robert was given a further two weeks' hard labour. This was followed by six months' hard labour because he was caught concealed under a carpenter's ship in 1851. Disorderly behaviour that winter led to one-month hard labour and leaving his gang led to two months' hard labour. Then, disorderly behaviour led to one, two, an unknown number of days, then three consecutive sentences of fourteen days of hard labour respectively. Then due to an illegible offence he was given six months' hard labour. Three offences of idleness led to three-, two- and then one-month hard labour. Then he was caught 'being dressed in ward with intention of breaking out ... and conniving with prisoners with intention of stealing a boat and escaping from the Island' in 1852. It was recommended that he be given eighteen months' task work before any period be fixed on his detention. He was then disorderly, disobedient twice, insolent and disobedient twice more, for which he received between three and fourteen days' solitary confinement for each offence. Then when he was caught wilfully destroying government property he was given fourteen days' solitary confinement. Robert was disobedient in 1854, for which he was given one-month hard labour; he interfered with police and was given seven days' solitary confinement; in August he was again disobedient and was given seven days' solitary confinement. He was absent in 1854 and was given seven days' hard labour. On the same day he was convicted of having money in his possession and was punished with two months' hard labour. This was his last recorded offence. In total he committed sixty-two offences. This is far above average.

Before his removal from England, Robert was a labourer; but in 1849 he was described as a tailor. He had therefore learnt a trade while under servitude. He was described as having 'slight made features sharp and pointed' in his Description List. Unfortunately, there is no record of any marriage or death in the colonies and he is lost after a relatively abrupt end to his offending in 1854.

Robert Spencer's case demonstrates how repeated offending often led to being moved between the different penal stations. While he begun in Point Puer, where it is likely he was taught the trade of tailoring, he ended up in Port Arthur after being convicted of theft and being given another transportation sentence. Despite repeated minor offences he seems to have been kept in Point Puer; it was only a 'serious' offence which resulted in him being moved to the secondary penal settlement of Port Arthur. Similarly, he was only moved to what was at the time considered the more severe station of Norfolk Island, after being convicted of theft from the dwelling house. Sustained offending led males to be sent to penal stations, but females were not usually sent to these stations and were instead sentenced to other forms of punishment.

Female juveniles

There were broadly the same three phases of female convict transportation as there were for males: the exile or open prison period 1803–1813, the assignment period 1814–1842 and the probation period 1843–1853. None of the female juveniles arrived in the first period, 56 per cent arrived in the second period, and the later period saw 44 per cent arrive. Therefore, while the number of female convicts transported may have increased with each new period, the female juvenile numbers did not follow this pattern (Kavanagh & Snowden 2015, 132). These broader management systems are important because they influenced the punishments administered. Kavanagh and Snowden noted that with each progressive system the female convicts were 'subjected to a more severe discipline' (2015, 132). In line with beliefs that the transportation system needed to become more regulated and disciplined during the probation period, female convicts were now to be subjected to 'successive stages of punishment commencing with a period of confinement and labour'. If the female convicts conducted themselves appropriately they would be able to earn a probation pass and become available for hire, earn a ticket of leave and a pardon (Kavanagh & Snowden 2015, 132). If they did not, they were subject to varying punishments. The most common of which was hard labour, with an average of 555 days per convict. Less common were extended sentences with only thirty-seven days extended sentence and seventy days' confinement to the cells on average per convict.[2] What hard labour consisted of was not always specified; if it was, it referred to the wash tub. Seven underwent between four and six weeks, and six females spent over six weeks at hard labour. Only 24 per cent of them were not sentenced to any form of hard labour; the majority were. While we are dealing with small numbers, thirteen spent at least one month at hard labour, and Ellen Miles spent over five and a half years in hard labour.

Case Study No.8: Ellen Miles (aka Smith/Jackson)

Born in 1827, Ellen was twelve when she was convicted at the Old Bailey. Ellen was sentenced to transportation for seven years for uttering counterfeit coin. This was not her first offence of uttering. Ellen was brought before the courts for uttering when she was just ten but her judgement was respited after she pleaded guilty. The *Taunton Courier* and *Western Advertiser* referred to Ellen as 'A Young Hopeful'. The article stated that at the Guildhall Ellen was charged with passing a counterfeit half-crown to a shop keeper. The article pointed out that Ellen was one of three sisters whose mother had died: 'all notorious utterers'. It further asserted that Ellen had been in custody thirty times and was discharged only the previous week, adding that she had been convicted at the Old Bailey previously and if convicted again she would be transported. Claiming he was unable to control her, Ellen's father suggested that it would be an act of mercy to transport her. Instead, Alderman Lainson discharged Ellen with a warning. While thirty custodial sentences could not be found, Ellen had been confined previously for fourteen days, and in May 1839 she was be kept in prison for six months at the House of Corrections Clerkenwell and put to hard labour. It was recommended by the court that she be made known to the Children's Friends Society. Its founder focused on diverting juveniles out of the penal system. Despite this recommendation, it was noted that Ellen's sentence was for 'too short a time' to send her to the Children's Friends Society. However, the reporters were correct. Ellen was transported after a further offence later that year aboard the female convict ship the *Gilbert Henderson*. Ellen was thirteen when she arrived in Hobart. Even at the age of twelve Ellen had been shrewd enough to attempt, albeit unsuccessfully, to use an alias. Ellen used both 'Smith' and 'Jackson' as her surname, presumably in an attempt to avoid her previous court appearances being connected to her, and in doing so avoid a harsher punishment.

Ellen's first offence in the colony was in 1840 which was being insolent and disobedient for which she received six days' solitary confinement. Consequently, she was removed from her assignment to the cells. The offences which followed include disobedience of orders, neglect of duty, absconding, absence, insolence, found in company with a man of the name of Richard Nichols, (gross) insubordination, misconduct in destroying a table and two mess kids, creating a disturbance in the gaol, and larceny under five pounds. There were eighteen offences in total. These offences led to punishments such as solitary confinement, but she was also put to hard labour in the crime class at the female factory, and when Ellen absconded she had her original sentence of transportation extended by six months. It was also noted that she should be detained in the house of correction for two months on probation. Initially after each punishment Ellen was reassigned. However, after her sentence extension Ellen spent the majority of her time imprisoned, until 1844 when Ellen was at the hiring depot. However, this did not stop Ellen being repeatedly reassigned after her following offences. Ellen spent time at Cascades and Launceston female factory.

There is no evidence that Ellen earned a ticket of leave; however, she was free in 1847 after eighty-four months in the colony. Ellen was a 'slightly poke-pitted', 'nurse girl' when she arrived in VDL, but there she grew up and applied for permission-to-marry in 1847, four months after her freedom. In 1848 Ellen was married at Melville Chapel to Thomas Watkins. Thomas had arrived in VDL on the *Runnymede* but was a ticket of leave holder when the pair married. Thomas worked as a costermonger at the time of their child's birth. Ellen was twenty-one when she married, and Thomas was only slightly her senior at twenty-three. Ellen could neither read nor write before her arrival in VDL but by the time she was married she was able to sign the marriage register. They had at least one child, whom they named after the father, born in 1847. Ellen would have had to spend twelve months in assigned service without an offence to be able to apply for permission-to-marry (Reid 2007, 136). Ellen's repeated offences led to her spending the bulk of her sentence confined. As such, Ellen married only when she reached freedom. Yet, she did marry and form a family almost immediately after freedom.

Ellen Miles spent an uncharacteristically long time undergoing hard labour when compared to others. Facilities for hard labour grew over time, but also the number of females in the colony increased over time. With a greater number of female convicts for domestic employment, there may have been a greater willingness for masters to send those who misbehaved for time-consuming punishments. While convicts who committed more offences were liable to be punished more than those who did not, the practicality and convenience of the punishment, in terms of the master and the infrastructure, must also be accounted for. Juveniles spent long periods at hard labour. They also committed many offences; but given the 'minor' and 'medium' nature of the offences, it is possible that their relative lack of skill and inexperience also increased their chances of being reported. This is reflected in the continued reassignment of female juveniles as demonstrated in the life of Ellen Murphy (*Case Study No.14*). There was no 'short and sharp' punishment for females such as flogging; punishments including hard labour and confinement in the cells were time-consuming. The majority (88 per cent) of female juveniles spent time in the cells. However, the length of time varied: one female spent only one day, whereas another spent 141 days (albeit not at one time). Moreover, all incidences of being sent to the cell, whether in solitary or not, have been included in this section. Despite Margaret Corbet having the longest-known servitude (thirteen years), she spent only five days a year in the cells on average. Five days was the average for all female juveniles who spent time in the cells. Whereas Ellen Miles served seven years but spent twenty days a year in the cells on average – which was the longest period in the cells. The average length of servitude was seven and a half years. Being sentenced to the cells or confinement would generally have meant being sent to the female factory.

The female factory

There were five female factories established in VDL between 1803 and 1853: Hobart Town, George Town, Cascades, Launceston and Ross. Housing only female convicts, they were places not only of punishment but also for the pregnant and ill (Cowley 2008, 53). Female factories allowed the female convicts to be put to labour and 'contribute to the colony'. These factories also served as places of reception and hiring when increasing numbers of females arrived. Like the males, the females would now be able to be classified according to behaviour: from the crime class, the second class, to the first assignable class. The hard labour included spinning, carding, washing or picking (Cowley 2008, 54–55). While conditions in the factories were often poor, females did not experience chain gangs, penal stations or flogging. Because of gender rules, punishments which were previously used on women including head shaving, iron collars (only one female in the sample experienced these punishments) and the stocks were phased out (Reid 2007, 136). Instead, female factories were the main stay of female punishment. While they were primarily envisaged as places of labour, this was not always the case due to lack of resources and overcrowding. Hobart Town factory (established in 1822) lacked hard labour because it neither had the equipment nor the space available. The 'difficulties in finding suitable punishments for female offenders', as one magistrate explained, eased over time as more infrastructure was built – but these too became overcrowded (Cowley 2008, 55). Because of overcrowding and escapes, which were identified by an 1826 enquiry, Governor Arthur established Cascades female factory in 1828. This led to the re-purposing of the Hobart factory (Cowley 2008, 55–56). From its opening, females were sent to Cascades from the ships to be assigned, instead of being assigned directly from the ships. Just after its opening, Colonial Secretary John Burnett published *Rules and Regulations for the Management of the House of Correction for Females*. The superintendent would be able to pass sentence upon these females and enforce 'cleanliness, quietness, regularity, submission and industry' (Cowley 2008, 59). Not considered as brutal as the male regimes, conditions were still poor and strict, and the children's death rate was very high (Brooke & Brandon 2005, 238–239). Cascades ran for twenty-eight years. The probation system was extended to female convicts due to the *Inquiry into Female Convict's Discipline* (Cowley 2008, 60). This inquiry highlighted the overcrowding, corrupt officers, poor nutrition and lack of separation between classes (Cowley 2008, 60). After 1841, the newly arrived female convicts would spend the first six months in probation on the *Anson* Hulk, where strict classification was followed. Meanwhile at the factories, a 'strict regimen of silence and task work' was introduced (Cowley 2008, 61). Despite this enforced discipline or because of it, riots took place. Cascades was the largest factory but there were others including George Town female factory which opened in 1822, and was used until 1834 in north VDL. Like Hobart, this factory was plagued by overcrowding, poor security and lacked hard labour. The situation was made worse when the spinning wheels were removed to Cascades when it opened (Cowley 2008, 57). Indeed, the newspapers expressed a wish for a factory to be built in Launceston, because it was believed that females wanted to be sent to George Town for a 'rest' (Cowley 2008, 58). Launceston female factory opened in 1834, and ran until 1855. It was only a few years until it too became overcrowded (Cowley 2008, 64). Ross factory was the last to open in 1848, and ran until 1855. Ross was opened because one was needed in the interior. Better designed, there was no overcrowding and it did not suffer from the same damp conditions as Cascades (Cowley 2008, 67). It is likely that the majority, if not all, sentences of hard labour resulted in a stay at a factory. All, apart from one female juvenile, spent at least part of their sentence in a factory. The exact period of time the females spent in each factory cannot be ascertained from their Conduct Records. However, where punishments are issued it can be ascertained that certain female juveniles did spend long periods of time within the factories. For example, Ellen Murphy spent long periods in the female factory, whereas for Mary Coleman it is not explicitly stated that she spent any time in a factory. It is probable that Mary did spend time at a factory while awaiting assignment and when she carried out her hard labour. Nevertheless, it is clear that her time within a factory was limited unlike Ellen Murphy. Their time in the factory would also have varied according to when they were confined and which factory they were sent to. In the larger factories, such as Cascades, there was a wider range of work, including spinning, straw plaiting, factory duties, housekeeping, working in the hospital, sewing, laundry and weaving. Those in the third and lowest class broke rocks and picked oakum (Hendriksen 2009, 5–6).

The issue of overcrowding in these establishments did not go unnoticed but despite being authorized, Governor Wilmot did not build a female penitentiary. Instead he continued to use the, much cheaper, *Anson* Hulk (Shaw 1966, 304). It was the practice, from 1843 to 1847, to keep new arrivals on the *Anson*, a hulk moored on the River Derwent, separate from those in the factories (Kavanagh & Snowden 2015, 132). While only five female juveniles arrived after 1843, there is evidence of only one spending (what was a limited time) on the *Anson*. Eliza White, who was sick en route to VDL, died shortly after arrival aboard *Anson* (*Case*

Study No.25). Since new arrivals were sent to the *Anson* for domestic training in a six-month probationary period, it is unclear why the juveniles were not recorded as being there. They may simply not have offended while aboard. As pointed out by Nolan (2013), the shift in convict management from assignment to probation was not as clear for female convicts as it was for males. For females the probation system was a combination of elements from the assignment system (Kavanagh & Snowden 2015, 145). As pointed out by Sir John Franklin in 1843, a 'great mass of women in the factories are those women who have committed crimes under assignment or [ticket of leave]'. Meaning, the factories were not full because these females could not obtain a position. Instead they had been returned to factories due to misbehaviour (Franklin 1843, 14). However, he does point out that 'respectable families' preferred convicts who arrived fresh in the colony and were not tainted by factory life, but they would take them if they had to (Franklin 1843, 14). Kavanagh and Snowden point out that, by 1846, more females were housed on the *Anson*, in hiring depots and in the female houses of correction than were in domestic employment. This was due to increasing numbers of convict women arriving in VDL and the depressed local economy reducing the demand for domestic labour and consequently the bargaining power of convict women (2015, 144). Yet, Meredith and Oxley (2005, 47) argue that unemployment was never the problem for females that it was for males. Indeed, the female juveniles, even after repeated (yet minor) offences, were frequently reassigned to different masters even after 1846. They may have been quickly returned on several occasions, but new masters were easily sought as can be seen in the case of Susan Campbell.

Case Study No.9: Susan Campbell

Born in 1828, when Susan was thirteen she was convicted of shoplifting four pairs of boots worth thirteen shillings in Kingsland Road in 1841. Despite being recommended to the penitentiary, Susan was sentenced to seven years' transportation. Susan did not act alone. Her accomplices Jane Draper, aged fourteen, and Mary Gill, thirteen, were also found guilty. While Susan and Jane were given transportation sentences, Mary was sentenced to four days' confinement. The former two were known by the court to have previous convictions. In fact, Susan and Jane had been accused of committing crimes together before. Earlier in 1841 they were accused of committing larceny but 'no bill' was found. They were later transported together on the *Royal Admiral*. Susan's father was William and she had four brothers. She was a nursemaid, who could read but not write, and a member of the Church of England prior to transportation.

Susan departed in 1842 and arrived four months later in Hobart. During the voyage Susan suffered from ophthalmia but was discharged cured within eight days. Susan did not commit her first offence until February the following year when she was assigned to 'Babington'. Because of insolence she was given one-month hard labour in the house of correction. This sentence was then extended by three months due to gross misconduct and abusive language. However, by October Susan was placed in the assignable class but she was still breaking regulations – leading her to be given fourteen days' solitary confinement because she used indecent language. In 1844, Susan was assigned to 'Lake' but due to an absence was given ten days' solitary confinement. In 1845, she was admonished for misconduct. Then, in February while assigned to 'Baker', Susan was accused of stealing a one-pound promissory note. Susan was committed for trial but was discharged 'for want of evidence'. Yet, as was often the case she was still 'sent to the factory [in] Launceston on probation for six months'. By 1847 she was assigned to 'Collins' but was absent without leave and consequently given one-month hard labour. Then in October, when assigned to 'Langmaid', she was absent from her service and was given fourteen days' solitary confinement. When assigned to yet another master, Susan misconducted herself but was only admonished. In 1848, while assigned to 'Hortle', she was given seven days' solitary confinement. This was the last offence in her Conduct Record. Susan had a total of ten offences, but only one was non-regulatory and was discharged. Still, Susan was repeatedly returned from her assigned service and repeatedly reassigned to different masters. This demonstrates that not all females had trouble gaining a position even when poorly behaved.

By 1848 Susan was free. There is no evidence of Susan marrying but she did migrate, from Launceston to Melbourne aboard *Yara Yara* in 1852. A Susan Campbell was tried for vagrancy in Melbourne in 1858 who was confined for three months. This Susan was also involved with a 'house of ill-fame' (*The Age* 20 November 1858, 6). However, this connection is uncertain.

The first ten female juveniles who arrived in VDL, in the assignment period, were all assigned within a year. After the switch to the probation system, they were still assigned but at a slower rate. However, it is only possible to know whether these females were assigned if they had committed an offence. At which point, along with their offence information, their status and where they were based were included. Therefore, these female juveniles may have been assigned at earlier dates but did not offend until later. Certainly, if they were badly behaved their assignment was prevented, as in the case of Ellen Caley (*Case Study No.13*). Because Ellen was badly behaved on the voyage over in 1842, it was noted that she should be confined in the house of correction for twelve months' probation on arrival. However, after repeated offences at Brickfield house of correction, she was still assigned at least as early as 1844. Female juveniles did not have more skills or experience than their adult female counterparts (*see* Chapter 5). Yet, female juveniles were readily assigned even during economic downturns and female immigrant influxes. While they were relatively quickly assigned, they were often returned after minor offending and then re-assigned to someone else.

No female juveniles were re-transported, and only two had their sentences extended. Even these two juveniles, Jane Draper and Ellen Miles, only had their sentences extended by six months. This is not an insignificant period but in comparison with the re-transportation sentences of male juveniles it is a short period of time. It would appear that even for the juvenile female offenders who had a greater number of offences, it was not in the interest of the colonial authorities to extend their servitude. While females certainly committed fewer offences, and less serious offences than their male counterparts, there seems to be an implicit punishment practice of not extending the sentences of female convicts. This may be because, given that their offences were generally 'minor' and 'medium' level, it was more practical for them to free the females so they could marry. In doing so, these females would no longer be a financial burden to the colonial government. While females were exploited for government work when in the factories, due to reasons of infrastructure there was no gain in increasing the number of females in the factories. Indeed, the greater number of sentence extensions came under the assignment period. During the assignment period females would have been more likely to have spent this extended period under assignment to free settlers, instead of burdening the overcrowded government institutions. Males, on the other hand, could more easily be put to productive use within the colony. Moreover, it was certainly true that marriage was seen as 'the best instrument of reform' for females and so family life will be explored in Chapter 6 (Brand 1990, 91).

Conclusion

The male and female juveniles were generally petty but persistent offenders pre-, and immediately, post-transportation. Yet, they did not go on to a life of crime and their offending was not serious. Given their youth and inexperience with regard to skill, it is probable that while under assignment their masters were more likely to report 'minor' and 'medium' (status) offending than they would an adult with more skill. In this way, a master would not be concerned about the time-consuming punishment juveniles might be subject to, and the interruption of work that would result. Indeed, it may have been their aim to procure a more skilled, experienced or simply a stronger worker as a replacement. Not only would masters be willing to have juveniles replaced as servants, but also the ingrained culture of child chastisement would have influenced the same outcome. Similarly, in institutional settings there was always another convict to take over their work. Moreover, surveillance and punishment would have been more refined in the institutional settings. The experience of punishments varied per convict and because of these variations in practices and institutions, and the relatively small sample size, trends are difficult to uncover. However, generally juvenile convicts were punished more than adult convicts, and punishments were gendered. What punishments juveniles received is related to the *ad hoc* management system in place for their age and sex (and not necessarily the broader management systems adults were subject to, that is the assignment and probation systems). Life was not only different for a juvenile convict than for an adult convict, but it was also different for male and female juveniles, and directly related to both their worth as workers, and the ability and inclination of penal authorities to punish them.

5

Education, training and employment

The post-transportation employment of these juveniles is important when considering whether they settled in society. This information was gathered from Australian newspapers, criminal records and their children's birth records. Integral to that employment is their pre-transportation education, training and skill, which were gathered from their Description Lists and Conduct Records. Their employment in the colony will also have been affected by any post-transportation education and training. This is because the skills and education they experienced as juveniles would have affected what type of employment they were able to obtain in adulthood. It will also be important to consider the colonial economy, average wage rates and changing populations – which in turn would have affected the employment market that the juveniles were competing within. Since juvenile convicts were not necessarily treated the same as adult convicts, it is important to begin this chapter by outlining the development of the 'special' management of juvenile offenders and to put these juveniles in the context of their colonial servitude.

Unskilled labour for males in the colony relied on physical strength. Based on the Description Lists, which include information on height and age, Nunn (2015, 59) points to the 'typically slight build of juvenile convicts' which made them 'problematic as an immediate source of labour'. The male juveniles sampled for this research had a similar height profile to other juveniles who were transported and were not especially short as compared to other juvenile convicts. Indeed, as Nunn argues, it is not that juvenile convicts were smaller than free juveniles elsewhere either. Instead, these juveniles were inadequate physically because of the 'primacy of physical labour' within VDL and were inevitably not as strong as full-grown adults. When juveniles were sought for employment in newspapers, free settlers often specified Australian-born children, as they believed urban-born juveniles were unsuitable for the harshness of the Australian bush (Sidney 1847). The types of industrial jobs that employed large numbers of juveniles in England did not exist in the colony (Nunn 2015, 63). Consequently, they were difficult to assign and many had to be kept at Hobart prisoners barracks (Slee 2003, 5). There were exceptions; juveniles with agricultural or commercial skills were employed. Yet, with 'the convict ration being fixed at a minimum level, little opportunity existed for making the assignment of juveniles a more tempting proposition' (Jackson 2001, 7). With increasing numbers of juvenile convicts financially burdening the colonial government since 1827, the issue came to a head in 1833. The Assignment Board's concerns increased when sixty boys were unproductively grouped in the barracks. The Board recommended that a separate barrack for boys be built at Slopen Main on Tasman's Peninsula to work on the land (Slee 2003, 5). The task was passed onto the commandant of Port Arthur Penal Station, Charles O'Hara Booth, who established what came to be known as Point Puer, adjacent to Port Arthur (Jackson 2001, 7; Slee 2003, 6). Booth was given no additional resources. Still, by 1834, temporary barracks were built and the first sixty-eight boys were accommodated. More permanent structures quickly followed (Jackson 2001, 7).

While not wholly humanitarian in nature, these schemes, which grouped male juvenile convicts in one place, were not necessarily considered to be for immediate economic gain either. Goods produced at their workshops were sold through government stores but there is no indication of whether they successfully offset institutional costs. Indeed, when a consignment of leather goods from government stores was returned to the barracks as unsaleable, the superintendent of convicts sent a letter to Andrew Murray (superintendent of the Carter's Barracks) asking 'can not the Boys get back the ill made articles … which nobody will buy and be employed in remaking them in a proper manner!' Shortly after the government stopped sending leather to the institution for training. Steadily the government reduced training support forcing Murray to redistribute boys into cheaper employment areas. Murray concluded, 'In whatever way, they may be employed, full allowance should be made for the destruction of material, the inferiority of their work, and the small quantity performed'. As Nunn notes, Murray was arguing that considering the boys only in terms of their existing labour value would inevitably be economically unprofitable (2015, 67). Point Puer was under the same economic pressures from the Colonial Office. But unlike the Carter's Barracks, nearly everything it produced it also consumed. Nevertheless, Booth was aware that in order to present its efficacy, he would need to demonstrate economic productivity.

As such he calculated the 'notional value' of the juvenile convict labour of 1837 as being £1,134.19s.7d. The figures presented are unconfirmed (Nunn 2015, 68). As Nunn (2015, 68) points out, Booth had a vested interest in demonstrating the economic efficacy of the settlement *he* established. It is difficult to reconcile this production rate with the information contained in Benjamin Horne's report for the lieutenant governor, John Franklin, only six years later which outlined the 'natural poverty' of the area. Nevertheless, the Molesworth Commission accepted Booth's figures and reproduced them in the parliamentary report.

The move to establish Point Puer might have been largely driven by pragmatic concerns, but it also coincided with emerging ideals for the rehabilitation of juveniles through retraining, along with their segregation from the 'more intractably criminal adult counterparts' (Jackson 2001, 7). A widely held belief at this time was that adult criminals were 'beyond redemption', but juvenile offenders might be saved. Moreover, it was thought that by rehabilitating youths, wider society could be improved (Slee 2003, 1). Still, from correspondence between Booth and Arthur, it is clear there was no radical move from what was already operating for adult convicts and initially they were governed under the same rules as Port Arthur. However, Arthur's perception of the role of Point Puer and his discrimination dependent on age are important. Arthur believed that association with criminals, poverty and homelessness were the causes of juvenile delinquency. By holding this belief, that boys learned crime through association, Arthur accepted that juvenile convicts *could* be reformed (Slee 2003, 6–7). An important step in juvenile justice, Point Puer was not the first time convicts were treated differently. In 1803 apprenticeships for juveniles were introduced in NSW but they were unsuccessful (Brooke & Brandon 2005, 131). Similarly, Carter's Barracks in Sydney had implemented separate training for approximately one hundred juvenile convicts, but this ended by 1835 (Brooke & Brandon 2005, 131; Nunn 2015, 59). In a response to the assignment problem, in the late 1820s to early 1830s, apprenticeship programmes were established for a small number of juvenile males at penal stations within VDL, including Macquarie Harbour and Port Arthur (Jordan 1985, 1092). However, the separation of juvenile offenders in the Australian colonies did not happen in isolation (see Chapter 2). Point Puer was not the first establishment to separate offenders according to age and implement 'special' training and education, but it was important. How much Point Puer, and transportation more generally, actually affected the lives of the *male* juveniles will be discussed in this chapter along with the females, for whom there was no such institution.

Education

First let us consider the education of children generally in the nineteenth century. As shown in the work of Rosalind Crone (2015), parents often decided whether their children would acquire literacy skills. In her work on prisons and education she was able to demonstrate that local schools were usually how this was achieved. Formal schooling could also be combined with informal methods of education through home schooling, but it was less common for the latter method to be used alone (Crone 2015, 487). Traditionally, historians have argued that over the course of the nineteenth century the number of schools, and those attending schools, increased, so that by the establishment of government board schools in 1870, the majority were already receiving a formal elementary education. National government surveys conducted (in 1818, 1833 and 1851) support this conclusion. However, attempts by contemporaries and by historians to count schools and scholars have been criticized. Nineteenth-century surveys tell us about elite attitudes to education, but not about working-class experiences of education. Similarly, literacy information gathered within the prison system (such as Conduct Records and Description Lists) could also be viewed as limited. Nonetheless, as Crone (2010) argues, 'by providing micro level data on the schooling of discreet groups alongside their levels of literacy, ages and sometimes occupations', these records offer a more comprehensive overview of the range of schooling options that certain groups were exposed to over a period of time and the results of that exposure (Crone 2010, 30–31). Conduct Records do not include where literacy skills, of any level, were learnt. However, we can ascertain if the juvenile convicts had already acquired either reading or writing skills before they entered the criminal justice system.

The drive to educate the masses from the turn of the nineteenth century, evident in the increasing range of schools for the children of the poor, was largely supported by a series of investigations highlighting the links between low educational attainment and crime. Thus, not only was the need for elementary instruction for the masses recognized, but so too was the need for the provision of education for those who had already begun offending. The government signalled its commitment to the education of criminals in the official instructions issued to surgeon-superintendents of convict ships in 1815 (to establish schools for juveniles) and 1832 (to instruct all convicts) and in the Gaols Act of 1823. This commitment was 'mostly rhetoric as the government lacked power to enforce these provisions, especially in local gaols, the presence of these clauses encouraged experimentation' (Crone 2012, 49–50). From the mid-nineteenth century 'there were an increasing number of schools instructing pupils in both skills', meaning reading and writing, and this was reflected in the prison population (Crone 2015, 491). Indeed, compulsory education was utilized for criminal or potentially criminal juveniles after 1856, and even education of adult prisoners was included in the prison regime in convict and, later, local prisons (Crone 2012a, 49). Importantly, by matching the literacy rates of prisoners with those of the respective county populations and socio-economic groups, Crone found that the achievements of male prisoners were probably representative of those of the male working class (2010, 37). Was this the same for the juvenile convicts transported to VDL? It is important to uncover the changing literacy levels of the juvenile convicts: Did they arrive in the colony already able to read and write, or was this something they learnt in the convict system itself? And how did this affect their ability to secure later employment?

Male juveniles

The Description Lists and Conduct Records of these juveniles tell us their pre-transportation literacy levels. As such it is possible to track any improvement. Only 45 per cent of the male juveniles had their literacy information noted in their Conduct Records; 27 per cent could read only, 56 per cent could read and write, and 18 per cent had neither skill. Nine males improved in their literacy from pre- to post-transportation. For example, one convict could only read on arrival in the colony, but by the time of his marriage he was able to sign the marriage register. The marriage registers provide a near 'universal, standard and direct measure, of the ability to sign one's name', which the majority of the population would be required to undertake. Because literacy comprises of two skills, the ability to read and write, and because until at least the mid-Victorian period these skills were largely taught in sequence, the reading skill being imparted first—the act of signing the marriage register—indicated some accomplishment in both skills; however rudimentary. Yet, this means we cannot capture those who only learn to read within the marriage register, and this is why criminal records (which record different stages of literacy) are so useful (Crone 2010, 3–4). Moreover, not everyone underwent formal marriage. Another juvenile convict could neither read nor write when at Parkhurst Prison, but by the time he arrived in VDL he was recorded as able to both read and write. There are some discrepancies between the information reported on literacy in different institutions. For example, one convict could both read and write on the hulks but when reported on in his Conduct Record (which was later) it stated he could only read. While human error on the part of the recorder, as well as dishonesty on the part of the convict, is possible, it is also probable that different literacy standards were held at different institutions. On the crowded hulks methods of obtaining information may have been less rigorous than information gathered for the Conduct Records before transport disembarkment. As pointed out by Crone (2010), historians have questioned the methods of testing used by different individuals in different penal institutions. Both V.A.C. Gatrell and T.B. Hadden have pointed out that there was no Home Office directive on how or what information was to be recorded. Therefore, it is often unclear whether prisoners underwent tests in reading and writing or whether self-report data was sufficient (Crone 2010, 5). Still, a clear pattern does emerge whereby, as noted by Maxwell-Stewart (2016, 422), men were less literate when they entered the hulks than on arrival in VDL. This is because great emphasis was placed on schooling. And as Crone (2010) and David Philips (1977) have argued, even though the adequacy of classification varied over time and between prisons, 'the categories applied were sufficiently large and loose for it to be unlikely that there was any serious distortion of the true position in the results obtained' (Philips 1977, 161). Both reading and writing classes were held on the hulks and on transport. An example of the changes in recording is shown in the case of Richard Young.

Case Study No.10: Richard Young

Born in 1827 Richard was fourteen when he was brought before the Old Bailey for stealing from his master. He was found guilty of stealing four pairs of shoes valued at 10s.6d and sentenced to seven years' transportation. This was not Richard's first offence. He had been previously convicted for deserting an apprenticeship which resulting in three weeks' imprisonment and being flogged. Richard also stole one can and one gallon of beer worth 3s.4d, and 8s.8d in money, from a Luke Wootton. He pleaded guilty and was given four days in Newgate in 1840. He was further convicted of stealing six pairs of leather soles, an apron and a handkerchief valued at 7s.3d from the same master he later stole shoes from; George Wood. It was stated that he was fifteen during that offence (which does not fit the time line) but juveniles often lied about, or did not know accurately, their age. Richard had four brothers but there is no information about his parents – suggesting he had none. He is described as having scars on his left cheek and forehead. Before arrival in VDL he was a Protestant (he later became a Roman Catholic) and he was described as 'orderly' aboard the hulk and by the surgeon-superintendent on transport. The hulk officials recorded that Richard could read and write. However, his Conduct Record states that he was only able to read. It is likely that this was due to differing standards in information gathering. By the time Richard was twenty-two he could both read and write.

Richard was transported directly to Point Puer aboard the *Lord Goderich*, in 1841. It was not until 1843 that Richard committed his first offence which was misconduct. This was a common, minor offence and he was given five days' solitary confinement. Richard did not offend again at Point Puer. However, in 1854 Richard was charged with stealing a horse, valued at thirty pounds. The animal had been entrusted to Richard, who was in the prosecutor's service. However, Richard sold the horse to a blacksmith for eighteen pounds (*The Courier* 1854, 2). For this offence Richard was re-transported for life and committed to ten years until he could earn a conditional pardon. Richard was a free man when he was convicted of this offence but he claimed to be 'Thomas Collins', presumably to hide his previous sentence of transportation. Richard committed no more offences.

Richard was trained in shoemaking at Point Puer and was described as an 'orderly good shoemaker'. In 1845 it was recorded: 'Shoemaker can earn his living'. He earned his first ticket of leave in 1845 and was free by 1848, after seventy-five months in the colony. After his reconviction it was advised that 'no remission of his probation can be allowed'; however, in 1857 it was recommended that he 'now [be] classed as a passholder', and later it was recorded; 'will be allowed four months' deduction of time'. In October that year he was awarded his second ticket of leave. Unfortunately, he was pronounced insane by the medicine board at Port Arthur in 1859.

Prior to transportation Richard was described as a 'labourer', at Point Puer he trained as a shoemaker. Not only did he learn the trade sufficiently to earn a living, he also appears to have increased his literacy skills. Richard grew from 53 inches when fourteen, to 64.5 inches by twenty-two. He committed only one regulatory offence and one serious offence. Richard also married and had at least two children. Unfortunately, no further information about his family life is known. Despite successful training and education, and beginning a family and work life, the outcome of Richard's life was not a successful one. Richard died of mania at Saltwater River in Port Arthur in 1862, aged forty.

While there are limitations to the literacy data gathered, and the literacy levels of many of the convicts are either still unknown, or any information of their improvement or stagnancy remains unknown, it was found that at least 35 per cent of all the males could read and write, and 11 per cent could read (excluding the two males who died on transport). According to Godfrey and Maxwell-Stewart (2016), males convicted in London disproportionately claimed that they could read and write compared to those convicted in other English counties. This relationship was less evident amongst female convicts; nevertheless women convicted in London were still amongst the most literate convicts. It was possible to test the accuracy of these literacy claims. The less literate a population, the more likely it is to report ages in rounded years. The heaping of ages at decimal and mid-decimal points can be measured using a Whipple Index. The closer a Whipple Index score to one hundred, the fewer signs there are of age heaping, and therefore the more literate the population. Male convicts convicted in London have the lowest Whipple scores of all British and Irish convicts transported (Godfrey & Maxwell-Stewart 2016). In comparison, in England 41.6 per cent were illiterate in 1830. Specifically, 33.7 per cent of males were illiterate, and 49.5 per cent of females were. This remained fundamentally unchanged at least until 1846 (Hooper 1954, 303).

Point Puer education

All convicts had the benefit of some education if they were kept on the hulks and on the voyage over. This is because both secular and religious training were considered the very basis of the reforming process (Jackson 2001, 8). This was especially true for young male convicts, which is evidenced in the management of those at Point Puer. Educational training at Point Puer was even extended to the Crime Class by Lieutenant-Governor Franklin (Jackson 2001, 8). (The Crime Class held those who committed a crime and were sent to Point Puer as punishment, unlike the rest of those at Point Puer who were not sent there for secondary punishment.) In the earlier period (1834–1837) instruction consisted only of plain reading, writing and basic arithmetic (Hooper 1954, 56). Poor accommodation along with low staffing levels and deficiencies in supplies led to practices falling short of intentions (Tuffin 2007, 19). For instance, the Lancastrian System, which is a monitorial system, could be implemented only once the right accommodation was constructed in the late 1830s. Even then it was only partially used and by this time the system had been widely over taken elsewhere by the 'modern' system of education which grouped students by age and taught in the lecture method (Humphrey 1997, 34). Education was also limited by the exposure period. In Point Puer's early years, juveniles attended school for only one hour each night. However, by 1843, they attended school for 3.5 hours on alternate days (Horne, March 1843). The school was divided into thirty-two classes, monitored by the teacher and two convict overseers, and assisted by forty juvenile convict monitors (Tuffin 2007, 20). In addition to inadequate space, supplies were also problematic. Writing in 1839, Thomas James Lempriere, Commissariat Officer at Port Arthur in 1839, complained that the teacher's efforts were hampered by limited 'papers, pens, slates and books' (Lempriere 1954, 96). Horne concurred with this sentiment in 1843:

> The Class books are such as have been laid aside in good Schools in Britain for several years. There is no apparatus for illustrating lessons except one very small black-board seldom used … there is not so much as a Map of the World or Palestine in the School. In the more advanced classes the only book used for reading lessons, except a spelling book, is the Bible. (Horne, March 1843)

There were two reports written on Point Puer. The first was written by the insider Commandant Charles O'Hara Booth, in 1837, which was followed by Benjamin Horne, a prison inspector sent by the British Government, in 1843. Booth asserted that the system resulted in juveniles becoming 'proficient in the 3R's' (Burton 1986, 8). Whilst Booth was happy with the system, Horne was not. Horne believed Point Puer should be an institution

> where criminal boys may for a certain period undergo the punishment … at the same time they may also be so instructed in religious and moral duties and so trained in habits or order and industry leading to a considerable probability of at least a portion of them becoming good and useful members of society after the period of their punishment has expired. (Horne, March 1843)

With this in mind, Horne's standards were not met and his report was damning (Jackson 2001, 8). In comparing Point Puer with Parkhurst Prison, he found the former wanting:

> With regard to the school the conclusion to which I have reluctantly come is that it is of little benefit to the boys themselves in a secular point of view and that as a means of religious and moral improvement it is almost worthless. (Horne, March 1843)

Notwithstanding Horne's good intentions (demonstrated by him staying on as headmaster), largely because of his untimely death in 1843, many of the report's recommendations were not implemented. However, changes were made. Inappropriate communication was reduced, and playtime which Horne disapproved of, was removed, and the juveniles had 7.5 hours' labour and 2.5 hours of instruction (Burton 1986, 10). There was little exposure to contemporary teaching methods, and there were large classes of two hundred attendees with convicts employed as teachers from Port Arthur. As Horne complained to

Franklin: 'One of the prisoner teachers goes round ... and a boy thus stands the chance of receiving the benefit of his instructions at the rate of one two hundredth part of an hour once in two days' (Horne, March 1843). The monitorial system was still used under Horne but more care was taken in selection: where possible ticket of leave holders and third-class pass holders were employed (Burton 1986, 11). It is difficult to uncover how successful Point Puer's educational endeavours were. However, there is a suggestion that there was increasing efficacy over time (Anonymous 1836; Hooper 1954, 68). Still, Horne, headmaster for only three months, was the only trained teacher Point Puer ever had (Tuffin 2007, 20). Nevertheless, there was an effort made to educate juvenile convicts at Point Puer in order to ready them for freedom, even if practice fell short of expectations. The aim was to instil reformation from crime and to increase their chances in the job market. A market which, for working-class juveniles, did not need them to be advanced scholars. While such education may seem rudimentary, these convict juveniles were given the opportunity to learn. Female juvenile convicts, on the other hand, had no 'special' penal settlement established for them.

Millbank, where many of the female convicts were held awaiting transportation, did attempt to educate its charges. However, the matron recorded that there was no enthusiasm in learning to read and write. Millbank staff briefly taught arithmetic but the experiment failed (Beddoe 1979, 77). While the range of books was limited and inappropriate, Millbank had a library made up of religious works and volumes on the history of Carthage, Greece and Rome (Beddoe 1979, 78). Female convicts were also educated on-transport, which presents a contrasting picture of their improvement and enthusiasm. As described in Elizabeth Lang Grindod's account of the *Garland Grove* voyage to Elizabeth Fry, Grindod reported that the voyage went well despite the fact that eight women died en route. Nevertheless, she also added that by arrival they had taught the children who were old enough to read, and of the fifteen female convicts who were unacquainted with the alphabet, ten 'improved aptly'. Some could only read imperfectly but they improved, and others could read but not write and they 'gladly embraced the opportunity of learning' (Beddoe 1979, 117). Unfortunately, there is little information on the pre- and post-transportation literacy of the female juveniles. Only 65 per cent of the female juveniles (excluding one female who died on transport) had literacy information recorded in their Conduct Record: three (27 per cent) could read only; three (27 per cent) could read and write and five (45 per cent) could do neither. Only three of the females were known to have improved in their literacy. This gave a total of six females who could read and write in adulthood, which was evidenced through them signing the marriage register. Whereas convicts transported to NSW between 1826 and 1840, and the population at home, had similar levels of literacy. While less than half of females marrying between 1825 and 1840 could sign the marriage register, 45 per cent of female convicts tried in England could read, and a further 34.6 per cent could also write. The tests are not identical, since the indent information is questionnaire data while the marriage registers provide a practical test. However, other questionnaire-style data exist for paupers and migrants. Compared with the literacy rate of only 50 per cent for adult paupers in 1838, 80 per cent of female convicts were literate. Free female migrants arriving in Australia in 1838 had a literacy rate of 79 per cent. Therefore, England's female convicts represent female English workers generally (Nicholas & Oxley 1993, 728). Surprisingly, female prisoners in a study by Crone (2010) had a greater experience of schooling than their male counterparts. Despite a 'variety of sources from the nineteenth century suggesting that the male sex-privilege often meant that sons rather than daughters were afforded priority in the provision of schooling among working-class families' (Crone 2010, 32). The female juveniles are less literate than these comparison groups pre-transportation but clearly further research in this area is needed. It is doubtful that their youth is a factor as most of the females were older than schooling years by the time they were transported. This is a small sample but when the whole lives of the female juveniles is accounted for, at least 62 per cent could both read and write or just read, which is lower than all comparison groups excepting paupers. During the early years of industrialization, Nicholas and Oxley's data on literacy indicate that English women experienced falling living standards. Only 10 per cent of transported females born in 1795 were unable to read, while over 20 per cent of those born in 1820 were totally illiterate (1993, 746). The birth date of the female juveniles, which ranges from 1808 to 1832, must therefore be taking into account when addressing their relatively low literacy rate. All of the juveniles were born during the Industrial Revolution; this may begin to explain their lower literacy levels. Since there is very limited information of the literacy levels of the female juveniles' post-transportation, it cannot be known if the three females who improved in their literacy were alone. This is largely because once females married the colonial state was uninterested in them as economic assets and instead wanted them to produce the next colonial generations. That is not to say they were not economic assets, only that the government did not consider them so, or at least keeping tabs on their educational attainment was not deemed necessary. Firmer conclusions would need a larger sample. But would either sex have been educated if they arrived as a free immigrant, or was it their status as convicts which resulted in their education – flawed or otherwise?

How does the education of male and female juveniles compare with the free immigrant juveniles arriving in the colonies? The educational training of juvenile convicts must be put in context with the free population. There are no official records pre-1828 concerning government schools. In 1824 there were two government schools but the details are unknown. By 1828 statistical returns show that there were eight schools with 419 attendees. By 1835 there was an increase of 262 per cent in schools and 180 per cent in attendees while the population had only increased by 118 per cent (Anon 1836, 4–5). For example, in Hobart and its surrounding suburbs there were two daily schools, and one belonging to the church had thirty-one male, and nineteen female, attendees. The number admitted since the opening totalled 1332. Of the daily scholars, twenty-four also attended on Sundays. While the government rented the school house at £115.10s per annum, twenty-six of the juveniles paid 7s.6d weekly. This implies that many of the juveniles attended without charge, making it possible that some children from the lower classes, from the early 1820s were educated. While having to work or do domestic chores would still have been a barrier for many lower-class juveniles in the colony, those fortunate to be able to attend were taught spelling, reading, writing and arithmetic (Anon 1836). The statistical returns from 1828 to 1854 show that the number of government schools in VDL increased over time. In 1841 there were 906 males attending the schools and 753 females, giving a total of 1659 (Ewing 1843, xiii). By 1842 there were an extra 834 more children than in 1839 (Ewing 1843, xiv). This does not include either Point Puer's educational endeavours or infant schools. There were, for example, two infant schools in Hobart Town and one in Launceston by 1836 (Anon 1836, 4–5). This also does not include private schools, which in the same period 'made a greater increase'. From relatively few private schools in 1828, by 1835 'they were established in almost every Township, and Hobart Town had several' (Anon 1836, 5). There is limited information for Roman Catholic Church schools. Despite no returns, it is known that in December 1835 a Hobart, Roman Catholic–associated school had forty-five male, and twelve female, attendees (Anon 1836). From 1866, at least, there was also a provision of Ragged Schools in the colony, for example Watchorn-Street Ragged School and Lower Collins-Street Ragged School. The latter had an almost equal split of female and male juveniles registered with a total of 363, and an average daily attendance of 218 pupils.

Through exploring the relative educational opportunities in both Point Puer and free juveniles, it is *impossible* to assess the quality. Nevertheless, there were opportunities for free juveniles to be educated as early as 1824. Certainly, the number of free juveniles attending these schools increased over time. However, from the statistical returns it is impossible to assess the class (meaning the economic status) of attendees. Yet, we do know that some attendees were subsidized by the government. This implies these juveniles were from the lower classes. Therefore, while not all working-class free juveniles would have been educated, some were. As for convict juveniles, it is possible to demonstrate that (from the later date of 1834) juvenile convicts sent to Point Puer were given basic education. Indeed, they were encouraged to learn by not only having time set aside, but also having incentives held out to those who progressed. Those who carried out their menial labour tasks and learnt basic schooling were able to move into the trade training class. This suggests that while some free immigrant children and colonial-born free juveniles had the *chance* of education, their convict counterparts were *strongly urged* to do so. It is also important to note that even if juveniles from the lower classes were educated at home in England or in the colonies, this education would have ended when it was time for them to begin work. Whereas the convict juveniles were educated well into their, what we would now term, teenage years for as long as they remained at Point Puer. Nicholas and Shergold (1988, 9) point out that the English convicts transported to NSW were better educated than the working population at home. Three-quarters of the English who arrived in NSW could read and/or write; a significantly higher percentage than the average for all English workers (58 per cent) could sign the marriage register. Moreover, economists who have viewed education as a process of human capital formation found that 40 per cent literacy rate is the threshold for economic development. Australia's convicts easily attained this threshold, and the *male* juveniles were comfortably among this group (Nicholas & Shergold 1988, 9). Unfortunately, less information is known about the females.

Trade training

As well as scholastic education, practical skills were of importance to later employment. This chapter will now move on to assess the trade training of Point Puer and whether juveniles benefitted from such training later in life. Of those male juveniles who arrived in VDL, only twenty-nine are evidenced to have spent time at Point Puer. Often, only if a juvenile committed an offence while at the establishment was it noted where they were based. However, there were a further twelve males who arrived on juvenile-only transports and so it is very likely that they too were sent to Point Puer. This would give a total of forty-one juvenile males who were sent to Point Puer. However, given the difficulty of determining which juveniles spent time at Point Puer, it is difficult to know which juveniles benefitted from trade training. It was in an attempt to deal with the difficulty of assigning juveniles, in the early days of the Port Arthur settlement (1830–3), when it was a 'timber-getting camp', that a number of juvenile males were sent there and instructed in trades. It was hoped that these juveniles would 'become capable of rendering essential services to the public, and of afterwards earning for themselves a reputable livelihood' (Ross 1831, 273). From 1831 through to the establishment of Point Puer, boys were employed in a variety of skilled trades including sawing, shingle-splitting, shoemaking, boatbuilding, nailmaking, carpentry, brickmaking, blacksmithing and limeburning (Anon, September 1833). As early as the 1830s these juveniles were trained in trades considered useful to the colony. This arrangement at Port Arthur continued even after Point Puer's establishment, within trades including shoemaking, nailmaking and boatbuilding (Tuffin 2007, 10), thus highlighting the fluidity of the concept of Point Puer as a juvenile convict establishment. Initially the routine at Point Puer followed that of the adults at Port Arthur. Juveniles carried out chores necessary for establishing the settlement (Slee 2003, 7). There was one major difference and this was the early emphasis on trade training at Point Puer. Once the workshops were built the training began. The original intention of the Assignment Board was to employ juveniles in cultivating soil and then to draft them into the Colonial Marines. Instead, it was decided that trade training would produce useful workers (Slee 2003, 9). The official statistical returns detail the number and trade types taught in 1835 (and the number of pupils): carpenters (20), labourers (149), shoemakers (35), tailors (18), blacksmiths (6) and sawyers (14) (Anon 1836, 7). This training scheme expanded over the years: in 1846, for example, there were 490 boys at Point Puer involved in training as shoemakers and tailors (85), boatbuilders (13), carpenters and coopers (36), brickmakers (22), brick layers (16), bakers and cooks (11), stone masons and quarrymen (24), nailors (16) boats' crew (4) and sawyers (17). Other boys were employed in more general positions which included washermen, wardsmen, gardeners, carters and labourers (Slee 2003, 9).

Not all juveniles at the establishment would have benefitted from the opportunity of learning a trade. Placement in the workshops 'was reliant upon their religious and scholastic progress' (Tuffin 2007, 12). Their behaviour was also integral: the provision of trade training was used as part of the reward system. Entry into trades was contingent upon cooperating in menial, hard labour (Slee 2003, 39). The proportion of those within the trade classes, as opposed to those carrying out unskilled labour, grew from 1836 to 1849 (Hooper 1954, 124). Assignment was held out as an incentive for juveniles who excelled at their trade (Slee 2003, 39): 'The boys are not permitted to leave the establishment until they are acquainted with their trades, nor even then unless their conduct has been good' (Anon, August 1846, 122). During the 1830s, boys who showed themselves to be 'good and useful mechanics' were assigned at Hobart Town (Booth, July 1837). Therefore, advancing in trade was a requirement of release from Point Puer: 'the boy ... remains at Point Puer inevitably till he is old enough or is sufficiently master of his trade to obtain his own living' (Hampton, August 1846). Pride was taken in training these juveniles as alluded to in a letter from Booth to an enquiring settler. Booth informed him that 'all our best mechanics have been sent up to headquarters' but recommended two juveniles, Thomas Leighton a carpenter and George Boswell a Blacksmith, who he described as 'very useful' and 'well-disposed lads' (Hooper 1954). While many were placed in the trade class, there were practical limitations. A letter to Lieutenant-Governor Arthur from Commandant Booth in 1834 reveals that juveniles who were supposed to be employing their time as tailors lacked the necessary materials to do so. Instead they were clearing the grounds. It has been suggested that given the inconsistencies in instruction, trade training was poor and the skills taught were not necessarily helpful in finding employment in the colony. Particularly since there was a lack of agricultural training (Humphrey 1997, 36). Still, attempting to direct trade training to post-release needs was ahead of its time. Common in similar institutions at this period were meaningless tasks including picking oakum (Slee 2003, 39). Moreover, in 1843, the trade training was described as superior to that taught at Parkhurst by Horne (Horne, March 1843). There is also evidence of the skills of these juveniles. For example, the fittings and intricate stonework incorporated into the grand church built at Port Arthur, in 1836, still partially stands as a testament to their skill (Booth, July 1837b). This is not to forget the metalworkers who produced nails, tools, eating utensils and building fittings that have been lost to history (Tuffin 2007, 24). Despite not all entering the trade class, all juveniles were taught how to use the hoe and spade for 'raising produce for the sustenance of themselves and their fellows' (Booth, July 1837b).

Steps were made to improve Point Puer in line with Parkhurst through, among other changes, building a purpose-built penitentiary. However, before the new penitentiary could be occupied, the situation in the colony changed. There were an increasing number of juveniles sent to VDL from Parkhurst Prison, rather than from the hulks. Those that were sent out to Point Puer were either the worst behaved, or those coming out under 'juvenile emigration'. In this scheme, juveniles from Parkhurst were sent to VDL to serve time at Point Puer before entering the colonial workforce as passholders (Humphrey 2008, 32). When the probation system commenced in 1840, juveniles arriving in VDL were sent to probation stations other than Point Puer (Hooper 1954, 11). Furthermore, those that were directed to Point Puer often only spent twelve months there before being transferred (Hooper 1954, 12). Still, there were instances when juveniles not considered skilled enough in their trade were kept back even after 1840. For example, Booth remarked: 'As to the recommendation of the commandant, this boy is to be detained at Point Puer until more proficient in his trade.' This was in reference to 'Irish' William Fannin. Despite having spent twelve months' probation at Point Puer, he was kept back *not* due to bad behaviour but because he needed further training (Hooper 1854, 125). Nevertheless, there does seem to have been a push to remove boys from Point Puer but this was not necessarily at the expense of their training. For example, juveniles (mainly taken from the *Hindostan* in 1841) were removed to be attached to a gang employed in the erection of the New Magdalen in 1843. They had spent two years and seven months at Point Puer (Hooper 1954, 137). They were not removed because they were proficient in their trades. Not only were not all of them employed in the trades in which they had been trained at Point Puer, but also the comptroller-general stated that part of the reason for their removal was so they could be 'perfected in their trades before they are called upon to provide for themselves' (Hooper 1954, 137). Therefore, the sentiment of training these juveniles in trades remained unchanged, but the method was not. No longer was it deemed necessary for juveniles to remain at Point Puer to be trained and educated, it was now acceptable to send them out into the colony earlier. However, there was some difficulty in this by 1847. It was reported that while those proficient in their trades were discharged from Point Puer, many others remained 'for long periods in the hands of the government at the Depot near Hobart Town' and increasing numbers were becoming free-by-servitude with little chance of obtaining situations (Hooper 1954, 162–163). Still, the colonial Government would sometimes make a direct request for Point Puer labour. For example, in 1843, the director of Public Works applied for thirty juveniles to be sent to Hobart to learn the trades of masonry, bricklaying and carpentry (Montagu, June 1843). Ultimately, Point Puer became another probation station reserved for juveniles. However, after 1843 only the youngest boys were sent there; those over fifteen were sent elsewhere (Hooper 1954, 26; 139). Under the new system, to avoid contamination with adult probationers, juvenile convicts were sent to the now juvenile designated probation station at New Town Farm from 1842 (Hooper 1954, 121). It became the established practice to send boys recommended as proficient in their trades at Point Puer to this boys hiring depot (Hampton, August 1846).

Quantifying the success of the Point Puer training, or lack thereof, is difficult. However, Hooper did find some interesting, albeit short-term, life-outcomes for the juveniles transported on the *Frances Charlotte*. This ship was the first juvenile-only designated ship. The outcomes for these juveniles were varied but the majority were positive. Unfortunately, three of the youngest died between 1838 and 1840. A further three juveniles had the dubious honour of being the only juveniles in Point Puer history to successfully abscond to the mainland; they were recaptured. Another three were sent to Port Arthur for insubordination. While these nine juveniles were unsuccessful in the short term, twenty-four others obtained a ticket of leave within four years, two received conditional pardons before their sentence expired, and the rest became expirees (Hooper 1954, 8). In 1842 David Burn stated that 'several instructed there [*at Point Puer*] were already earning comfortable livelihoods in various parts of the colony, and numbers have feelingly acknowledged to Captain Booth the blessings they thence derived' (cited in Humphrey 1997, 35). These words must not be taken uncritically. However, while many visiting officials commented on the low educational value of Point Puer, even Horne asserted juveniles took assigned positions in trades learnt at Point Puer (Slee 2003, 13). While positions within the trades section were limited by resources and teaching skills, and were only available to half of the juveniles at any one time, some did benefit (Jackson 2001, 8). While not the initial instigator and while its successes are questionable, successful rehabilitation became a long-term goal (Slee 2003, 10). As pointed out by Lempriere, the aim of Point Puer was to give juvenile convicts the opportunity of 'learning a trade, of enabling them at a future period to earn a respectable livelihood' (Lempriere 1954, 89–90). Point Puer may have been one of the pioneers of the juvenile justice system, but it eventually fell behind in education and treatment in terms of the reformers expectations. Still, while criticized by many, John West found it 'refreshing to find that kindness and coercion were united in the discipline of Point Puer; an oasis in the desert of penal government' (Newman Unk, 4). Burn, meanwhile, questioned 'how many of England's poor but virtuous children would be overjoyed with the full provisions, excellent lodging, and comfortable clothing ... beneficial instruction – of Point Puer!' (Burn 1842, 3). For many contemporary observers Point Puer was a remarkable experiment.

With fewer convict juveniles arriving in VDL, the Point Puer population reduced from 800 in 1842 to under 200 by its closure in 1849 (Humphrey 1997). Cascades was instead used for the decreasing numbers needing accommodation (Hooper 1954, 167). Not all of the male juveniles ended up in Point Puer and it is unknown how many benefitted from trade training. Despite the flaws and criticisms, when compared with the immigrant population and those at home, this training was unique. Such juveniles would have had to rely on family connections to gain training and education at home. The level of instruction was behaviour dependent but these Point Puer boys were encouraged to learn; but did they go on to gainful employment?

Employment

Male juveniles

The juveniles' pre-transportation trades varied widely: gunmaker and brass polisher (1); farmers boy (1); shoemaker (14); farrier (1); willow worker/basket maker (1); labourer (40); punter waterman (1); errand boy (5); bookbinder (2); rough work (1); tailor (14); none/boy (10); look after hours (1); carters boy (1); lath render (1); carpenter (2); cooper (2); mariner (1); paviour (1); stable boy (1); poulterer (1); painter (1); bricklayer (1); brickmaker (1); unknown (12). In total there are sixteen different types of 'trade'. While a declaration of their trade in their Conduct Record does not mean they were employed in said trade at the time of their crime or trial, it does give an idea of the variety of different skills that these juveniles brought to the colonies. As argued by Maxwell-Stewart (2016, 422), the employment listed on the Conduct Records is reasonably reliable. Using literacy data, it is possible to 'check on the integrity of occupational information'. The most literate convicts were those with professional skills, followed closely by shopkeepers and dealers. The least literate were labourers, miners and agricultural workers. Some trades considered to be low skilled had fairly high literacy rates, reflecting job requirements. Errand boys, for example, needed to read addresses (Maxwell-Stewart 2016, 422). This is backed by Crone's (2010, 35) research which found that more male prisoners identified as skilled workers were sent to school than those identified as unskilled labourers. Notably, their proficiency in their listed trades usually remains unknowable. It is likely, given that the majority listed more than one skill, combined with their youth, they were not 'masters' of their trades. There were ninety-five separate skills listed for seventy-eight male juveniles which demonstrates the fluidity of their employment. It is perhaps unsurprising that the most common trade listed was 'labourer'. Not only did it cover a variety of tasks, it required less skill. Unfortunately, the employment is unknown for forty-six of the juveniles pre- or post-transportation. Seven of these males did have information recorded in their Conduct Record but they were recorded as 'boy' – indicating they did not yet have employment (*Case Study No.11*). Post-transportation, there were 42 per cent whose trades are unknown (this excludes three who died on transport).

Case Study No.11: Matthew Cantlin (aka Cantlon)

Matthew was baptized in 1816 by his parents Margaret Knight and John Cantlon. Unfortunately, in 1831, when Matthew was fourteen, he was convicted of simple larceny. He stole six shillings from a shop but in the trial he denied the charge:

> I was going with a boy to Tottenham to help him carry a parcel, as I was out of work – I went to the prosecutor's shop, and saw a man coming out – I asked him for a halfpenny orange, thinking he belonged to the shop; this witness then came out, and said I robbed the till – I denied it; she made a dart at me – I ran up the town, and this gentleman took me; she said she had lost 4s.6d., that she had had 5s.6d., and there were two sixpences left – the gentleman then said he had found 6s.; she then said she had had 7s., and she thought this was hers.

Despite Matthew's denial and having no previous convictions, he was found guilty and sentenced to seven years' transportation. A petition was made by Matthew's mother, which asked for him to be sent to a penitentiary and be taught a trade to be more useful to society. She further stressed that his father had died, that he had no previous convictions, his youth, and his previous good character; but to no avail. Matthew was transported aboard the *Southworth* in 1833. This Newington-born male was reported to have been 'good' aboard the *Euryalus*, and 'orderly' on transport.

It was not until 1835 that Matthew was recorded as committing an offence and this was a status offence. He had been 'out after hours' and was only admonished. Matthew was assigned when he committed this offence and was assigned to the same person when he committed another. Matthew assaulted his master's brother in 1836. This time he was returned to the government for reassignment. In 1837 he went 'into town without leave' but was only reprimanded. At this time, he was assigned to 'Conster'. This was his last offence. In total he committed only three offences, two of which were regulatory. For the assault of his master's brother he was only reassigned and not punished. There may have been an unrecorded mitigating factor.

Not only did Matthew have few offences, he also set himself apart. Matthew received his ticket of leave in 1837 after just forty-three months: *'to receive a T Leave on the Kings Birthday in August … for his exertions upon the occasion of a fire which recently took place in Murray Street Vide Lieu Dec sup 31/5/1837'.* Matthew's Conduct Record lists his trade as 'boy', implying he had no formal training. This is backed up by his mother's request of training. Unfortunately, it is unclear what tasks he undertook during assignment and whether there was any attempt to train him but he did not go on to any artisan trade after freedom. Instead he is recorded as being a police constable in 1836, a post he resigned from in 1838. His employment thereafter is unknown but he did marry in 1839 to an Elizabeth Buchannan. There is no record of any children. Matthew migrated from George Town to Port Phillip on the *Swan* in 1846. He died in 1854 in Victoria when just thirty-eight.

There is no evidence to suggest that Matthew spent any time at Point Puer or received any trade training. Instead he seems to have been assigned very early on despite his lack of skill. This case highlights that not all juveniles arriving after the establishment of Point Puer were subject to its education and training. Nevertheless, Matthew was able to gain respectable employment, marry and migrate.

While Matthew was assigned, overwhelmingly juveniles were not assigned. For example, of the fifty juveniles aboard the *Lord Lyndoch,* only eight were initially assigned. The characteristics that seemed to increase the likelihood of a juvenile being assigned were age and height. While there are also skill correlations, Nunn (2015, 65) points out that so few juveniles had trades that when 250 juveniles arrived between 1836 and 1837, 'other more significant factors mask any obvious skilled-labour selection process'. Of the three juveniles who claimed to have a trade, all were assigned, but what employment they were assigned into is unknown. Similarly, those who were apprentices pre-transportation were also more likely to be assigned in the colony but they were also older. Nunn also found height was a factor: 'While the records show that apprentices over five feet were more likely to be assigned than unskilled workers of the same height, taller unskilled workers were more likely to be assigned than skilled workers under five feet.' Of the eight boys who were assigned on the *Lord Lyndoch,* all were seventeen and over. The average height of those who were assigned was 5"1' compared to those not assigned who were 4"8' (Nunn 2015, 65). Therefore, age and height were important considerations in assignment. It is not certain whether skill was not important, only that generally speaking juveniles had less.

Gorton and Ramsland (2002), and Kociumbas (1997), argued that the juveniles that were transported came with trades and skills in colonial demand. For example, Gorton and Ramsland argued that the study of children sent to NSW reveals a pattern of children employed pre-transportation, thus enabling them to bring with them 'skills crucial to the colony'. However, Nunn found that of the 272 juveniles transported to VDL between 1835 and 1836, 50 per cent had their occupation listed as 'Boy', and therefore did not have a recognized skill. A further 14 per cent were identified as 'Labourer's Boy', and 8 per cent who had been sentenced as juveniles, but arrived as seventeen-year-olds, were identified as 'Labourer'. The skills of juveniles, like those of adults, were detailed precisely. If a juvenile worked as a 'boy' within a particular employment area, that employment context was also recorded. For example, 'tailors' boy'. It is unknown what 'boy' meant; whether there was a causal connection or an informal apprenticeship. Yet, formal apprenticeships were identified by having the number of years noted: William Gadsby (tailor two years); William Mason (poulterer eighteen months); George James Wick (tailor two years); Edward Robottom (shoemaker four years); John Jordan (tailor 3.5 years); Henry Hawthorn (cooper twelve months) (*Case Study No.12*). In Nunn's sample there were only eight juveniles identified in this way (Nunn 2015, 60). Of the juveniles there were 6 per cent who were recorded with this detail. Nunn (2015, 60) found only three juveniles he considered as having a trade; a leather dresser, a harness-maker and a copper-plate printer. This overview is consistent with what is known of juveniles repeatedly before the British courts. Magistrate Dyer reported to the Select Committee on Policing (1828):

> The ordinary trades exercised in the Metropolis do not afford a sufficient demand for boys in the shape of apprentices. Some others are provided for as pot-boys, errand boys and in other menial situations; but there still remains a considerable surplus who have no means of getting a livelihood. (cited in Nunn 2015, 60)

Similarly, Shore notes that 81 per cent of juveniles at Parkhurst were described as having no trade. By the nineteenth century, apprenticeships were declining. Those entering apprenticeships were usually fourteen (Shore 1999a, 40). Bearing in mind the ages of juveniles in this research, it is not surprising that few had recognized trades. While Nicholas (1988) contends that adult convicts were specifically selected for transportation *because* of their employment skills, Nunn points out that there is little evidence that the same was true for juveniles (2015, 61). Yet, even using the strictest consideration of a trade, therefore ignoring any description which included 'boy' (e.g. 'tailor boy') and ignoring manual labour jobs (e.g. 'brick layer'), 39 per cent of juveniles described themselves as having a trade. Twenty-five per cent were tailors and shoemakers, and there were more varied trades including a lath render, a farrier and a gun and brass polisher. Proficiency cannot be guaranteed and less than half were described as having trades, and given the youth of the group, they would not have been well advanced in their trades. Having skills on arrival in the colony does not translate to those skills being in demand, but the majority of these Londoners had worked and many of them had worked within skilled trades. This is despite the emphasis on the poor skills of London convicts in much of the literature about the nineteenth century. Godfrey and Maxwell-Stewart (2016) point out that there is no evidence that Londoners were disadvantaged in colonial labour markets. Certainly the juvenile convicts arrived with knowledge of work, but were they disadvantaged in the labour market? How were the juveniles employed in the colonies?

As these juveniles grew up in the colonies, did they increase their skill base and did they gain employment? As was expected, the range of trades increased as compared with pre-transportation. This information was uncovered from newspapers, their children's birth records and criminal records: unknown (41); not applicable (3); watch (2); hawker (1); pauper (1); tailor (6); police constable/field police/water police (6); shoemaker/bootmaker/bootcloser (9); publican (2); bookbinding (1); boatman (1); labourer (9); cook (1); farmer (2); general dealer (1); carpenter (4); sawyer (2); sailor/seaman (4); flower seller (1); bullock owner (1); fireman (1); manufacturer (2); mason/stone cutter (3); overseer (1); drayman (1); beggar (1); mechanic (1); miner (1); servant (1); fisherman/oysterman (2); general servant (1); carpenter (1); shepherd (1); cooper (1); woodsplitter (1); lodging house owner (1); making grass mats (1); clerk (2). There were forty-four different trade types found, and there were eighty-five separate employments listed, between fifty-six juveniles. Again proficiency remains unknown, but the increased fluidity of employment within the colony is evidenced. This demonstrates their ability to adapt to the needs of the colony to earn their living. While the highest concentration of post-transportation employment was listed as 'labourer', there were only 11 per cent who were labourers in adulthood compared with 42 per cent pre-transportation. This highlights the more specialized nature of many of the occupations taken up by these juveniles in the colony.

Very few juveniles are known to have gone on to become remarkably successful but there are a couple of examples including Phillip Maine (formerly a clerk) and James Alder, who both oddly became manufacturers of gingerbeer and soda water, and then both went into insolvency. The former migrated to Melbourne and the later to Geelong. James Alder became a 'confectionary maker'. He was granted his confectioners licenses in 1848. In 1854 he was a sodawater, lemonade and gingerbeer manufacturer in Geelong charging six shillings per dozen. In 1860 he put an article in the newspaper thanking his patrons for thirteen years of support. In 1861, James retired from his business due to ill-health and advertised all materials connected with the business for sale. Consequently, the extent of his business is known; one soda machine, one first-class bottling machine, six draught horses, three carts, three vans, one dray, one water cart, two carriages, harness and saddles, etc., five water tanks, two copper boilers and still casks and vats, etc., as well as the bottles and various ingredients and 'every requisite for carrying on one of the largest businesses in the colonies'. While he succeeded in building a large business, he was insolvent by 1865 to the sum of six pounds' liabilities and £102 assets. Only some of the debts were proven but it is unclear how much. James died just three years later. Despite a disappointing end to these businesses, and despite the rareness of the initial success, these examples illustrate that it was possible for these juveniles to break class barriers. More commonly juveniles worked in trades and were often fluid in their approach to employment as Henry Hawthorn's case demonstrates.

Case Study No.12: Henry Hawthorn

Born in 1829, Henry was thirteen when he was sentenced to seven years' transportation. In 1842 he was found guilty of simple larceny – he stole 5.5lbs of beef valued at three shillings from a shop. In his defence he declared: 'I never took it; and never saw anything of it'. He had been *acquitted* for the theft of a silk handkerchief. Henry's parents lived in London with his two brothers and three sisters. Originally Henry was from Ireland, he was a Protestant and could read and write. He was reported as 'indifferent' in the gaol, and 'bad' aboard the *Euryalus* (where he had trouble with his health) and 'no offences, not employed, good conduct' was recorded by the *Anson* surgeon-superintendent. He grew from 4"9' aged fifteen, to 5"4' by the age of twenty-three.

Henry was transported in 1843 and was approximately fifteen on arrival. In the colonies Henry went on to commit a number of offences. His first offence was in 1845 and was minor in nature – 'misconduct in making use of obscene language' – for which he was given one-month hard labour and it was recommended to include the tread wheel. He then absconded in 1846 and was given six months' hard labour and was recommended to be downgraded to the crime class. In the same year it was recorded: 'disorderly conduct in assisting a fellow prisoner to take a knife from the hall' which resulted in his existing sentence of hard labour being extended by a month. Then he 'Misconduct[ed himself] in wilfully cutting a piece of board without authority' for which he was sentenced to seven days' solitary confinement. Next, he misrepresented his abilities leading to ten days' solitary confinement. After being absent without leave, he was given ten days' hard labour in chains. When he absconded in 1847, he was given six months' imprisonment and hard labour in chains. For the same offence the following month, he was given the same sentence but for eighteen months' duration. However, after absconding the following month he was only admonished. Henry's next record was not until 1848, when he was accused of larceny under five pounds – but he was discharged. He was at this time at Launceston prisoner's barracks. One month later he was accused of the same crime but this time he was given eighteen months' hard labour and imprisonment and was further recommended to be sent to Port Arthur. Then when he misconducted himself by taking his trousers off without permission, he was given ten days' solitary confinement in 1849. When he threw 'a dead kid at an overseer' at Cascades he was given three months' imprisonment with hard labour in addition to his existing sentence.

Henry's next offence was more serious than all his previous offences – he was convicted of burgling the house of Rev Frederick Holdship Cox. He stole a writing desk and other articles including wearing apparel in 1850. Henry committed this crime with Noah Renshaw, and Samuel Levy was indicted for receiving. Both Renshaw and Levy were prisoners, unlike Henry who was free-by-servitude. The jury found the prisoners guilty and Hawthorn and Renshaw were re-transported for life, and Levy for fourteen years (*Hobarton Guardian, or, True Friend of Tasmania* 4 December 1850, 3; *The Courier* 3 December 1850, 3). When confined in the police station Henry escaped. The constable on duty had accidently left the door open and consequently received six months' hard labour at Turnbridge for gross misconduct (*Hobarton Guardian, or, True Friend of Tasmania* 9 November 1850, 3). Henry was sent to Norfolk Island when he was apprehended, and given a five-year probation period. Henry was still only twenty-three.

At Norfolk Island he committed many minor offences. For idleness in 1851, he was given fourteen days' hard labour. He was then given the same sentence for an illegible offence. Then because he wilfully destroyed his kettle he was given three months' hard labour. When he was disobedient in August, he was given a further three months' hard labour. He was given the same sentence again in November for possessing tobacco. This offence and sentence was duplicated in 1852. When he was disobedient in April, he was given a further three months' hard labour. Then when he had sheep skins in his possession in November, he was given the relatively minor punishment – in relation to the others – of fourteen days' hard labour. He was given this sentence again for using improper language. In 1855, he was disobedient and given thirty days' hard labour but it was also recommended that he not reside in the district of Fingal. He absconded in 1857, and was given hard labour. He was back in Hobart at this point. In 1859, Henry absconded again and was given two months' hard labour – at this point it appears he had earned his ticket of leave and was residing in Launceston. This was the last offence recorded in his Conduct Record but it also states that his ticket of leave was revoked in 1861. He had only earned his ticket in 1858.

His ticket had been revoked because he did not report to muster. However, he was apprehended in 1862. Henry, who had been working as a shepherd and was then thirty-three, was accused of 'leaving a flock of sheep at Mike Howe's Marsh unprotected and absented himself altogether by proceeding to Kingston, Avoca'. Henry acknowledged the offence. The prosecutor stated that the defendant had never complained of dissatisfaction or given notice of leave and that he took with him rations, leaving the sheep to fend for themselves. Henry pleaded guilty to the offence against the law of Masters and Servant Act. The bench sentenced him to a penalty of ten pounds and costs (*The Mercury* 9 December 1862, 4). Unable to pay, he served one-month imprisonment, during which he escaped from the Oatlands Gaol Party. He was employed repairing the foot paths and asked permission from Constable Hill to step aside. It was granted, and he did not return (*The Mercury* 19 December 1862, 5). He was again found and brought before the Warden and Councillor Roe. He was arrested at Campbell Town and admitted to absconding, stating, 'he hardly knew what caused him to do so'. Henry was sentenced to three months' hard labour at Hobart Town. Mr Gumley, the gaol keeper, enquired whether any step would be taken against the defendant for having made away with a full suite of prisoners clothing (the clothes he was wearing). The bench informed him that a detainer was lodged against the defendant (*The Mercury* 31 December 1862, 4).

Henry had originally earned his free certificate in 1850 and had a number of different employments in his life. Pre-transportation Henry had been a labourer but also a cooper for twelve months, and a shoemaker. Yet in the colony he had worked as both a carpenter and a shepherd. Henry exemplifies the fluid employment of these juveniles. It was possible that this was out of necessity because of a lack of employment related to his skills. There is no record of a marriage but he died in NSW, in 1865, aged just thirty-six.

There is no overwhelming evidence that those who spent time at Point Puer and whose post-transportation trades are known learnt trades there which allowed them to gain colonial employment. Three became labourers. While two became sawyers, a trade they very likely learnt at Point Puer, both had had skilled trades pre-transportation; one had been a poulterer for eighteen months and the other a tailor. It is likely that in the colonies work as a sawyer was more readily available, and so this skill allowed them to gain employment. Three became shoemakers, but two of those had been shoemakers' pre-transportation. Of the two juveniles who became tailors in the colony, one was recorded pre-transportation as a complete tailor who could 'sew a coat well', and the other *did* work as a tailor in the colony but he *died* when working as a labourer. Moreover, one of those shoemakers later went on to become a general servant. However, there was also a farmer, a stone cutter and a carpenter (the latter of which became a lodging house owner) who could have learnt their skills at Point Puer. Another juvenile, John Press, was a labourer pre-transportation and became a tailor, a trade he *did* learn at Point Puer. He became proficient enough in this trade to be sent to New Town Farm and described as a 'good tailor'. Additionally, there was also a grocer and an oysterman. While they may not have been trained in these trades at Point Puer, they may have been helped into their trades by educational attainment there.[1] One of the juveniles, who could already both read and write pre-transportation, went on to became a clerk at Cascades, whereas pre-transportation he had worked as a brickmaker. This is an improvement. It is worth noting that in London, despite being able to read and write, it would have been very unlikely that he would have become a clerk. It was being in the colonies which enabled him to take up the occupation, even if the skills were at least partially learnt at home. The only conclusion here is that there were mixed results but that they were not unfavourable. The juveniles used a mixture of their pre-transportation skills, and those skills they picked up in the convict system (on assignment and/or in Point Puer), to earn their colonial livelihood.

It has been argued that domestic workers and unskilled urban workers brought skills less well suited to colonial needs. Consequently, these convicts had to adjust and learn new skills when they were assigned to unfamiliar employment in agriculture or the public service. Nicholas and Shergold (1988, 10) found that when these convicts became free they utilized pre-transportation skills and rejected their colonial employment such as building roads and clearing land. There are only seven known cases where a juvenile worked in the same trade they had worked in pre-transportation and this includes two labourers and three others who are also known to have worked in other trades in the colony.[2] This may be because, as juveniles, these convicts had less time to become skilled in, and attached to, their pre-transportation trades. Was it the type of, or lack of range of, the juveniles' pre-transportation skills which made it necessary for them to shift trades in the colony? Nicholas and Shergold (1988, 9) found that convicts brought useful skills to NSW. The proportion of convicts in the skilled, semi-skilled and unskilled occupational categories was roughly the same as the English workforce in 1841. They found that convicts transported to NSW came from the same occupational population as English free workers. While there was an urban-skill bias, the wide range of skills convicts brought suited the building of a new colony. This wide skill range was reflected amongst the convicts transported to VDL. However, the urban bias is particularly evident in the juveniles from London, and they were further disadvantaged due to their youth with regard to size and work experience. Adult convicts inevitably arrived with more skill, and a greater variety of skill, than juvenile convicts. This is inevitably a disadvantage to juveniles, but within the context of the economy and with the 'special' management that juveniles received, the majority seem to have fared well on the labour market. What were the effects of the economy?

Economy

As the economy changed over time, the labour market fluctuations affected the transportation system. Free settlers, convict adults and juveniles were all affected. In the 1830s when land was opening up, the supply of convict labour was short of demand (Hooper 1954, 156). VDL developed from a prison farm on subsistence to a colony with an agricultural and pastoral economy in 1820, after just sixteen years of occupation. Yet, the colony was still a small settlement of 5,500. The only exports were grain and salted meat, and internal trade depended on government demand. A total of 2588 convicts and 2880 free colonists (of whom only 714 *arrived* free) survived under these conditions. Yet, by the 1850s, Hobart challenged Sydney as the Australian commercial centre (Hartwell 1954, 11). In this time, both manufacturers and trade grew. For example, there were five mills in 1824 but by 1835 there were forty-seven; an increase of 840 per cent (Anon 1836). However, the comparative wage rate from 1839 to 1842 shows a slight decrease due to increased mechanic numbers (Ewing 1843, xiii). This affected both free and assigned workers, including juvenile convicts. In 1837 when Point Puer contained 233 juveniles and labour was in demand, 39 juveniles were sent down to Hobart for assignment (Hooper 1854, 158). However, this demand did not continue and the *Mandarin boys* serve as an example. The fifty-one *Mandarin boys* (named after their transport) arrived directly from Parkhurst Prison in 1843. They were to be regarded as free immigrants and provided with employment and accommodation without necessarily making their convict origins known (Hooper 1954, 107). Their guardian was charged with finding work related to their Parkhurst Prison training. This sample cannot represent convict juveniles arriving under 'normal' circumstances. While they were technically free they were transported against their will, they were trained in trades in Parkhurst Prison, they underwent its disciplinary regime, and they were aided and supervised during their colonial settlement. Notwithstanding these different (dis)advantages, what this sample does allow is an understanding of the difficulty of gaining colonial employment in the period (Hooper 1954, 107–108). Despite being 'free', their behaviour was closely supervised and disapproved of. They absconded from work, thieved among themselves and were generally insubordinate. First they were given solitary confinement, and when their behaviour persisted they were flogged. Many of these punishments were for crimes that 'normal' free settlers would not have been punished: status crimes (Hooper 1954, 109). Therefore, this group was unique. Nevertheless, of interest here is their struggle to gain situations. Early 1844, thirty-seven had gained positions in private service, ten juveniles were transferred to the prisoner's barracks, two were under sentence in the house of correction, one remained in quarters but were described as good and the last had absconded (Hooper 1954, 111). It is possible that it was their behaviour which discouraged employers as they were described as follows; satisfactory (fifteen), vacillating between good and bad (six) and the remaining thirty 'as manifesting propensities positively bad'

(Hooper 1954, 111). Another factor was the condition of the labour market. There was little demand in the colony for their services.

During 1839–1840, VDL experienced a short boom which collapsed at the end of 1840 and was followed by five years of depression. The boom was due to increasing trade with Dollap District and South Australia. Exports of wool and whale oil were higher than at any time pre-1850. Credit expansion was allowed by the colonial banks and land sales doubled (Hooper 1954, 158). This 'boom' period led settlers into speculations using borrowed money. Interest rates rose resulting in bankruptcy. Colonies imported more than they exported, and their finances were strained (Brand 1990, 24). The burst was also thought to be caused by the withdrawal of £40,000 by the commissariat, and the setting up of the colonial bank requiring coin for its initial reserve from its co-bankers. This was sufficient to begin the deflationary movement (Hooper 1954, 159). Essentially the banks needed to call in debts but settlers could not pay. This, all at a time when the new convict probation system was being launched (Brand 1990, 24). An economic depression, a 40 per cent increase in the convict population (thanks to the cessation of transportation to NSW), the new untested probation system, the inexperienced Lieutenant-Governor Wilmot and unsympathetic London superiors – all added up to 'financial ruin' (Shaw 1966, 299–301). What-is-more, the labour shortage during 1840–1 had led Franklin to promote free immigration (it had earlier been suspended). Unfortunately, when the convicts, who had been taken off the labour market by the new probation system, finally emerged from the probation gang seeking waged work – there was none (Shaw 1966, 279–281). The external job market was critical. Neither the settlers nor the colonial government could afford to pay the convicts according to Lord Stanley's (Secretary of State for the Colonies) new terms. To prevent starvation and crime, Wilmot kept some probation passholders in government service. With increasing unemployment Stanley eventually agreed to allow conditionally pardoned convicts to seek work on the mainland (Shaw 1966, 299–301). It was too little too late. By 1850 VDL had a well-developed economy with a pastoral and agricultural core producing the export staples; wool and wheat. Simultaneously, the growth of domestic industry and 'the tiny beginnings of a basic industrialism' (a coal mine and a few foundries) was gradually liberating the colony from complete dependence on external trade. Since 1820 agriculture had expanded and increased in efficiency, the wool industry was mature, but the fisheries were declining (Hartwell 1954, 13). Labour, convict and free, was plentiful after 1830. Government policy encouraged settlement, at first by giving away land and later by selling it cheaply. Thus VDL progressed into a commercial economy (Hartwell 1954, 13). However, as noted, by 1843 conditions favourable to the employment of convict labour of any type had disappeared (Hooper 1954, 115). This is highlighted by the changing demand for assignees. Whereas in 1835 there had been 2740 assignees and a demand for 3130 more; by 1846 there were 8500 qualified to seek employment, and 3500 did not find situations (Hooper 1954, 115). Wilmot suggested that, as well as the Parkhurst boys, the juveniles who had undergone trade training at Point Puer were also struggling to gain employment. Demand for their services had fallen (Hooper 1954, 119).

When we compare the *Mandarin Boys* with the thirty-nine *Moffatt Boys*, who arrived at the earlier date of 1834, there are different outcomes. They were kept separate from 'contaminating forces' both on transport and at Point Puer, but they were convicts. Within just three years most were forwarded to Hobart Town for assignment (Hooper 1954, 126). Ten were given a certificate of freedom by 1840, and by 1841 six earned their ticket of leave and entered the service of free settlers. However, two did die at Point Puer (Hooper 1954, 127). These juveniles arrived before the economic depression had fully taken hold which may have aided their move into employment. It must be highlighted that we are not comparing like for like. While the *Mandarin Boys* were described as badly behaved, the juveniles from the *Moffatt* were generally well behaved: twenty broke no regulations and only seven or eight were tried once or twice after arrival (Hooper 1954, 126). It is likely that the *Mandarin Boys'* bad press was influenced by an expectation of exemplary behaviour which was not met. They were not particularly bad, but they were not as well behaved as was expected of juveniles chosen to be the privileged 'exiles'. Still, what the disparities in their struggle for employment highlight is that the arrival date was integral to success when entering the employment market. A different pattern emerges for female juveniles.

Female juveniles

There is far less variety of skill demonstrated by females, as compared with the males, pre-transportation but this was expected: house servant/maid (5); prostitute (3); nurse maid/girl (10); wash/get-up linen (1); needle girl (2); unk (2). There were twenty-one separate trades listed for sixteen females, but only five different trade types. The most common employment listed was that of nurse maid: meaning they nursed children. Less skill variety does not mean the skills they brought were any less important. Moreover, it is possible that many were kept home to look after house and family, and as such skills learnt were not necessarily included in Conduct Records. Very little is known of their post-transportation trades: unknown (10); nurse maid/girl (4); housemaid (2); prostitute (2); needle girl (1). This is because most of the females married. This is not to say they did not work. Not only would they have managed their households and taken on child rearing, but also they may have worked to supplement the household income. Unfortunately, such endeavours were not recorded. Seventy-six per cent of the females in Godfrey and colleagues (2017) study 'were either supported by husbands who were the main wage-earners, were unemployed, or were engaged in earning a little money in marginal and insecure urban occupations such as charwomen, street sellers or hawkers'. Working women very rarely had the opportunity to enter the skilled subsection of the working classes. Roberts's (1995) oral history of working-class women in the late-nineteenth and early-twentieth centuries found that women's employment opportunities were largely limited to work before marriage, which included domestic servants, shop assistants and factory workers. Therefore, the reduction in employment for female juveniles from their pre- to post-transportation lives reflects patterns of working-class women in Britain. Additionally, the post-transportation employment of male juveniles was often recorded on their children's birth certificates. Such documents took no interest in female employment. Contemporaries saw females as wives and mothers. Officials recording trades in the Conduct Records were actively seeking knowledge of female skills. At no other point were the female convicts, or indeed free females, trades and skills actively sought (excepting sometimes on conviction). When females married their skills ceased to matter for recording purposes, except within the unique circumstances of the Conduct Record. Consequently, it is difficult to find details of post-transportation employment. It is known that domestic roles were the most common type of employment for females in the colonies. Commonly, the juvenile females worked as nurse maids. The occupational structure of female convicts transported to NSW, between 1826 and 1840, was compared with female occupations in the 1841 English and Irish census by Nicholas and Oxley. Using Armstrong's Social-Skill Classification, they found that 78 per cent of English female convicts and 83 per cent of English female workers were in the skilled and semi-skilled categories. This is not surprising since most convicts were employed in domestic service which is classified as skilled/semi-skilled work (1993, 725). When contemporaries did discuss female employment there was often a concentration on their (what was contemporaneously seen as) 'immoral' behaviour; meaning prostitution. Only three of the female juveniles worked, at some point, as prostitutes (see *Case Study No.13* Ellen Caley [aka Hunt]).

Middle-class contemporary commentary held sway on the historiography of female convicts well into the twentieth century. Prostitution was a particular interest of contemporaries and historians. Even Wood (1922), along with Shaw (1966), Clark (1987) and Robson (1976), believed female convicts were generally prostitutes. However, Wood did paint them as less guilty than the British seamen and officers for their services. While this relieves female convicts of guilt, it paints them as victims. Meanwhile other historians, based on 'little more than contemporary remarks' painted female convicts as morally abandoned (Oxley 1996, 6). Robson (1976) did attempt to find the number of female convicts who were prostitutes by relying on reports made by gaolers and surgeon-superintendents, and occasionally the women themselves. He estimated 20 per cent of the convict women sent to VDL had been prostitutes. Yet, as Oxley (1996, 6) pointed out, he failed to recognize that the social superiors writing these records often confused cohabitation and promiscuity with prostitution. What is more, even though 80 per cent of female convicts were not prostitutes, as determined by himself, he still concluded that female convicts were a 'bad lot'. Contemporaries' contempt for the morals of these females was cemented in 1790 when the *Lady Juliana*, a First Fleet ship, was labelled the 'floating brothel'. There were rumoured to be liaisons between the female convicts and the male officers. At this time, women were seen as a dichotomy between virtuous purity, and wild and abandoned. For instance, the Molesworth report concluded that with scarcely an exception the female convicts were 'drunken and abandoned prostitutes'. Yet, as Brooke and Brandon (2005, 100–111) pointed out, the contemporary stereotyping of female convicts as 'wild, drunken, sexual commodities' did not reflect the majority. Prostitution was judged to be evidence of immorality. Consequently, prostitution and badness were confused and women who misconducted themselves were often wrongly characterized as prostitutes (Oxley 1996, 7). This concentration on convict women as prostitutes resulted in other aspects of their lives being overlooked. Even the concept of prostitution employed was limited because it was conceptualized in terms of morality rather than work (Oxley 1996, 7). Thankfully, in the 1970s and 1980s with the second wave of feminism, the stereotype began to break. Dixon (1975) and Summers (1975) brought women back into focus. Nevertheless, they did not go beyond the stereotype of females as prostitutes and reinterpreted the ideas instead of questioning its validity. Prostitution, like marriage, was part of the female patriarchal condition in which women traded sexual services for economic support. Focusing on sexual exploitation highlighted systematic discriminations but robbed women of their agency. Females in Dixon's colonial story ended up being 'the victims of victims'; an outlet for male hostilities bred from male servitude. Summers's work also 'presented a dismal status for women at the mercy of the imperial whoremaster' where prostitution was foisted onto them due to a lack of official accommodation and support. However, Summers did argue that these female convicts did not willingly accept their fate (Oxley 1996, 8). Later Sturma (1978) used Robson and Clark's findings on female crimes and pre-transportation occupations to locate them in their economic context. Then, both Robinson (1988) and Beddoe (1979) demonstrated that not all female convicts were 'drunken whores'. Increasingly, it has been acknowledged that some female convicts did engage in prostitution, but it was viewed as work. Not an all-encompassing life-choice, but an economic option which women could turn to and mix with ordinary work – and sometimes crime. 'Prostitution, harassment and sexual abuse were part of many women's working lives but they were not measures of female immorality' (Oxley 1996, 9). This will be shown in the following case study.

Case Study No.13: Ellen Caley (aka Hunt)

Ellen was born in 1829, and was just twelve when she was sentenced to transportation. She was convicted under the name of 'Caley'. However, she was also known as 'Hunt', 'Jane Kilrone' and 'Ellen Caylon'. Ellen was tried in 1841 for pickpocketing a handkerchief worth forty-eight pence in St. James' Park. In her defence she simply stated: 'I did not do it'. When sentencing Ellen and her accomplice, Charles Cotter, the *Old Bailey Proceedings* recorded:

> Cotter*-Guilty Aged 16.-Transported for Ten Years-Convict Ship
> Caley†-Guilty. Aged 12.-Transported for Ten Years-Penitentiary

The words 'convict ship' and 'penitentiary' both refer to where the two would be held prior to transportation. Since Charles was male he was placed on the hulks, whereas Ellen would be placed in a penitentiary. While the star indicates that Charles had a previous conviction, Ellen had also previously been confined for seven days for breaking windows. Ellen was originally from Bloomsbury, London, and was a Roman Catholic who could neither read nor write. Her gaol report described her as 'bad convicted before', and similarly the surgeon-superintendent described her as 'bad'. Ellen had a tattoo of 'JD' on her left arm. Ellen had both a father and a brother before she was transported aboard the *Royal Admiral* in 1842.

Ellen arrived in Hobart aged fifteen. However, given her stated age at trial she would have been thirteen; yet another juvenile who misled the court about her age. The surgeon-superintendent's description likely arose from her misbehaviour on transport. As a result of this behaviour Ellen was confined in the house of correction on arrival in Hobart. In 1843, due to disorderly conduct, she was given six months' hard labour. She had been at Brickfields hiring depot but was then moved into the penitentiary's third class. When she was absent without leave in 1844, whilst assigned to 'Evans', she was moved to Cascades factory and given three months' hard labour as punishment. For misconduct, when assigned to 'Frederick' in 1844, Ellen was given fourteen days' solitary confinement. Then Ellen misconducted herself 'in being in a brothel and presenting herself free' in 1846 and was given three months' hard labour as punishment. At this point she had earned a ticket of leave. The following October Ellen was recorded as 'idle and disorderly and earning her living by prostitution' and was consequently given six months' hard labour. Misconduct in 1847 led to three months' hard labour. Being drunk and using indecent language in March led to a ten-shilling fine. Misconduct just ten days later led to ten days' solitary confinement and an order 'not to remain in Hobart Town or Launceston'. The following month it was again recorded: 'misconduct being a common prostitute' and Ellen was given ten days at the Hobart factory, had her ticket of leave revoked and was then to be sent to the Ross factory. When Ellen did not proceed to Bothwell according to her pass in 1848, she was given one-month hard labour at Hobart factory.

In 1849 Ellen gave birth to an illegitimate child at the nursery and named him James. Now at the Ross factory, she was insubordinate in March and given three months' hard labour. In November, Ellen was given four days in the cells at Ross for assault. In December, when Ellen was in Launceston without a pass, she was given three months' hard labour. When, in 1850, Ellen was found to be living in a disorderly house and was given one-month hard labour. Ellen was out after hours in June and was consequently given one-month hard labour. For the same offence in November she was given two months' hard labour. In February the following year she was out after hours and given fourteen days' hard labour. When Ellen was caught 'disturbing the peace using obscene language' she was fined five shillings. Next she was out after hours and given one-month hard labour. She was given another five shilling fine for using obscene language. Ellen was again out after hours in April, then being out after hours and disturbing the peace in May resulting in two months' hard labour, and disturbing the peace in December gained her another five shilling fine. There were no more offences recorded against

Ellen's name after this point. Ellen had spent time in Cascades, Launceston and Ross factories.

Ellen had earned a ticket of leave in 1845 which must have been revoked because she earned another in 1847. This latter ticket of leave was revoked in 1848, but she was again awarded a ticket of leave in 1849. Ellen was free-by-servitude in 1851, at which point there were no more offences recorded against her name. Ellen was a 'nurse girl' pre-transportation and it is likely she worked in different domestic roles while in the colonies while on assignment – but the Conduct Record only gives information on her work as a prostitute. There is no record of Ellen marrying, but she did seek permission-to-marry George Wilson in 1849. This permission was revoked because George was unable to support a wife (she was the only juvenile refused permission). Nevertheless, there is some evidence to show that Ellen had three children. The birth of James Caylon is recorded in her Conduct Record. This illegitimate child was born in 1849 in Campbell Town, Ross Factory. There is less certain evidence that she had two further children: one female child named Jane Maddox or Hunt was born in 1855 and was admitted as an orphan in 1862 to the Girls School New Town, Tasmania and was later apprenticed to William Gunn in 1870 at Broadmarsh, Tasmania until 1875; and a male child named George (Maddox/Maddon or Hunt) who was born in 1859 and was also admitted as an orphan, in 1862, to the Infant School New Town, Tasmania. He was later apprenticed in 1873 to Mr Muscatt.

This case study demonstrates that while we do not know information about the whole of Ellen's life, and she did work as a prostitute for part of it, it was *not* her whole life. It also demonstrates the authority's concentration; they do not outline any details about her assignment employment but instead record various connections to prostitution.

Reid (2003, 3) argues that female convicts were systematically assigned to settlers based on their pre-transportation occupations and skills, and they were *not* a 'squandered resource'. And that there was a move away from viewing the female convict role as marriage and birthing, which persisted in the early days of settlement, to being increasingly seen as a source of unpaid labour. Like men, a shortage of labour meant that in the past women had been able to bargain and gain indulgences both from the state and in assigned service. However, the escape routes for female convicts, whereby marriage meant assignment to their husband and therefore removal from forced colonial labour, closed over time (Reid 2007, 132). In the early-1820s almost 60 per cent of female convicts were married within two or three years of arrival (Reid 2003, 10). From 1829 regulations put in place by Governor Arthur meant that not only was the route to marriage slowed, but also female assignment became increasingly ordered and regulated (Reid 2003, 10). Female convicts were increasingly seen as a bonded labour force which resulted in them becoming subject to heightened servitude, discipline and punishment (Reid 2007, 154). As Reid points out, demand for female convict labour was neither static nor universal. It shifted between 1820 and 1850, when convict labour was reformed and streamlined (2003, 3–4). Arthur, in response to a proposed new management scheme which would have made settlers take one female convict for every two/three male convicts, stated that there had not 'during the last three years in this Colony, been any difficulty in assigning to the service of settlers such female convicts as ... were assignable' (Reid 2003, 24). This continued even under the economic depression:

> Of those who arrived on the *Garland Grove* 27/1 last, with 1 single exception the whole number obtained situations within 6 weeks from the date of arrival. And that person was 68 years of age. Out of the 1,000 women who have been transported to this colony during the last 18 months, in the last 6 ships, 709 were engaged within one week of the date of their arrivals, of these 6 ships 3 were from Ireland, and many of the women out of them were completely useless for any household purpose. Thus in the case of the *Waverley* – although many applications were initially made they were withdrawn once they knew it was from Ireland. But even under such unfavourable circumstances 30 gained a place within a month. (Franklin 1843, 12)

Out of the English women three-quarters were engaged within a month of their arrival. Such a demand demonstrates that female convicts were readily assigned despite the arrival of free immigrants. Franklin further adds that the factories would always have a population if the ships of female convicts sent over contained 'lame, aged, mentally helpless and incapable, pregnant, nursing, mothering women' (1843, 13). Economic growth stimulated demand for female convict servants from the mid-1820s onwards and consequently the majority of female convicts were assigned on arrival. If they remained unemployed on arrival it was generally due to, as Franklin pointed out, ill health, pregnancy or child-care responsibilities, and not through lack of demand for their labour (Reid 2003, 4–5). Demand was not limited to newly arrived female convicts. On average just under three-quarters of females eligible for assignment at each muster were assigned. The remaining females were usually at the female house of correction due to behaviour. For example, in 1832 of the 284 women confined to the Hobart house of correction, just 18 were awaiting assignment. With the growth of the economy from 1820 to 1830 there was increasing demand for female convict labour and contemporary complaints about the shortage of convict servants and the high price of free female labour. In 1825 all the females who arrived on the *Henry* were assigned within days except one infirm female and three nursing mothers. Governor Arthur even detained the *Mermaid* female convict ship (which was en route to Sydney) because VDL needed female labour (Reid 2003, 6). This demand persisted, for example, in 1837 when the *Platina* arrived newspaper reports complained only one-third of applications could be fulfilled (Reid 2003, 7). By 1835 free female wage rates had risen to between twelve and thirty pounds per annum. Wages were even higher in Launceston and the surrounding district, where labour shortages meant female wages were comparable with male wages. Despite their unfree status, female convicts also benefitted from these labour shortages as it increased their bargaining power over issues including work hours, rations and leisure time. From 1832 to 1837, assisted emigration led to 13,000 additional female colonists. However, they only supplemented, and did not replace, convict labour. This is evidenced through the convict appropriation rates which remained consistently high throughout the assisted female emigration period. Evidence even suggests that some employers preferred convict labour. As John Price, Chief Police Magistrate, commented, 'few good house-servants come out free ... good servants are often transported' (Reid 2003, 8). Moreover, female convicts, as opposed to free females, could be sent to the less desirable interior. Consequently, the colonies core labour force remained that of the female convicts despite the arrival of free migrants (Reid 2003, 9).

The first ten female juveniles arriving in VDL in the assignment period were all assigned within a year. After the switch to the probation system, the female juveniles were still assigned but at a slower rate. However, it is only possible to know whether they were assigned if they committed an offence. At which point their status and where they were based were included. Therefore, these females may have been assigned at earlier dates but did not offend until later. Certainly, if they were badly behaved their assignment was postponed as in the case of Ellen Caley (*see Case Study No.13*). There seems to have been little difficulty in assigning them, even after frequent offending. As Meredith and Oxley (2005, 47) point out, unemployment amongst female convicts was never considered the problem it was for males at certain points. However, new masters were often used after former masters presumably refused to 're-employ' them. These female juveniles were less skilled or experienced than their adult female counterparts. Yet, they were assigned even during the economic downturn and increased female immigration. It may be, as Reid argues, that despite *changes* in demand for female convict labour, the demand remained. Or perhaps skill and experience were not the only criteria used to select servants. Certainly female juveniles did not suffer from the assignment problems that juvenile males did. Female juveniles were often re-assigned after being returned to the government for minor offenses (see Chapter 4). The male convicts had a greater variety of trades and skills than females, but this was expected given the male-dominated nineteenth-century labour market. Unfortunately, there is limited information available for the post-transportation work activities of the female juveniles largely due to their early marriages which resulted in the employments of their husbands taking precedence in any recording. It is evident that despite misbehaviour while under sentence their services were still sought by free settlers. We do not know the nature of the work but it is likely to have been domestic.

When the probation system was implemented, initially wages were fixed at nine pounds per annum for males and seven pounds for females. Rations, accommodation, medicine and medical attendance were also included. From 1844 the wages were made flexible and therefore subject to bargaining between the colonial authorities and employers. At the time there was a high rate of unemployment among passholders. Meredith and Oxley suggest authorities hoped employers would be encouraged to take convict workers because they could pay lower wages. However, when the economy recovered, demand for labour increased and so did convict wages (2005, 48–49). 'This swing in favour of convicts was quickly tempered' (Meredith & Oxley 2005, 49). In 1847 changes to hiring regulations included: convict passholders no longer being able to refuse employment at reasonable wage rates (which was then seven pounds for an adult male); and they could not refuse employment unless they had another employer to go to; whereas the passholder used to be able to appeal to the comptroller-general to terminate contracts, they now had to lodge formal complaints against their employer with the police magistrate and could be punished for unfounded complaints; employers were no longer required to give ten days' notice of contract termination; if a passholder obtained a ticket of leave they had to remain there for fourteen days; convicts too sick to work were no longer required to be paid; and if they needed hospitalization the employer could terminate the contract. Nevertheless, male wages drifted upwards. Ending October 1847, the average male passholder wage was £10–4–0d, a rise since 1844 of just under 4 per cent per annum. Male passholder wages increased to a peak of £11–13–5d in 1848.

In the same period, female passholder wages averaged £8-4-0d, an increase of 17 per cent (Meredith & Oxley 2005, 49).

The requirement of paying passholder wages led to the compilation of 'Registers of Employment' (Meredith & Oxley 2005, 50). Unfortunately, while this register tells us where convicts were employed, to whom and for how much, the nature of employment was not included. The average pay rate for male juveniles was approximately nine pounds per annum per contract. The highest pay rate was twelve pounds and the lowest eight. There were only two females and three contracts, and the average pay rate was approximately six pounds, the highest rate being nine pounds and the lowest five. While wages were neither fixed over time nor constant among workers, these figures suggest that the male and female juveniles were paid more than the minimum allowed, but less than the average convict. However, the median for males in Meredith and Oxley's sample, from 1848 to 1857 is ten pounds and this is the same as for the male juveniles. For females, for the years 1848– 1849 the median was nine pounds. Moreover, four males earned over the median and seven earned the median. The median for the female juveniles was five pounds. However, given there were only three contracts, and only two females, the sample is too small to draw wider conclusions. Suffice it to say that one female earned a good wage, while the other was paid below average. Meredith and Oxley point out that their sample contained many juveniles who had lower earnings. However, the 'juveniles' in this research were adults at this point. The average age for males was twenty-six; the oldest being forty-five and the youngest eighteen. Both females were nineteen. Meredith and Oxley also point out that a positive skew resulting from a comparatively small proportion of high-wage earners pulling the mean well above the median. Among the middle 50 per cent of male passholders, annual wages varied by three pounds (around 30 per cent), but among the men as a whole wages ranged from five pounds to an extraordinary £109.50 (2005, 53). Skilled workers extracted higher pay and this was true for both sexes (Meredith & Oxley 2005, 58). Consequently, these juveniles were not extraordinarily skilled or unskilled – they were average. The most common place for female passholders to be employed was Hobart (58 per cent); both Jane Draper and Emma Driver were contracted in Hobart. Domestic work was also the most common employment – it is likely that this was the work undertaken by these females. Males were most commonly employed as agricultural and pastoral workers and were most commonly found in the interior (58 per cent) (Meredith & Oxley 2005, 60). While percentages differ, the majority of the male juveniles were also assigned to the interior; twelve were contracted to the interior and one to an island (54 per cent), and eleven were contracted to Hobart and its suburbs and Launceston (46 per cent).

Free workers were usually paid considerably more than convict workers in VDL in the 1840s and 1850s. Meredith and Oxley present several comparisons. Hundreds of bounty immigrants arrived in VDL, and 625 arriving between 1841 and 1843 had their annual wage rates from initial contracts recorded. Single labourers were the lowest paid; the minimum wage was 8 pounds and the average was £12–15–0d. Unmarried male farm servants had an average of sixteen pounds. No married farm servant had less than fourteen pounds and their average was twenty-seven pounds. Unmarried groom wages started at ten pounds (an average of nineteen pounds), and married grooms at fifteen pounds. Single carpenters and gardeners could begin at twelve pounds and fifteen pounds respectively, if married, sixteen and twenty-five pounds. Married gardeners and married shepherds received the highest average annual wage of £37–17–2d and £36–10–0d. The lowest wage for a single female domestic servant was seven pounds annually, with an average of £12–15–7d. Dairy maids started at eight pounds and averaged £10–10–0d. Dressmakers received an average of thirteen pounds, with the lowest at ten pounds. At this time, passholder convict wages were fixed at seven pounds per annum for females and nine pounds for males. Although a few free immigrant workers received a 'convict wage', the great majority of free wage rates were at least 50 per cent higher than convicts (Meredith & Oxley 2005, 63). The juveniles' wages therefore compare unfavourably with the free immigrants arriving in the colony. Despite fluctuations caused by the gold rush, convict labour was always cheaper, more so in times of rising wages. The free labour market was more sensitive to changing demand levels, and was not constrained by government interventions (Meredith & Oxley 2005, 64).

While employment has been the concentration for this chapter, unemployment must also be addressed. At least ten juveniles died at a pauper establishment – one was female. Three were married, including the female, and three are known to have had children. While some had formed new families, the lack of wider familial connections in the colony meant that they lacked a support network in old age. Strutt (1887, liv) pointed out in the statistical returns that the total number of paupers only represented 1:167 of the VDL population. Eight per cent of the juveniles became paupers compared with 0.6 per cent of the total population (free and criminal). Unfortunately, there are no figures on how many paupers were emancipists. But as the statistical returns demonstrate (Strutt 1887, liv), while both populations declined, broadly speaking, as the number of prisoners decreased the number of paupers increased. As such, it has been argued that many of the aging prisoner populations moved categories; from prisoner to pauper (Piper 2010, 1047). Therefore, it is likely that the majority of paupers were emancipists, and the juveniles are over-represented in the number of paupers.

Conclusion

Nunn notes that 'historians have been prone to overstating the economic value of juvenile labour to avoid the conclusion that juvenile labour lacked any real economic significance' but adds 'of course, neither of these positions is accurate' (2015, 69). These juveniles were able to survive and settle into the colonies. A key part of this is their education, skills and employment. As the pre- and post-transportation employment of juveniles demonstrates, the males arrived in the colony with few skills compared with adult convicts, the free population at home and free emigrants. Even with the added training many received at Point Puer, there is little evidence to suggest that those males went on to trades learnt *only* at the establishment. However, that is not to say they did not benefit from the educational and trade refinement (and indeed it saved them from being mixed with the adult convict population). These male juveniles were encouraged to learn and perfect their trades and it is possible that they learnt transferable skills in the establishment. Certainly many of the juveniles had a fluid approach to employment in adulthood. While this may have been out of necessity, possibly due to not being a master of a trade or economic hardship, it still allowed them to earn their living in the colonies. It is likely that it was *because* of their colonial experience that they were able to do this. Due to a combination of their pre-transportation skills, trade training and varied assignment tasks, they were able to be fluid in their employment allowing them to survive in the colony. The majority of the juveniles remained among the 'working classes' but within respectable trades. Unfortunately, due to contemporary lack of interest in female skills and trades, there is limited knowledge of adulthood female employment. This is compounded by the fact that most of the female juveniles married very early in their colonial lives. This is not to say they did not supplement their husbands' income, only that there is no evidence of it. However, many of the women did go on to have children, which contemporaneously speaking was their expected role in the colony after freedom, and *at the time* would have been the measure of their success.

Male juveniles suffered from initial disadvantage due to a lack of skills, work experience and small physiques which worked against them; but 'special' management aimed at training and educating worked for them. Many did not marry in the colony and this combined with a lack of extended family (due to their forced migration as juveniles) led to the juveniles to be over-represented among paupers. With no extended family they ended their days in pauper establishments. Nevertheless, while most did not live extraordinary working lives post-transportation, male juveniles lived average working-class lives in a variety of different trades despite their early-life upheaval. For females it is clear that on the assignment market their limited skills did not prevent them from being assigned, and while we know little of their post-transportation employment, their post-transportation familial lives will be further explored in the next chapter.

6

Family life

Exploring the family life that these juveniles later formed is important in gaining a rounded understanding of their whole lives and whether they were able to settle in the colonies. This chapter will explore factors that influenced their family life including their age and whether they were free when they wed. Additionally, were their marriage partners convicts, emancipists or free settlers? And what were the age and occupations of their marriage partners? When assessing whether they had settled familial lives, it is important to do so in relation to the conditions in the colony and the practices of its inhabitants by taking into account, for example, the economy and population shifts. From the behaviour of the juveniles themselves, to the decisions of the administrators and the conditions of the penal colony into which they were removed to, were these juveniles able to form 'settled' colonial lives and which factors inhibited or facilitated this process?

Marriage

Sociologists, including Becker (1981), Goldscheider and Waite (1986), Kalmijn (1998) and Oppenheimer (1988), argue that 'both marriage formation and partner selection can be expected to depend upon preferences and opportunities' (van Schellen et al. 2012, 548). It has been argued that those with low levels of self-control seek immediate gratification, and that same trait, which leads them to commit offences, would make them less likely to marry. Simultaneously, those who commit offences limit their opportunities to marry because a criminal record can make them less attractive to marriage partners and offending reduces their chance to meet potential partners (van Schellen et al. 2012, 548–549). This latter point refers to incarceration but it would follow that being transported and having ones' movements restricted would have had the same effect. This would lead to those with criminal backgrounds having less chance of marriage. Indeed, van Schellen and colleagues found that the 'seriousness of a criminal history is strongly related to outcomes in the marriage market' (2012, 564). Particularly for male offenders, incarceration was associated with even lower marital chances than just having a criminal record. Suggesting that, for men, opportunity was more important. But they also found that offenders did not refrain from marriage altogether. Instead, they were more likely to marry criminal spouses than to remain unmarried. This may not only result from their own preferences but also a lack of opportunity to meet non-criminal spouses (van Schellen et al. 2012, 564–565). For juvenile offenders in particular, Sampson, Laub and Wimer (2006) found that an early age at first arrest, arrest in the previous year, the total number of arrests until the previous year and the length of incarceration in the previous year all reduced *male* marital chances (van Schellen et al. 2012, 550). Sampson and colleagues (2006) studied only male juvenile offenders, but since criminality reduced females' opportunities more, it is reasonable to assume that the same would apply to them. Following this thinking, the juvenile convicts who were studied in this research were disadvantaged in their marital prospects. They were all certainly young upon first offence, their offences were all contemporaneously speaking serious, and their punishment was long in duration, and involved removal to a new society and often incarceration (if not incarceration they were at least limited in their movements in assignment). With this in mind, were juvenile convicts able to form families in the colonies? Before this can be answered, it is important to explore the barriers and facilitations which were unique to the time and place of colonial VDL.

Every convict couple had to take two steps in order to marry in VDL. First, they had to apply directly to the principal superintendent of convicts, or otherwise to the local police magistrate who wrote to Hobart himself. Second, they had to get permission from a clergyman (Atkinson 1985, 25). From the 1820s males who had previously been allowed to work for part of the time for wages to support their family could no longer do so. Now they had to have a ticket of leave. Married male convicts were also increasingly unlikely to be given permission to live with their families. Only in very exceptional, and under very strict, circumstances did Governor Arthur allow convicts to live anywhere other than in the convict barracks or in their assigned service. Also from this point, men had to supply written testimony of their ability to support a wife as part of their petition. This meant that men generally had to wait longer to marry (Reid 2007, 139). From 1829 women could not marry until they had completed one year in assignment without committing an offence (Lamont 2014, 4–6). Both males and females could be denied permission by the governor, due to bad behaviour, and in the cases of men because they were unable to support their proposed wife (Brand 1990, 91). By 1845, convicts now only had to be free from offences for six months (Kavanagh & Snowden 2015, 184). Nevertheless, permission-to-marry was conditional on the extent of the sentence served, which differed over time, and was always dependent on behaviour. Of those female juveniles who married, thirteen sought permissions while still a convict. Only one of these females was not given approval. Ellen Caley (*see Case Study No.13*) was refused permission because her potential husband was unable to financially support her. Ellen Murphy (*Case Study No.14*) and Caroline Watson applied for more than one permission. On average it took sixty-seven months to apply for a marriage permission (the shortest period being 10 months and longest being 219 months). Of the females who were granted permission-to-marry all, but one, were full convicts and the remainder was a ticket of leave holder.

Case Study No.14: Ellen Murphy

Born in 1817, Ellen was thirteen when she was sentenced to seven years' transportation. Ellen committed simple larceny in 1830: the theft of four printed books worth twenty-one shillings from a shop. In her defence she stated:

> The gentleman asked us how much we wanted, and we told him – he said we must send our mother, and we said would our eldest brother do – he said Yes; we were to meet the young men the next morning at the same place – we went for the books, and were detained.

Her accomplice, Margaret Corbett, was also transported on the same ship, the *America*. No-one petitioned on Ellen's behalf, unlike her accomplice, whose parents accused Ellen of being a bad influence on Margaret. Ellen was indicted twice in the same session, and in the previous year had been indicted for theft but 'no bill' was found. Nevertheless, both Margaret and Ellen arrived in Hobart in 1831 after four months' voyage. Ellen was a Roman Catholic 'nurse girl' but could neither read nor write. Her report from Newgate recommended that she be sent out of the country, and the ship surgeon-superintendent reported that she and her accomplice were 'rather idle'.

It was September 1831 when Ellen committed her first offence in the colony. Already on assignment, Ellen disobeyed her master's orders but was only reprimanded. The following month Ellen, due to general neglect of duty and insolence, was returned to the government and put in the second class of prisoners. In 1832 Ellen was 'out at a late hour last night and endeavouring to pass herself off as a free woman'. For this offence Ellen was placed in a cell for six days and removed from her assigned service. Assigned yet again, Ellen was absent again, but she was only reprimanded. Under the same assigned service, she was out after twelve o'clock. This was reportedly the fault of her master but she was returned to the government for re-assignment to a more suitable master. This was followed by more absenteeism and being out after hours, leading her to be repeatedly returned to the government for reassignment. Nevertheless, she *was* repeatedly reassigned. She was then drunk and disobedient which saw her receive the punishment of seven days on bread and water in a cell, and later she assaulted a Margaret White for which she received her worst punishment to date; one month in George Town Factory in 1833. After a series of more absences and absconding she was repeatedly placed in the 'crime class'. However, each time after her punishment finished, she was reassigned. By 1839 it was recommended that she not be assigned 'in this district'. Ellen's last offence, misconduct, was in May. Ellen had spent time in Cascades, George Town and Launceston factories but still earned her ticket of leave by 1840. Two months later she was married to George Manning (or Mannering/Mainwaring).

George was also a convict, transported aboard the *Aurora*, but was a ticket holder when the pair wed at Westbury. George had arrived in 1835 and began his employment in the colony as a labourer before becoming a farmer, dying in 1893. However, through investigating Ellen's marriage permission documentation it is revealed that she had already applied to marry other men. In 1837 she was granted permission-to-marry Ephraim Digby, an expiree, and in September 1839 she was granted a second permission-to-marry Henry John Wallis, another expiree. This suggests the choice that female convicts had on the marriage market. Notably, this latter permission was given after her permission was granted to the man she did marry, George Mannering, whom she was granted permission-to-marry in March 1839. Nevertheless, it was George that she married and they went on to have eleven children.

Ellen also had an illegitimate child named Joseph Murphy, born in 1834/1835. Ellen was the only 'Ellen Murphy' at Launceston factory when Joseph was born. The only other 'Ellen Murphy' under sentence at that time was assigned elsewhere. The father of this child was 'Joseph Barnett'. Ellen died in October 1870, aged fifty-two. After her ticket of leave was earned, Ellen Murphy committed no further crimes and went on to have a large family in relative obscurity. It is unknown whether Joseph joined that family.

There was a high approval rate for both male and female juveniles seeking permission-to-marry. To put this into context; in VDL in 1838, there was a 94 per cent approval rate but only 188 marriages were recorded. Atkinson found that in some cases minds were changed due to a better offer. For example, a female would be in a better position by marrying a free man than a man who was under ticket. Implying that they were not necessarily 'moved by deep and binding affection, one individual for another' (1985, 26). While this may not always have been the case, perhaps this was the case for Ellen Murphy (*Case Study No.14*). Perhaps Ellen was 'hedging her bets' on the marriage market by seeking permission-to-marry several different men. Marriage permissions are informative and demonstrate the relative freedoms of males and females to seek formal relationships while under sentence. Fewer males sought permission-to-marry. Excluding the nine juveniles who were known to die under twenty, only 20 per cent sought permission. All of these proposals were approved. However, there is only evidence of fifteen approvals resulting in marriage. On average it took these males ten years to apply for permission-to-marry (the shortest period being nine months and the longest being twenty-three years). Of these juveniles who were granted permission, all were at least ticket of leave holders. No full male convict was granted permission-to-marry, or even sought it, in this sample. Also of importance are the actual marriages; when and with whom.

Unfortunately, while finding a marriage record and birth record can tell us that an individual married and had children, it cannot be said that those without a record did not. In the 1860s 50 per cent of married women experienced nine or more births (Doust 2008, 10). However, Maxwell-Stewart found that convict women tended to have fewer children because they were delayed by the convict system. Nevertheless, we still would have expected these *juvenile* female convicts to have gone on to have more children than they appear to have had due to their relative youth on arrival. Similarly, it is possible that marriage records for individuals may not have survived. The law on marriage was unclear in VDL until the 1830s. From 1810, the government ordered that chaplains keep a record of all marriages, christenings and funerals of both convict and free persons. Yet, only marriages concluded in the Church of England had to be registered 'on pain of financial penalty' between 1825 and 1839. This does not include marriages concluded in other churches, including the Roman Catholic Church. As such, many marriages and births were not recorded (Lamont 2014, 4–6). In 1836 British Parliament passed an Act for Registering Births, Deaths and Marriages in England in order to make up for the inefficiencies of Parish registers. A registration act was then passed in VDL in 1838 after being introduced by Governor Franklin. VDL was the first British colony to do so. Every birth, marriage and death of the free population (including emancipists) was to be included – the convict population was to be excluded and their life events recorded in a separate register. The first births, deaths and marriages were registered in November 1838 (Kippen 2002, 43–45). Yet, despite the Act, registration was not completely followed. For example, in 1847 John Abbot (Registrar, and Deputy Registrar for Hobart in 1840–56) noticed that there were 2041 baptisms and only 1531 registered births (Kippen 2002, 49). While such registration in Tasmania improved steadily over the course of the nineteenth century, birth registration was only fully registered by the 1890s (Kippen 2002, 58). Consequently, not all births can be found. It is equally possible that while they did not formally marry they instead cohabited or had a common law marriage. Therefore, not only would these partnerships be lost to history, but also even formal marriages. Nevertheless, what we can do is uncover the circumstances of, and minimum number of, marriages and family formations, of those that were documented.

Eighty-nine per cent of female juveniles are known to have married in the colonies, two of whom married twice. This is very similar to the 90 per cent marriage rate of female convicts transported to VDL uncovered by Maxwell-Stewart and colleagues (2015, 242). It took an average of five and a half years for the female juveniles to get married (the shortest period being 11 months and the longest 232 months). The average age that they married was nineteen (the oldest being twenty-five and the youngest sixteen). The average age gap between the female juveniles and their spouses, who were in every case older, was eleven years. However, the gap ranged from two years to twenty-two. Of the partners chosen by these females, 53 per cent were convicts (one of which was on a conditional pardon), 13 per cent were emancipists and 33 per cent were free. While this latter group were free when they married, it does not follow that they were not emancipists. Kippen and Gunn argue that convict females were less likely to be married or to be able to marry than their free counterparts (2011, 393). Further adding that 'convict women were not so highly prized' as free females (Kippen & Gunn 2011, 394). They argue this was due to both a lack of willing partners and impediments. The impediment of already having a husband was not an issue for these particular females, but they did have a high rate of minor offending in the colony which would have postponed them being able to seek permission at an earlier time. By comparing the offending of female juveniles sampled for this research, with a 1-in-25 sample of all female convicts transported to VDL (provided by *Founders and Survivors*) it was found the juveniles offended at a higher rate than female convicts generally. Whether the female juveniles made less desirable wives than their free counterparts, as Kippen and Gunn suggest, is more difficult to determine (2011, 394). Gordon Carmichael notes that there was 'a corporate image of debasement and promiscuity that largely disqualified female convicts as marriage partners (though not as sexual partners) of free settlers and, later, native-born males' (Carmichael 1996, 285). It makes sense, as pointed out by van Schellen and colleagues, that persons with the most attractive characteristics have a high likelihood of selecting each other as partners first, leaving the less fortunate to end up together (van Schellen et al. 2012, 551). Meaning in this context, that all things being equal, free persons would choose free persons before they turned to convicts as potential marital partners. Still, 35 per cent of the female juveniles' marriage partners were free at the time of marriage indicating that the female juveniles were not wholly undesirable as wives. They went on to marry convicts, emancipists and free persons. In VDL in 1838, forty-six convict women married free men and another fifty-seven to sixty-six married ticket of leave holders, leaving only ten to nineteen from a total of 122 who married men still in bondage (Atkinson 1985, 22). They appear to have had some choice in their marriage partners. Kippen and Gunn, and Carmichael's respective arguments that convict females had difficulty in tempting partners down the aisle is not reflected in the lives of female juveniles.

Without knowing the rate at which free females married after migrating to VDL it is not possible to know whether female convicts were less attractive partners. Nonetheless, despite the impediments faced by these female juveniles, which included gaining permission from government and church officials; going without offences for a given period; having a high rate of offending when behaviour was a condition of permission; and having less freedom to meet partners when held in factories (due to that offending) and to a lesser extent in assignment – they still married and mostly pre-emancipation. It has been argued that females' marital chances diminish after just one conviction, while males' chances are only affected following an extensive criminal record. Certainly females are less common within the criminal justice system, then as they are now, than males. van Schellen and colleagues suggest that because a 'criminal lifestyle is less common and [less] accepted for women', those with a criminal record become less attractive marriage partners in comparison to male convicts (2012, 564). Leaving beside the term 'criminal lifestyle', which does not reflect the majority of juvenile convicts under investigation here – the criminal 'taint' did not attach itself to the female juveniles in any meaningful way. van Schellen and colleagues point out that the offenders' attractiveness as potential partners may be even lower in a context where convictions and imprisonment are less common. Where, 'the negative signal of a criminal record is likely to be stronger, leading to even lower chances to marry'. They are referring to the relatively mild penal system of the Netherlands pre-1990 (2012, 552). The context in which these juvenile convicts were removed to was very different. The concentration of convicts was very high. For example, in 1830 90 per cent of the Vandemonian population was a convict, a emancipist or the child of a convict. It is likely that the commonality of criminality positively affected the female juveniles' marriageability.

Very little is known of the females' colonial employment but thanks to their children's birth certificates, the occupations of their children's fathers are known. Most of them went on to 'respectable' trades including a carpenter then later a publican, a printer then later a compositer, costermonger, butcher, servant then later a gardener and lastly a shoemaker. There are exceptions such as the husband of Margaret Corbett, who began married life as a shoemaker then went on to own a lodging house. However, he was described in the newspapers by police as a brothel owner. Nevertheless, the pair went on to have a large family. While another three of these females' husbands were labourers when they began their marriage, one became a farmer and another an inn owner. A further husband began married life as a carter then went into labouring. This is not to say there was no convict stigma experienced by female convicts on the marriage market, only to say that these female juveniles largely still married men of respectable trades whether there was stigma or not, and mostly before freedom. It is highly likely that the combination of low female numbers and common criminality worked in their favour. Only two females are not evidenced to have married including Susan Campbell and, as noted above, Ellen Caley who was refused permission-to-marry. It is possible that Ellen and Susan married and documentation has not survived. It is also possible that they cohabited instead. Ellen had an illegitimate child who was given a variation of her surname. However, her two later children were given different surnames which were likely to have been the name of the father who she may, or may not have, married (*Case Study No.13*).

Being able to marry without a ticket of leave, female convicts were often assigned to their husbands. This effectively made their husbands masters of them. While marital relationships at this time were patriarchal, this process added a new dimension to the inequality to the relationship (Shaw 1966, 219). The convicts' marital status could have an important impact on their assignment and the nature of the labour carried out. We cannot not know 'how far women were moved by a simple wish to be free of convict restraint, and how far they also hoped to share a life with their bridegrooms' (Atkinson 1985, 22). What Atkinson did find was that the initiative generally lay with the man. For example, in VDL Louisa Meredith (a free settler) described how men came to find wives among her servants. Women then either consented to the marriage or not (Atkinson 1985, 20). For female convicts, Atkinson (1985) argues that regulation of their behaviour was shifted from the state to the private sphere when they married. However, in this research there are incidents where regulation was left to the state despite their married status. Indeed, Caroline Watson (*formerly* Beaton), who was transported for simple larceny in 1834, was punished in the solitary cells for one month. Her offence was striking her husband in the presence of another man. For this she was regulated by being brought before the magistrate. In the same year Caroline was again sent to the solitary cells, this time on bread and water for two days for being 'absent from her place of residence and playing at cards in the house of Mr. Smith'. Her ticket of leave was also revoked. This demonstrates that some husbands were willing to use the regulatory power of the state within the private sphere of the home. Similarly, there is also evidence that the state interfered unwelcomely within the family sphere. Ann Malony was 'drunk and making use of very beastly language and in company of a common prostitute'. Consequently, she was sent to the wash tub for six months and it was particularly noted that she should not be returned to her husband until the governor's pleasure. Therefore, Atkinson's argument that the assignment of women to their husbands meant that they ceased to be convicts for all practical purposes does not always hold true. Atkinson even identified a case herself, where a husband prosecuted his wife for being absent from her assignment (i.e. as having left the marital home), whereupon she was sent to Parramatta Factory (Atkinson 1984, 22). Such cases point to the ad hoc nature of regulating female convict behaviour. Moreover, as Lamont (2014, 13) notes, this process had the potential to allow the state authorities intimately into the domestic sphere, monitoring the conduct of marital relationships in a way unknown in Britain at the time.

While direct comparison with the marriage rate of free immigrants arriving is problematic, we can compare the juvenile convicts to other convicts arriving in VDL. Of those who arrived in 1845 aboard the female convict ship *Tasmania (2)*, 69 per cent were involved in at least one permission-to-marry. These applications appeared, generally, within a few months of their six months' probation period ending. Seventy-six per cent of female juveniles sought permission (one of which was turned down). This is 7 per cent more than the *Tasmania (2)* convicts, but it is likely that the age and married status of the *Tasmania (2)* convicts contributed to this slight disparity (Kavanagh & Snowden 2015, 196). Therefore, the *youth* of the female juvenile convicts helped them in their ability to marry only in as far as they had not already married at home. A greater influence was their sex as will be shown when we turn to male juveniles.

That the female juveniles rushed into marriage is not surprising considering the female position. Few had access for very long periods of their lives to independent sources of income, few had a livelihood outside of marriage, few were in a position to leave a marriage if they wanted and none had the vote (Godfrey et al. 2007, 89). Add to this, the prospect of leaving the formal transportation system and having no social ties or support systems in their new colony. As pointed out in Godfrey and colleagues (2017) study, the image of marriage as being institutions that are intimately wrapped up in romantic love does not fully explain why females (or males) married in the nineteenth century. Marriages are not simply about romantic attachments. Among the educated classes there was by this period a belief in romantic attachment before marriage. Conversely, among the poor it was widely accepted that inclination could not reasonably be viewed as the sole motivation for marriage (Atkinson 1985, 27). Researchers, including Goffman (1963), have reported how partners also provided practical assistance. In addition to this, marriage had an economic aspect. Indeed, Godfrey and colleagues found evidence to support the view that during the late-nineteenth and early-twentieth centuries, marriage was sometimes as much about economic or practical necessities as it was about romantic feelings (2007, 87). This is not to say that these juveniles did not have romantic feeling, we cannot know without first-hand accounts, but it is to say that for the female juveniles it was both economically and practically in their interest to marry before their freedom. This is also likely to be true of adult female convicts, but arriving young and single meant that the female juveniles were often abler to take advantage of this process. This is despite, as previously pointed out, the higher offending rate of this group. Through marriage women freed themselves, and men colluded with them in establishing independent households (Atkinson 1985, 29). The story is very different for the male juveniles.

The evidence suggests that most males did not marry. Forty-two per cent of male juveniles married of those who survived until twenty, or of all the males (excluding two males who died en route) 39 per cent married. Three males are known to have married more than once (presumably following the deaths of their former wives). Where dates are available, the average length of time to marry after arrival was 135 months (the shortest period being 1 year and the longest being 445 months). Forty per cent of the partners chosen were convicts when married, and 0.08 per cent are known to have been free. Unfortunately, for 53 per cent of the females such information is unavailable. The average age of male juveniles (upon first known marriage) was twenty-eight. However, the range was wide, the youngest being nineteen and the oldest being fifty-one. The male juveniles were, on average, four years older than their spouses. However, three were between one and three years younger, one was seventeen years older, and four were either the same age or just one year older. Therefore, while they were generally older, the age differences varied widely. The average age of the females upon marriage was twenty-three (the oldest being forty and the youngest being seventeen).

As with the female juveniles, the males married both free persons and emancipists but a higher proportion of their partners were convicts when married. While some convict men did marry free women, it was rare in both VDL and NSW. Neither government was keen to encourage convict men without tickets to marry free women. For women, marriage was a means of controlling them, but for men other institutions of state were used (Atkinson 1985, 23). Indeed, none of the male juveniles married when they were convicts and they certainly did not marry free females at this point. For female juveniles their spouses were in every case older and the average was eleven years older. The male juveniles were disadvantaged because they were competing for partners with older and more established males, whom it seems were preferred. This is suggested by the female juveniles choosing older partners with relative job stability. As pointed out by Doust, while most immigrants making their way to Australia wanted to gain sufficient wealth in the colonies in order to support a wife, many did not achieve this (Doust 2008, 5). Positive abilities stressed for women were competence, decency and virtue but males had to be able to 'provide a decent livelihood' (Atkinson 1985, 25). Socio-economic resources or a partner with many resources were often preferred (van Schellen et al. 2012, 550). Consequently, juvenile males who arrived with fewer skills than their adult counterparts inevitably had to wait longer periods to marry while they established themselves economically. It was not that the male juveniles arriving were small or unskilled for their age. It was simply that they, as juveniles, had only just begun to learn trades. This meant that it took them longer to establish themselves in the colony. Similarly, many of the male juveniles were sent to Point Puer which meant that until they left, through assignment or freedom, they would not come across any potential partner. Opportunities therefore effected their marital prospects. James Hudson, for example, was twenty-seven when he married and only did so after migrating (*Case Study No.20*). According to Maxwell-Stewart, only 50 per cent of male convicts were named in the permission-to-marry registers (Maxwell-Stewart et al. 2015, 242). While many female convicts married, only a quarter of Vandemonian convict men appear to have found a marriage partner, although many chose to cohabit (Maxwell-Stewart et al. 2015, 245). Therefore, the male juveniles were not unusual in their lack of marriages when compared with male convicts more generally. The under-supply of women excluded most men from the process (Carmichael 1996, 283). This is likely to be why the marriage rate is lower than the 53 per cent of juveniles who went on to marriage in the 2017 study by Godfrey and colleagues.

Colonial context: Economy and population

The population of VDL increased from 1824 to 1835 by 27,640 persons – giving a grand total of 40,283 (Anon 1836). By 1842 the growth rate of the total population had begun to slow. Yet, the growth from 1835 to 1842 had still increased by 79 per cent (Ewing 1843, ix). As well as the inflow of convicts and immigrants, the number of colonial births also bolstered the population (Ewing 1843, xii), but this growth would not last. By 1866 it was acknowledged by Barnard (1867, vi) that Tasmania could no longer be directly compared with the colonies of Victoria and NSW. Both these colonies became far more prosperous than Tasmania: Victoria due to its gold mining industry and NSW due to its agricultural and pastoral successes. For the decade following 1857, the population of Tasmania increased at a rate of 16 per cent per year but the number of people arriving in Tasmania was exceeded by the number leaving by 1867 (Barnard 1867, vi). Many were 'able-bodied men' who did not return. This is because of the decline in Tasmania's prosperity and the mainland attractions. We now know the importance of females to the economy thanks to Deborah Oxley's (1996) work, but the focus in the contemporary reports was very much the issues arising by the loss of males. Bernard did point to an upturn in this trend of emigration. From 1863 to 1866 the balance of immigration and emigration was in favour of Tasmania (Barnard 1867, vi). However, even with this change in trend, for the males at least, he pessimistically added that 'most of these, however, will, no doubt, appear in the next year among the departures, as being visitors from other colonies, who would return thither in the early part of the present year' (Barnard 1867, vi). He was right to be doubtful.

The decline in the prosperity of Tasmania had led to a colony struggling for a population size despite the odd upturn. Tasmania was decreasing in popularity as a destination for assisted migration. In 1865 only ninety-two individuals arrived via the bounty system (Barnard 1867, vi). This dropped to just nine people in 1871 (Bernard 1872, vii). Between 1870 and 1871 there was a population increase at the rate of 1 per cent, largely due to an increase of births over deaths; however, the number of people who arrived in the colony in 1871 was less than those who left, leaving a loss to the population (Bernard 1872, vii). The imbalance of immigration and emigration continued in 1874. In this year, for example, emigration principally took place to the following places: 87.75 per cent to Victoria, 7.64 per cent to NSW and 3.93 per cent to NZ. Only 0.17 per cent went to the UK (Bernard 1875, viii). With regard to the juveniles, at least 44 per cent migrated: 24 per cent of the females, and 48 per cent of the males. The majority went to mainland Australia, one male returned home, another two went to California and several made their way to New Zealand. Fortunately, the downward trend which continued from the point of the cessation of transportation to VDL reversed, and things began to improve after 1877 with the inflow of migrants. This was largely due to the discovery of gold in West Tamar in 1869. Mining began in 1877 which preceded a population boom. From 1880 there were a number of positive changes in Tasmania. However, since the last temporary exodus from Tasmania, upon the discovery of the Victorian gold fields in 1853, the proportion of persons aged over sixty was abnormally high. This led to a relatively low birth rate compared with neighbouring Colonies, which enjoyed a greater expanse of territory, a lower population density and the consequent greater attraction to immigrants (Strutt 1887, ix).

Concern over marriage, or lack of it, was connected to the economy. In 1840 when the economy was relatively prosperous there were 457 marriages, but in the following year when the depression had fully hit it decreased by 50. Ewing saw this decline as a demonstration of the effects of the depression acting on the ability of people to marry (1843, xii). Marriage was a concern and so was the connected issue of the unequal proportion of the sexes: 'much misery and vice are likely to prevail in a society in which the women bear no proportion to the men' (Rev. Samuel Marsden *cited in* Smith 2008b, 5). In 1824, of the total population in VDL (including convicts, free settlers, the military and their families, and Indigenous Australians) 77 per cent were male. By 1835 this declined to seventy-one. Still, there were around seven males for every three females (Anon 1836). Then, when comparing the free settlers with convicts, as they are the most significant groups in terms of numbers, we can see they both increased. However, while the number of male convicts and that of free males were similar (with a slight preference to convicts), there were approximately nine free females to every two convict women in 1835 (Anon 1836). This is thanks to the relatively few convict women transported, combined with the call for young, free, female settlers. Though not as disproportionate as 1835, by 1843 there were then one hundred convict males for every forty-five convict females, and one hundred free male settlers for every fifty-four free female settlers (Ewing 1843, x–xi). While the influx of free female settlers had been great, the influx of male convicts had been greater. Even with the 200 per cent increase of females over the increase of males since 1824, the disparity remained (Ewing 1843, xi). Initial opportunities to circumvent assignment on the part of female convicts were largely grounded in the fact that men so vastly outnumbered them. As time went on the gap closed but 'the ongoing imbalance between the numbers of males and females almost certainly continued to endow women with a degree of bargaining power both at work and in the marriage market' (Reid 2007, 132). Historians have argued that this imbalance was 'profoundly disadvantageous to women' because it resulted in a 'masculine-dominated culture' but Reid argues that female convicts simultaneously benefitted from this imbalance (2007, 133). Not least by propelling themselves into marriage to escape the convict system. However, while the female juveniles married quicker than their male counterparts, the majority served most of their sentence first. There were exceptions, and those such as Ann Malony were assigned to their husbands. But it must be noted that Ann was the first female juvenile in the sample to arrive; arriving in 1825. Only herself and Sarah Hodge (*Case Study No.27*) arrived in that year – all others arrived after the implementation of increased regulations in 1829.

The importance in comparing the number of females to males lies in the number of potential marriages. Essentially, the wildly unequal proportion of the sexes would inevitably affect the number of relationships among both the free and convict populations. By the census of 1841 there were 268 single to every 100 married individuals. In the next year this disproportion had only decreased to 258. While this was not dissimilar to NSW, it was still a concern (Ewing 1843, xi). Much of this concern related to morality. The moral issues of building a society out of convicts were acknowledged by authorities from as early as 1787 when transportation to NSW began (Lamont 2014, 1). Brand argued that females were encouraged to marry under sentence as soon as possible, but males had to earn a ticket of leave and be employed. With the end of the assignment system and establishment of the probation system, females were building up in the factories (1990, 91). While we cannot accurately ascertain the number of marriages in this period, from 1810 onwards marriage was actively promoted as the 'normalized family form'. Marriage was advocated particularly for female convicts. While females were assigned as domestic servants, males were assigned as labourers thus maintaining 'gender distinctions in the performance of work'. Assignment on domestic service was *'an interval before marriage for the female convict'* (Maxwell-Stewart 2010, 1234). While female convicts were encouraged to marry, Reid argues that the rate of female convict marriage (in VDL after 1830) slowed as the economic value of their domestic labour increased. After the Bigge Report, there was an increase in demand for female convict labour as domestic servants in wealthy free-settler homes. In order to increase the supply of bonded labour, the state reversed its pre-Bigge policy of encouraging marriage as a way of reducing the number of government-supported female convicts (Maxwell-Stewart 2010, 1234). Therefore, despite initial encouragements by Governor Sorrel, in 1818, of females to marry, moving forward the government began to systematically assign female convicts and to place corresponding limits on their initial freedom to marry. In fact, as early as 1822, all the applications for convict men to marry the women arriving on the *Janus* were turned down and they were instead assigned (Reid 2007, 133). Permissions-to-marry were subjected to increasingly formulized administrative procedures and state scrutiny (Reid 2007, 138). The proportion of female convicts who were married while under sentence fell from 45 per cent in 1822 and 1823, to just 7 per cent throughout the decade from 1832. While females in the past could marry immediately after arrival, and therefore effectively leave the convict system, this practice declined from the 1820s. The majority of those who arrived from 1824 to 1842 would spend at least three to four years in assigned service. A profound restructuring of female convict experience occurred due to colonial demand for female convict labour and changes in state policy (Reid 2007, 138).

 The authorities wanted the female convicts to form 'legitimate connections with unmarried convicts'. In this way, female convicts could become appropriate wives and mothers, and these relationships would serve to combat 'unnatural crime' among both sexes (Brand 1990, 68). Yet, not all convicts formed 'traditional' relationships. For those many male juveniles, and those few females, who are not known to have married they may have cohabited or had a common-law marriage. For many in the nineteenth century, common-law marriage was accepted as a customary and binding form of marriage. Robinson suggested that, among the high number of single men and women arriving in NSW, there may have been many couples who were married according to common law but would have been considered single by the authorities. Discussion of colonial marriage has been distorted to a large extent by terminology and the failure to recognize common-law marriages and cohabitation as an accepted form of marriage (Kavanagh & Snowden 2015, 194). Frost argues that cohabitation was not 'one of blanket condemnation' instead it was 'complex and contingent on many factors' (2008, 1). Such couples may have thrown into 'disarray the traditional definition of marriage' but many of them insisted they were married in all important respects. They fulfilled spousal duties, shared the same last name, reared children and had lifelong commitments (Frost 2008, 2). Most couples, even those who did not marry, showed 'a desire for a ritual and a lifelong commitment' (Frost 2008, 4). Cohabitation in colonial society was not limited to convict couples. In her study of immigrant women, Rushen found strong evidence that some of the immigrant women found security through living with a partner who they did not marry, following the prevailing working-class tendency to delay formal marriage (Kavanagh & Snowden 2015, 195). Similarly, Kippen and Gunn point out that in the 'working classes of England, it was perfectly acceptable – and respectable – for men and women to cohabit and raise families in what were often long-lasting and stable relationships without the formalities of legal marriage' (2011, 398). In VDL in the second half of the nineteenth century, cohabitation continued to be accepted among some groups. Cohabitation may explain why marriages cannot be located for many (Kavanagh & Snowden 2015, 195). Indeed, many couples lived happily in 'respectable sin' for almost their entire adult lives, not going through a legal ceremony both when there was, and was not, an impediment to a marriage (Kippen & Gunn, 399). Moreover, marriage may have been recorded for individuals but documents lost or simply not found.

Children

In addition to the governmental concern with marriage, came concern with convicts having children under-sentence and out of wedlock. Female convicts who became pregnant were sent to the house of correction. After giving birth, mothers were permitted to wean their children but then they would be sent to a separate part of the prison to undergo six months' punishment. 'Suitably chastised female convicts were redeployed into assigned service, whereas their children were sent to what were euphemistically known as orphan schools' (Maxwell-Stewart 2010, 1234). Infants remained in the nurseries until they were old enough to go to the Orphan School at New Town – usually about two or three years of age. However, the convict mother, if granted a ticket of leave or freedom and could support the child, would have the child released to her (Kavanagh &

Snowden 2015, 220). Excluding one female who died en route, 71 per cent are known to have had children. The average number of children each female had was five (the highest number being eleven and the lowest one). While 71 per cent of the female juveniles had children in the colony, only 43 per cent of those who arrived on the *Tasmania (2)* are known to have given birth in VDL (Kavanagh & Snowden 2015, 218). The disparity here is likely to have been due to the relative youth of the juveniles on arrival. While most females went on to have quiet family lives which resulted in no reason to leave behind a written record, others notably struggled to keep and raise their children. There are two known incidences where children were placed in orphanages. For example, Ann Maloney's first born, Charles James Evans, was placed in an orphan school whilst both Ann and the father were in prison, and he stayed there between 1835 and 1845. He was eventually discharged aged seventeen to Charles Pulfer in Hobart. Ann's daughter, Sarah Ann Maloney/Evans, was born in Hobart in June 1833 and baptized in August at Cascades Female Factory. Just over one week after her birth, Ann was sentenced to three months at the factory. While Ann's husband was free, he had a disreputable character. Jane Callahan/Callaghan also had one of her children admitted to the Convict Nursery:

Case Study No.15: Jane Callahan (aka Callaghan)

Born in 1829, Jane was fourteen when she was sentenced to transportation at the Old Bailey. She was found guilty of simple larceny for stealing a shawl, valued at six shillings and a table cloth, valued at two shillings, from a shop on Commercial Road, London. In court she stated:

> I did not speak to him till I was at the station my mother had a row with another woman, and that was the way he knew my name I said if he knew my name better than I did he had better take it down I was coming up from Poplar, and had my little brother in my hand.

Despite a good character reference from a labourer in Whitechapel, she was given seven years. This sentence was probably influenced by her previous conviction which police constable K98, Cornelius Foay, testified to. He produced a certificate of the prisoner's former conviction from Mr Clark's office stating, 'I was present at the trial, the prisoner is the person'. The details were not included in the transcription but it probably referred to the three months' confinement she earlier received for stealing clothes. Jane's mother

Ann and brothers Charles, Eugene and Dennis were living in Whitechapel when she was transported aboard the *Woodbridge* in 1843. Jane was described as coming from Poplar, London, and was sixteen upon arrival in Hobart. She was a Roman Catholic and could both read and write. The surgeon-superintendent described her as 'indifferent' on the voyage. During the voyage she was ill, it was recorded that aged fifteen, Jane suffered from 'Psora' on the 17 August 1843 but was discharged five days later; then she suffered from 'Cond fever' three months later but was again discharged.

It was not until 1848 that Jane committed a colonial offence, when she was 'illegally at large' from February until March. Despite being her first offence, she was given three months' hard labour. At this point Jane was already married but was placed in Cascades factory to serve her sentence. While in the factory in April, she gave birth to a boy named John Beach (Beech) who was placed in the adjacent convict nursery. In September she was awarded a ticket of leave. In 1849, due to use of abusive language she was fined five shillings. Up until this point Jane had held onto her ticket of leave but lost it in September for absconding. Jane had no further offences recorded against her name. She was free-by-servitude in 1850. Pre-transportation she had worked as a housemaid but her colonial employment details are unknown.

Jane had married before she committed any colonial offences. She sought permission-to-marry William Beech in 1845 and it was approved. The pair married in April that year at St. George's Church of England, Hobart (despite Jane originally being a Roman Catholic). William appears to have arrived in VDL free and was just twenty-two when the pair married. He was originally a servant in 1845, but then went on to become a gardener in 1846 (a well-paid trade in the colony). Jane was still a full convict when they married. They are known to have had three children, as noted their first born was John. While John was placed in the convict nursery when Jane was at Cascades and was subsequently put in the orphanage in New Town, he was discharged to both parents aged three. Their second born was named after the father, William. He was born in Hobart in January 1846. And lastly Walter Beech was born in 1847.

There was a high rate of illegitimate births in VDL. While social dislocation, sexual exploitation and lack of knowledge of birth control were undoubtedly factors, they were not solely responsible (Kavanagh & Snowden 2015, 227). Kippen and Gunn state that 'it is reasonably clear that illegitimacy rates were high in the 1840s and early-1850s and that they fell precipitously when the convict system was dismantled' (2011, 400). Finding that the conditions of the convict system must be held primarily responsible for the high levels of illegitimacy at this time, Kippen and Gunn also note that very few illegitimate births would have escaped official notice because not only were unmarried pregnant females incarcerated for the offence, but also the child then became the government's responsibility. Free women were not compelled to register illegitimate births and so comparisons cannot be accurate (2011, 396). In penal VDL sexual behaviour was subject to a certain amount of official scrutiny. When females were under sentence, pregnancy was difficult to conceal. Importantly, pregnancy impacted on the female convict's ability to work and consequently they were punished for their pregnancy. Kavanagh and Snowden argue female convicts were valued as economic reproducers and that illegitimacy was accepted as part of the convict system (2015, 227). They argue that while illegitimacy was not condoned, it did not result in the same social stigma or loss of character leading to inability to obtain secure employment as it did in contemporary Britain, adding, 'It is not surprising then, that convict women had more than one illegitimate child' (2015, 228). It is impossible to ascertain if the female juveniles underwent stigma as a result of their illegitimate children. At least three did have illegitimate children: Elizabeth Jones, Ellen Caley and Ellen Murphy. Ellen Caley (*Case Study No.13*) did not go on to marry, and Ellen Murphy (*Case Study No.14*) did marry but there is no evidence her illegitimate child was a part of her subsequent family life. Whereas Elizabeth Jones married the father of her illegitimate child and went on to have further children after marriage (*Case Study No.26*). Yet, without biographical texts and diaries such an understanding of stigmatization cannot be sought.

Compared with the female convicts, far fewer male juveniles are *known* to have had children in the colonies; only 23 per cent are known to have had children. This is likely to be an under representation. The number of children varied widely from two to fourteen. As well as lack of registration, missing civil records for male and female convicts may not be missing in equal measure. Records were more uniformly kept on convicts and since female juveniles married while they were still under sentence, and males waited until much later, males are more likely to have missing records. It is of course very likely that the males also had illegitimate children but such incidences were not recorded. Since the births of children alone are difficult to uncover, anecdotal information of children, and especially their connection to their parents, is inevitably difficult to find. When such information is located it is usually tied-up in an extraordinary event as in the case of Anthony Barkwith and the tragic deaths of two of his children (*Case Study No.19*). Another example is when the children of John Press became involved in his criminal behaviour:

Case Study No.16: John Press

Born in 1831, John was only ten when he was sentenced to transportation. In 1841 he was found guilty of simple larceny for stealing three half-crowns, nine shillings and three sixpences. Despite his professed young age, he had been convicted previously. John was described as having been in the 'house of Correction often'; once for stealing a loaf of bread for one month, again for a similar offence and given two months, another two months for picking a woman's pocket, six weeks for a similar offence, and lastly three months and flogging for housebreaking. He had a father named John and a brother named William. John Jr. was transported aboard the *Lord Goderich* in 1841. On arrival he was described as thirteen and could read, he was a protestant and lived in Whitechapel. He had two dots between his thumb and forefinger on his right hand, and a mole inside his left arm and was slightly pockpitted. The *Euryalus* authorities reported that he was 'indifferent and artful', and the surgeon-superintendent recorded he was 'indifferent/flogged and punished several times on board'. Therefore, he did not have a great start but he was still immediately placed at Point Puer thanks to his youth.

His first colonial offence was not until 1844, when he was absent without leave and was given five days' solitary confinement. At this point he was under probation. He was granted a free certificate in 1848. However, he committed an offence in 1849. He stole two bottles containing lemon essence and six jars of snuff from his master – Mr John Henry De La Hunt. He pleaded guilty and was re-transported for seven years, one year of which was to be hard labour (*The Tasmanian* 1873, 4). The *Colonial Times* added that he had robbed Mr Hunt 'to a very great extent by abstracting medicines in small quantities at a time' (*Colonial Times* 1849, 2).

Now at Port Arthur, in 1849 John was reprimanded for disorderly conduct. When he altered his clothes he was given three days' solitary confinement. When he used improper language he was given 'one month imprisoned hard labour in chains'. Then because of misconduct in shouting and making a disturbance while under solitary confinement, he was given a further three months' imprisonment and hard labour in 1850. He absconded in August of that year and was given twelve months' hard labour in chains. Disorderly conduct in his cell resulted in fourteen days' solitary confinement in November. When he was a passholder in 1851, he did not proceed according to that pass and was given four days' solitary confinement. He was then convicted of larceny under five pounds and given an extended sentence of eighteen months' hard labour in chains. Shortly after, idleness resulted in a further four months' hard labour extension. Next he was idle and endeavouring to incite men to neglect work, which resulted in his sentence of hard labour being extended by a further two months. For misconduct in chapel during prayers, he was given seven days' solitary confinement. Idleness in 1853 resulted in another seven days' solitary. Next he ill-treated a fellow prisoner in June, and was given fourteen days' solitary. It was in 1854 that John was granted his ticket of leave.

John's offending career was not over. In 1867 he was convicted at Launceston for horse stealing and given four years' imprisonment. John was arrested by Sergeant Piercy of the Westbury Municipal Police and convicted of stealing the chestnut horse of John Davidson worth two pounds. Press and the horse were working at Deloraine Tramway works. Press was spotted with the horse, along with his wife, son and daughter, and was apprehended in Carrick. He stated he was lent the horse for one pound. John called his son to testify. Joseph, who was only twelve, was also committed to the gaol with him on the same charge – 'the boy without being questioned delivered what appeared to be a made up statement, to the effect that his father had paid Davidson £1 for the loan of the horse'. John Press was found guilty but Joseph was released on the condition that his 'mother take control of him' (*The Cornwall Chronicle* 18 September 1867, 5). The *Launceston Examiner* reported that the statement given by Joseph was a 'rambling statement, which the little fellow had evidently got to memory' (19 September 1867, 5).

By December John had absconded, was captured and was given nine months' hard labour on top of his sentence. He had absconded from the gang he was employed in at the Queen's Domain but was arrested by a sergeant of the New Town Territorial Police. However, he was free again in 1869. Next he was tried at the Supreme Court in Hobart Town, along with his wife Bridget, aged forty, who was also free-by-servitude. Both were acquitted of stealing sheep belonging to John Griffiths of Richmond. Other counts charged the prisoners with stealing meat and receiving '30lb of meat'. The prisoners were defended in court but there was confusion over what could be said because they were arraigned on a joint charge. At this point John was working for a butcher. *The Mercury* also gives a glimpse into the home life of this family as it added 'Mary Ann Press the daughter of the prisoners who deposed that her mother had run away from her father' (*The Mercury* 1873, 3). They were both found not guilty but Mary's comment suggests there was discord within the family.

John's next court appearance was in Brighton in 1873. Convicted of larceny he was given six months' imprisonment. Notably in a return of Brighton prisoners in 1873, all but Joseph were present: John Press was described, aged forty-seven, 5"5', labourer, formerly resident in Richmond; he was listed alongside his wife, Bridget, aged fifty, 5"1', no trade; and daughter,

Mary Ann Press, aged eighteen, free, previous conviction for larceny, trade servant and 5"5'. *The Tasmanian* reported that this was originally a charge for housebreaking. All three were accused of breaking into Joseph Ormond's house at Bagdad and stealing bread and beef but the police could not prove they broke in, and so they were only found guilty of larceny. John received six months' hard labour, Bridget one month and Mary just one hour (1873, 4). John was discharged from the house of correction by 1874.

While he offended frequently and indeed committed serious offences, he was also described as a 'good tailor' in 1842. He was skilled enough to be forwarded to New Town Farm for hiring without having committed any offences at Point Puer. Pre-transportation John was described as a labourer he had, therefore, learnt the trade of tailoring at Point Puer. Therefore, he had become proficient in his trade and had been behaving well. It was only when he was released that his offences began. He sought permission-to-marry Bridget Keady in 1854. This was immediately after he was awarded his ticket of leave during his second transportation sentence. It was approved, and they married in the Roman Catholic Church the following month. While John was Protestant, it is likely that given the choice of church, the Irish-born Bridget was Catholic. They were both twenty-five when they married. Bridget died in 1905 in Victoria and was buried in Coburg Cemetery in a Roman Catholic grave. She was born in 1829 Roscommon. Bridget was transported at the older age of twenty-three in 1851 for larceny. She also had previous offences, was single on arrival and had been a servant by trade. They had two children, Mary was born in Fingal, when John was a labourer, and died in 1928. Their son was named Joseph and was born in Ross in 1854. John Press's death cannot be located.

While John Press involved his children in his criminal activities, and George Pickering was violent towards his family (*Case Study No.2*), the family lives of the males were relatively uneventful – as was the case with the females. Still, many resulted in lineages, for example, James Hudson's death resulted in what was described as a 'large assemblage' at his burial at Balaklava Cemetery. This respected old resident left behind his wife, having been married for sixty-four years, he also left behind five living sons and one daughter, forty grandchildren and eighteen great grandchildren. The life James led left him repeatedly in the papers because of the legacy he left in his children and grandchildren – who mentioned him in the newspapers every time they announced family marriages and births (*Case Study No.20*).

Conclusion

Females were far more likely to seek permission-to-marry while under sentence than male juvenile convicts. Of the 20 per cent of males who did, they were *at least* ticket of leave holders, whereas the majority of females were full convicts. Yet, there was a high permission success rate for both sexes. Not only would factors such as the availability of a partner play a role in marriage rates, but also it is clear that the management of female and male convicts was different. Since males had to be able to support their wives, they could rarely marry while under sentence. Additionally, punishment and reformation rhetoric reflected contemporary gender roles. Meaning the authorities wanted to put men to work and females to marriage. While, as pointed out by Reid (2007), female labour was increasingly sought, it remained the fact that there was not enough infrastructure for effective female punishment. This is reflected in the lack of extended sentences for females – despite female juveniles' repeated offending. Contemporaries also thought the reformation of males was linked to marriage and family formation. However, the need for male labour *and* the ability to implement it was greater. Females were encouraged by the authorities and their situations to marry. If females married they would be removed, partly at least, from the mechanisms of the penal system. While this may have been the case, the majority of the female juveniles still served the majority of their sentences before they married. This is despite there being a greater number of potential partners for female convicts. Since the female juveniles offended at a higher rate than other female convicts in the colony, it is likely that this factor was a hindrance to earlier marriage. Nevertheless, they were still more likely to marry, and marry younger than their male counterparts. Maxwell-Stewart (2010, 1234) points out that existing studies have linked 90 per cent of transported female convicts to a colonial marriage, and these marriages mostly occurred *after* sentence. Therefore, unlike other female convicts, the female juveniles mostly married when they were still convicts. Female juveniles also generally married partners with respectable trades. It would seem that the taint of a criminal past was not an issue for these females in a penal colony which was largely populated by convicts, emancipists and their families. Even when taking into account their whole lives, females were more likely to marry than males. This 'makes sense' due to the colonial sex-imbalance, but it must also be noted that since the females married younger, and importantly while they were still under sentence, their marriage records are inevitably more easily located. It is true that many of the marriage records for male juveniles have been located after they migrated by time and space from their Vandemonian servitude. However, some may have married but evidence not found.

With the stipulations of marriage permissions, it is not surprising that the male juveniles did not seek to marry until they *at least* had a ticket of leave. Moreover, with so few females in the colonies these male juveniles had to compete for marital partners with well-established older males. Those males who did marry settled into colonial society with regard to middle-class expectations. However, it does not follow that male juveniles who did not marry were 'unsettled' – as it was relatively common for males not to marry. One in four male convicts married after arrival in Australia, the imbalance between the genders making it difficult for many to find partners. Of those that did marry the majority were skilled men on short sentences (Maxwell-Stewart 2010, 1234). While the male juveniles were not on notably long sentences, many had sentence extensions and were re-transported due to their markedly high offending rate. Equally noteworthy, while many eventually went on to respectable trades they did not arrive particularly skilled thanks to their youth, and so needed time to establish themselves.

The majority of female convicts went on to have children in obscurity although some struggled to hold onto their children and others had illegitimate children. These latter cases highlight the difficulty of colonial life for female convicts: their private lives were subject to colonial oversight. Having an illegitimate child was only an offence because they were convicts. Additionally, the offences which resulted in these females being sent to the factory and having their children removed from them were regulatory offences. For example, when Ann Maloney's children were taken into the orphanage Ann's offence was being found in the public house after hours. This resulted in three months' confinement. A free female would not have been punished for this. Therefore, these less 'settled' cases of family life highlight the struggles which female convicts had to navigate. While the family lives of a number of the male juveniles are notable by their unsettled nature, the majority were, like the female juveniles, relatively uneventful.

7

Death

It was not until 1838 that VDL adopted compulsory birth, death and marriage registration. Although this was only a year after England and Wales it inevitably means that for some juveniles such records are unavailable (Kippen & McCalman 2015, 345). Therefore, just as some will have married and had children but left no record, so too did deaths go undocumented. However, for those juveniles for whom death records are available we can explore the causes, circumstances and age-of-death. How did their lives end? This question will be addressed by comparing the mortality rate of this sample with the rates for the Vandemonian population, other convicts and free people in England. Did the juveniles die younger than the average Vandemonian? What were the causes of death; were they victims of disease, accident or did they die in old age? Was there a correlation between repeated punishment and early death for instance? Answering these questions will give us a clearer picture of their lives as a whole.

Male juveniles

More juveniles died aged between sixty-one and eighty than in any other age category. However, an alarming number (41 per cent) died under forty years of age, and 14 per cent were under twenty. This can be seen in Table 7.

The average age-of-death for male juveniles in this research (given survival to age twenty) and provided they did not die while still under sentence was fifty-nine. The average age-of-death for juveniles (given survival to age twenty) and including those who died under sentence was fifty-five. All male juveniles (who died under sentence and after freedom not given survival to age twenty) had an average age-of-death of 50.7. Given survival to sixteen (with no other consideration) juveniles had an average age-of-death of fifty-two.

Table 7 Male juveniles age-of-death

Age	(No.) Percentage
<20	14
21–40	27
41–60	18
61–80	36
>81	5
Unk	34

Table 8 Male average age-of-death comparison data

	Males Given Survival to Age 20		Not Given Survival to Age 20	Given Survival to Age 16
	Died after Freedom	All Deaths[a]		
Male Juveniles	59	55	50.7	52
English Convicts	59.1	56.1	unk	unk
All Tasmanian Males[b]		62	unk	unk
English Males[c]		59–60	unk	unk

Non-juvenile transportee data comes from Kippen and McCalman (2015) study.

a Including before and after freedom.
b Early 1860s.
c Males in England aging at the same period as convicts.

Only broad comparisons between these groups can be made here because there are a number of differences between them. However, what we can learn from Table 8 is that if juveniles survived until they were free their average age-of-death was similar to English convicts who were transported. While they have a one-year difference in life-expectancy when looking at all deaths, they – in both cases – did not live as long as Tasmanian-born males, or those males in England. Furthermore, when including all male juveniles (including those who died under twenty) the life-expectancy is markedly lower than all comparison groups. Simply put, many of the male juveniles died very young and this consequently brings down their average age-of-death. Survival until the age of twenty was used in Kippen and McCalman's study and so their study inevitably does not include those who died young. Nevertheless, the average age-of-death of the London juveniles given survival to sixteen was calculated, and found to be still lower than all other comparisons. It *was* expected that the juveniles in this sample would over-represent the number of young deaths for juveniles transported as convicts. This is because, inevitably, the younger a juvenile died the more readily a death certificate could be found because they were more likely to still be under the supervision and/or control of the colonial state. They were less likely to have changed their names or moved away making them easier to trace in this research. However, even when allowing for survival until after freedom their average age-of-death is still lower than free Tasmanians and the English at home. Yet, specifying survival until freedom does bring their average in line with other English convicts.

Kippen and McCalman's (2015) study found death details for 42 per cent, whereas for juveniles there was a 66 per cent success rate. What these relatively low success rates mean is, the results may be distorted if the convicts not traced had different characteristics and mortality patterns when compared with those convicts for whom deaths were found. The deaths of convicts uncovered by Kippen and McCalman (2015) were less likely to be found for those with characteristics they associated with higher mortality (e.g. those born in industrial/urban areas or with more conduct offences under sentence). This means that the mortality estimates calculated from the sample, who were traced to death, are likely to be lower than those from the full sample. If all deaths had been traced, the life-expectancy estimates for convict men would probably be lower, and the difference more marked between the survival of convict men and the general Tasmanian male population (Kippen & McCalman 2015, 363). Specifically, Kippen and McCalman (2015, 355) found that those who were older on arrival and under a longer sentence were more likely to be traced to death. And, those born in London were less likely to be found. They attribute this to their 'streetwise' nature and therefore greater likelihood to adopt aliases when leaving Tasmania (Kippen & McCalman 2015, 355). Many convicts did indeed change their names but whether London convicts were more likely to have done this is unknown. It is also possible that individuals disappeared from the records due to no further convictions or migration. Indeed, migration was common. While those who were lost to follow-up may have changed their names and/or migrated, they may also have simply not appeared in any records. Emancipists would only appear in official records if they followed certain life-paths. It they committed no further crimes, and did not form 'traditional' families which were documented, they cannot now be found by historians. Although it is possible, we cannot conclude that they did not appear in the records because they changed their names. Moreover, if they were not later associated with the convict ship which they were brought out on, certain identification is sometimes impossible due to common names. According to Kippen and McCalman (2015, 362), survival after sentence depended on being able to find respectability through a 'reformed character' through a reference provided by a patron or the learning of respectable deportment, which enabled the ex-convict to 'pass' in respectable society. They suggest those who stayed in Tasmania would consequently have less chance of reinventing themselves; those who left the island after sentence were abler to disappear into the crowd of free immigrants and gold-seekers. While Kippen and McCalman largely point to respectability, which may have played a part, more pragmatically there were greater employment opportunities on the mainland. What is certain is that migration to the mainland decreased the likeliness of locating the death certificates of emancipists.

Comparing the juveniles with convicts who were sent from all over England, including rural areas, is an issue. This is because Kippen and McCalman found that convicts born in industrial districts and large towns had higher mortality rate than rural born convicts; by 14 per cent (2015, 353). This is relevant here because the juveniles came from London. The juveniles only had a slightly lower average age-of-death than all convicts arriving in VDL. This suggests that if rural juvenile convicts were added to the sample the average age-of-death for juveniles would rise. However, this ignores the fact that if juveniles died under sentence they would, like all convicts generally, die markedly younger than free persons. Furthermore, it does not account for those juveniles who died before they reached twenty. Consequently, the death rates of those held in Point Puer, which only held juveniles under twenty can be turned to. From 1834 to 1839 the death rate in proportion to the populations contained at Point Puer decreased. There was an increase in the death rate between 1839 and 1840, which then reversed for Point Puer as it did for the free population, from 1840 to 1841 (Anon 1836, 7). Between 1840 and 1841, on average there was one in sixty-two deaths per free Vandemonian. For juveniles in Point Puer in the same period the death rate was lower. It should also be noted that Point Puer contained only juveniles who were not expected to die save for disease or accident, unlike the free Vandemonian population which contained the elderly. It is also noteworthy that 2 per cent of juvenile convicts at Point Puer died between 1834 and 1841, but of the juveniles in this research, 13 per cent died under twenty in the same period. Juveniles sent to Point Puer had a lower mortality than convicts at Port Arthur, those at home in England and those free in the colony of VDL. Yet, this was not the case for the sample of juveniles in this research. Why these juveniles died disproportionately young will be explored further through turning to the causes of death.

Cause of death

The cause of death can shed light on a convict's way of life and standard of living. For many this information is unavailable. Until 1895, in Tasmania, certification of cause of death by a registered medical practitioner was not legally required. Even when cause of death has been provided it often lacks detail (Kavanagh & Snowden 2015, 245). Nevertheless, of the juveniles whose causes of death are known (51 per cent) 4 per cent were executed, 16 per cent were accidents, 35 per cent were caused by disease, and 35 per cent were natural causes or old age. Tracing the life of James McAllister (*Case Study No.17*) was enabled because of his visibility in the records which resulted from his execution. It was because of James's high-profile crime and resulting death that the newspapers detailed his history which enabled his identification. It is possible that if it were not for this 'newsworthy' incidence he would not have appeared in the newspapers, this combined with his migration would have made him increasingly difficult to find in the records. Nevertheless, James was traced from cradle-to-grave.

Case Study No.17: James McAllister

The life and crimes of James McAllister began representative of the whole sample but there the similarities end. He was one of only two juveniles to be executed in Australia. Born in 1827, James was brought to trial in 1842 for stealing sixty pence, aged fourteen. He was sentenced to seven years' transportation while his accomplice, aged sixteen, was sentenced to two months' imprisonment. There were no former convictions mentioned in his trial, but his Conduct Record states that he stole loaves for which he received three weeks' confinement, and a waistcoat for which he spent another fourteen days in the house of correction. Also of note is that he was admitted to a workhouse twice immediately preceding his Old Bailey appearance and was described as having 'no home'. His Conduct Record confirms what this phrase suggests; while he did have two brothers and two aunts in London, he had no parents at this time. He was employed as a mariner and/or labourer at some point but clearly he had a difficult start. As such he could neither read nor write and was also hesitant in his speech. Even at the time of his death he was described as being able to read and write very imperfectly. With regard to behaviour he was described as 'orderly' aboard the *Euryalus*, and 'good' by the ships surgeon-superintendent during the voyage. James only waited five months until he sailed aboard the *Asiatic*. Arriving in Hobart in 1843, James was put on probation for two years at Point Puer. While some juveniles filled pages with their offences while under sentence, James committed just one offence (there were only two others who committed one offence). His offence was: 'Misconduct in being concealed in the enclosed yard of Mr. Johnson for some unlawful purpose', in 1849, whilst a ticket of leave holder. This was six years after his arrival. This ticket of leave had only be earned that year. He was given three months' hard labour and ordered not to reside in Hobart Town. He finally received his certificate of freedom in 1850 after seventy-six months in the colony. It would seem to be a great start but just five years later he found himself in Melbourne Gaol awaiting execution for the murder of Jane Jones.

James had made his way to Melbourne working as a labourer and a carpenter. The papers also stated he had adopted the 'most disreputable means of getting a living since he has been in this colony'. He was at that time running a lodging house but the newspapers suggest that this lodging house was a house of ill-fame (this confirmed by the dying words of Jane Jones). He was not married and had no known children, but he had cohabited for two years with Jane. He shot Jane at the Exchange Hotel in 1855 and she later died in hospital of her injuries. Jane made a statement before she died where she pointed out that the prisoner was not the father of her child and that he shot her because she refused to live with him. Jane had left James to live with Thomas Chisholm, an article clerk. Jane had informed Chisholm that James had ill-used and threatened her. Jane and Thomas had to move lodgings because they saw James watching Jane. On one occasion he stopped her in the street and took her child from her and struck her. Consequently, James was summoned before the City Police Court and he was ordered to give the child back to the mother.

On the night of the incident James levelled a pistol at Thomas and fired. Fortunately for him, the bullet merely grazed his temple sending him falling backwards. Unfortunately for Jane, James then shot at her too. James tried to run but being stopped by a waiter he declared, 'I am the murderer'. It was noted that Jane was hit in her shoulder but she also had a bullet lodged in her spinal cord, which caused paralysis and death. Jane was only twenty-two and was described as 'of plain appearance', while James was described as 'respectable looking'. At trial the defence admitted the act but argued it was only manslaughter because he could not be held responsible for his actions because he was provoked. The provocation, they argued, was that James was furious because the deceased was essentially his wife and had eloped.

Then in seeing the man who had taken her, he was unable to control his actions. The judge disagreed, pointing out that he could see no provocation for manslaughter and there was nothing to suppose they were as good as married. The jury returned a verdict of wilful murder against James and he was executed at Melbourne Gaol aged twenty-six.

Approximately five hundred persons were present outside the gaol during the execution. Nobody but the officials were allowed to be present in the walls. He apparently approached his death with resignation in consonance with his general behaviour since his condemnation. He was said to have conducted himself with humility and apparent penitence, and expressed no hope of pardon in this world. There was reported to have been a cast of his head after death taken by an artist – Mr Pardoe.

While James McAllister is unusual because he committed a very serious offence and he was executed, the fact that prior to this he only committed a few minor offences while under sentence correlates with criminologists' beliefs that serious offenders are not usually recidivists (Godfrey et al. 2010). Importantly, the majority of juveniles were not executed but instead died of old age or disease. Thirty-five per cent of the deaths were attributed to diseases including brain, heart and liver disease, cancer, pneumonia, cholera, bronchitis, consumption, mania, progressive paralysis, stricture of the urethra and nephritis, apoplexy, anasarca and pyaemia. For example, John Burke (*Case Study No.18*) died of disease of the heart and Anthony Barkwith died of bronchitis. Both juveniles died of disease but led very different lives.

Case Study No.18: John Burke

Aged eleven, John was convicted of simple larceny in 1836 for stealing sixty-three brushes worth sixteen shillings. Despite being recommended to mercy by the prosecutor himself, he was sentenced to seven years' transportation. After four months on the *Royal Sovereign*, he arrived in Hobart in 1838. Generally, his offences while under sentence were status offences such as gambling and being absent but he did assault a Jack Williams in 1842. He is described throughout this time as being at Port Arthur. However, given that he is not recorded as committing any non-regulatory offences at this time, there was no reason why he would have been sent to a secondary penal establishment. It is probable that he was in fact at Point Puer. By May 1842 he is listed as being in the Invalid Party. His last offence was in June 1842, another minor regulatory offence, while still at the Invalid Party. It was in July 1840, when in government employment, that he was first known to be admitted to the hospital, but he was released five months later back to the Invalid Party. Again in 1841 he was admitted to the hospital for ophthalmia. He became blind. He was free-by-servitude by 1843 and no more is mentioned about him in the Conduct Record. He died in March 1879 aged fifty-four, in Tasmania, without marrying. The newspapers stated he died before reaching the hospital. They further described him as a 'blind beggar'. It was not the first time John had been in the newspapers. In 1855 *The Hobarton Mercury* praised the police for their efforts in clearing 'troublesome mendicants' from infesting the streets. In particular, they brought a blind 'delinquent' man before the bench named John Burke, 'well known in the town as a very imprudent beggar'. They described his conduct before the magistrate as 'disrespectful in the extreme'. He was sentenced to three months' imprisonment with hard labour to which he exclaimed 'that his liberty has been sacrificed by the false swearing of the constable' (December 1855, 3). In reporting his death, *The Cornwall Chronicle* stated:

> [He was the] youngest of our stock of blind men, and the quietest. He usually took his stand on Saturday night, near Messrs. Smith and Hutchinson's meat establishment, in Brisbane street, and offered to sell matches which nobody seemed disposed to buy. About 5 o'clock yesterday Burke called at Mr W. H. Westbrook's residence, Patterson Street, where he had frequently obtained assistance and as Mr Westbrook noticed that the poor man looked very ill he sent for a car and communicated with the police, Sergeant Green soon arrived and conveyed Burke in a car to the hospital. When Burke was taken out he requested Sergeant Green to take him outside before going into the hospital. Sergeant Green complied with his request and on returning to enter the hospital Burke lay down on the green and after a few gasps expired. We are informed the cause of death was disease of the heart (March 1879, 2).

This is a story of someone who struggled in the colony and had to turn to begging to survive due to his inability to find work because of his condition. Other juveniles died of disease after longer more settled lives.

Case Study No.19: Anthony Barkwith

Anthony Barkwith lived a long life. He was baptized in Kent in 1822 and was put on trial in 1837 for housebreaking. He stole one watch, two rings, one brooch, one pair of ear-rings and cash. The total value of the stolen items was 1728 pence. This, in comparison with the other juveniles, was a serious offence. However, he was only convicted for stealing up to five pounds, thus saving him from the death penalty but giving him fourteen years' transportation. His father, of the same name, petitioned on his behalf. He pleaded that he, and his thirteen-year-old son, had been abandoned when Anthony Jr. was aged five by his mother. Anthony Sr. was then left with seven dependents. He stressed his son's exemplary good character, and that he was a youthful dupe of others. He even referenced a case which followed Anthony's, which saw 'youth' taken into account as a mitigating factor, and that he had been given no time to gather good character witnesses. By this point he had clearly gone to a great effort and had even persuaded the prosecutor to sign the petition along with others – but to no avail. Anthony Jr. was transported on the *Royal Sovereign* in 1837, arriving in January the next year.

Anthony was sixteen when he arrived in Hobart, a world away from Deptford Green. He had been in the house of correction previously but his behaviour on the hulk and voyage was reported as 'good'. He had a total of thirty offences in his Conduct Record. This is above average; however, these were mainly regulatory and minor offences. He was at one point violent towards his overseer and he several times absconded, but these were his most serious offences. He spent the majority of this time in Port Arthur. Again, given that he committed no serious offences it is likely that he was specifically in Point Puer. He earned his ticket of leave by 1840. However, he was then recorded as being in the employment of W. C. Gatehouse, in 1843, and neglecting his duty as well as making away with things that did not belong to him. Consequently, he was put on the public works in 1844. There were no more offences after this time. He was recommended a conditional pardon in 1847, which he received in 1849.

Anthony married Harriet Hodge who was transported on the convict ship *Tory* in 1850. Harriet was a house servant and twenty-six when they married (Anthony was thirty-one). They went on to have at least three children. It is through the birth certificates that we can track Anthony's changing employment. Back in London he was a 'look after hours', but in 1850 he was a labourer when his wife gave birth to a male child. Unfortunately, this child, his namesake, died in 1853 aged just two years and ten months. By December 1854, when Harriet gave birth to Elinor, he was a shepherd. There was a third child who died in a mining explosion in Victoria in 1890 – but the birth details are not available. As a result of such information we also know that Anthony had made his way to Bendigo, Victoria, where he died of bronchitis at sixty-nine. While Anthony died of bronchitis, he died relatively old. He was honoured in the *Bendigo Advertiser*:

> Death of an old resident – an old Bendigonian passed away on Saturday Anthony of little Ironbark. The deceased had been ailing for about 12 months previously from bronchitis, which ended months previously, which ended in his death. He arrived in Bendigo in the early fifties, and followed mining pursuits until his health broke down ... he was employed at the old hustlers reef mine for 20 years. The deceased's son was killed 9 months ago in the Johnson's Reef Company's mine through a blasting explosion. (7 May 1891, 2)

While Anthony did not die in a mine explosion like his son and he died above the average life-expectancy, it is possible that twenty years in the mine contributed to his ill-health later in life. It is now widely acknowledged that bronchitis is correlated with working in the mines (Laney & Weissman 2015). As the case of Anthony Barkwith demonstrates, not all juveniles led tragic short lives and died due to accidents and executions but it is easy to become caught up in these shocking cases. It is easy to dwell on the case studies of juveniles who died so young, before they even reached freedom, because they are poignant. However, many of the juveniles went on to live long lives and 35 per cent died in old age or of natural causes. Moreover, as already pointed out, those who died younger were easier to find and so over-represent the number of juveniles dying untimely under sentence. James Hudson (*Case Study No.20*) not only lived a long life, but he also lived a settled life away from crime.

Case Study No.20: James Hudson

James died late in life, aged ninety-one, surrounded by family. Born in 1819, James was convicted, when he was thirteen, of theft. He had stolen a soldering iron worth eighteen pence. Consequently, James received a sentence of seven years' transportation. James pleaded guilty, which may have been related to the fact that he was prosecuted by his father, Joseph Hudson. His father was a whitesmith, while his mother had died by this point, and he had at least one younger sibling. James waited twenty-one months on the *Euryalus* before his transportation following his trial. This long wait may be attributable to an acute, bacterial skin infection he suffered from on the hulk. He also suffered from icterus during the voyage but was soon discharged cured from the surgeon-superintendent's care. James was reportedly 'ordered' and 'good' while in confinement and had no previous convictions.

Arriving in 1833 on the *Isabella*, Hudson notched up only two very minor offences while under sentence. The first being 'neglecting to deliver his pass and with making a false statement' for which he received one month's hard labour and was removed from his service to Port Arthur, and the second was insolence for which he was admonished. He committed no non-regulatory offences and received a ticket of leave in 1837 after forty-eight months in the colony. James made his way to Adelaide and there married Mercy Abbot at the Native School Encounter Bay, in 1846, after 147 months in the colony. He was twenty-seven when he married Mercy, who was ten years his junior. He worked for some time as a whaler but after his marriage he settled down to the trade of shoemaking. He later turned his hand to farming. James made the papers on numerous occasions. In 1855 he was religiously converted under exceptional circumstances. James and his family attended congregation in a barn. Also in attendance was an intelligent four-year-old boy who often entertained by mimicking the preacher. This boy suddenly became very ill and it was thought he would not recover, 'and in his childish way he gave evidence of a knowledge of spiritual things as only one taught of God could do'. This led to James's conversion. James then went on to help many by 'God working through him'. He secured a modest competency and settled in Whitwarta. The author of James's obituary wrote that from the letters he had received from James he knew he was of pure Christian sentiment and had extensive knowledge of God's work. James and his wife Mercy went on to have twelve children and James died in South Australia in 1910 aged ninety-one. His death resulted in a 'large assemblage' at Balaklava Cemetery. James was described in the papers as one of the oldest residences of Whitwarta, and was widely known and esteemed. He left behind his wife, having been married for sixty-four years, and five living sons and one daughter, forty grandchildren and eighteen great grandchildren. One son sadly only survived his father by four days which left his aging mother having to rush from the burial of her husband to the death bed of her son. Nevertheless, the life James led left him repeatedly in the papers because of the legacy he left in his children and grandchildren – who mentioned him in the newspapers every time they married or had children.

While 35 per cent of juveniles, including James Hudson, did not die of external causes an equal number did. This was more than expected. Male juvenile deaths due to external causes, both under and after sentence, was 20 per cent. However, for those who survived sentence this decreased to 12 per cent. Yet this is still higher than for the whole convict population, who survived until freedom (Kippen & McCalman 2015, 355–356). Male mortality under sentence from external causes was around 4.8 annual deaths per 1000 population. Moreover, external mortality for the total Tasmanian male population aged twenty-five to thirty-four (in the early 1860s) was significantly lower at about 1.8 annual deaths per 1000 population (Kippen & McCalman 2015, 360). Of the juveniles, 56 per cent died under sentence of external causes compared with 12 per cent of those who survived to freedom. Kippen and McCalman (2015, 355–356) found that for convict males who died under sentence, around 20 per cent died from external causes, ranging from drowning and falling trees, to execution. External causes include deaths attributable to an accident, suicide, assault or execution. The juveniles' external causes of deaths only included accident and execution. However, the *actual* proportion may be higher because the causes of death are known for only 53 per cent of those who died under sentence (and only 46 per cent of causes of death are known for all the juveniles). This high proportion of external causes may reflect the dangerous nature of the work both under and after sentence. This is demonstrated below in the case study of Charles Henson (*Case Study No.24*). Since there is an increased rate of mortality under sentence, death under sentence will be turned to. Fifteen per cent of the male juveniles died while under sentence.[1] They were aged between thirteen and twenty-six. Two died on the voyage over, including John Long and John Winford, and another two died within months of arriving.

Case Studies No.21: John Long and No.22: John Winford

Born approximately eight years apart, both denied their offences and both spent time on the *Euryalus* before being transported. Despite Long stealing a handkerchief worth thirty-six pence, and Winford stealing three pairs of shoes worth ninety pence, Long was given a life of transportation while

Winford was given seven years. Long died of cholera aboard the *Surrey* and Winford died of anasarca aboard the *Elphinstone*. Anasarca, or extreme generalized oedema, is a medical condition characterized by widespread swelling of the skin due to effusion of fluid into the extracellular space. It is usually caused by liver failure (cirrhosis of the liver), renal failure, right-sided heart failure, as well as severe malnutrition or protein deficiency. An increase in salt and water retention caused by low cardiac output can also result in anasarca as a long-term maladaptive response.

Long was sentenced to transportation after being convicted of pocketpicking, but before this he had already been convicted of simple larceny aged thirteen and confined for three months after being recommended to mercy on account of his good character. No such recommendations came on the second conviction and he was given a life of transportation. Not only did he have a prior conviction he was also described as 'mutinous' by the hulk officials. While it is indeed possible that John Long contracted cholera aboard the ship there is no evidence of this and no one else aboard the ship died. However, the fact that the ship set off in the middle of winter would not have helped his health. Largely due to the focus of emptying the overcrowded hulks, voyages were often sent regardless of the season. It was only in 1836 that convict ships were banned from sailing in the middle of winter to reduce the chances of disease due to cold conditions (Brooke & Brandon 2005, 110). This change came four years after John Long's death.

John Winford was baptized in Shoreditch in 1828 and went on to be convicted of shoplifting. Winford was recorded in the Settlement Paper, in 1829, with his mother Matilda and siblings; an unbaptized baby, Matilda aged two, the eldest Sarah (who was an illegitimate child of a different father) was eleven, and he was at the time five. They were deserted by John Winford, a dyer, who went to the country to work. There was trouble over the settlement of John Winford junior's grandfather's house but it is unclear what the dispute was. However, there was an order of removal from Saint Matthew, Bethnal Green Parish in 1831. John Winford junior therefore did not have a very easy start in life. Before his transportation sentence, he had already spent ten days in the house of correction. Yet his father does not seem to have completely deserted him as he wrote a petition for the mitigation of his son's sentence. John senior was living at this point at '5 Friars Mount opposite the new church, Church Street, Bethnal Green'. His mother, Matilda, is recorded in the 1841 census as also living with John senior and the children (now six siblings) in Bethnal Green. It would appear that if John senior did desert his family, he came back. It is also

> possible that during a time of hardship when they could not make ends meet, the family decided to say this was the case in order to receive relief in the workhouse. Nevertheless, it is clear that given John Winford's uncertain start in life his nutritional intake was likely to have been particularly poor even before embarkation aboard the transportation ship, and while the voyage and consequent diet (salted meat) certainly would not have helped his health, it cannot be said to have been the sole cause of his death.

The British government wanted to keep the punishment of transportation as cheap as possible. As such there were 'numerous complaints about the conditions of convicts during the voyage'. Reluctance to make improvements on the grounds of economy led overcrowding of transports to be inevitable. Convicts were also not closely supervised beyond the bare minimum of preventing mutiny. The convicts' health was said to deteriorate during the voyage, in part, due to poor rations (Meredith 1988, 17). Before they were transported the surgeon-superintendent, in theory, decided who was healthy enough to transport. This would exclude any convict who had an infectious disease or was deemed unfit in any way (Brooke & Brendon 2005, 174). The criteria for selection were also supposedly based on age: males between fifteen and fifty, and females over forty-five were not to be transported (Meredith 1988, 14). These guidelines were not always followed, as it is known that juveniles under fifteen were transported. After 1815 there was a surgeon-superintendent placed on every convict ship, who was responsible for the health and discipline of the convicts. It was thanks to the surgeon's exertions for good hygiene that health improved on convict ships. As noted, these surgeon-superintendents were also responsible for picking the convicts who were fit to sail. However, naval surgeons complained of the impossibility of this task and argued convicts hid their illnesses to get a place on a ship, and the hulk authorities tried to get rid of their more troublesome charges by transporting them regardless of their condition. This was of course denied. Certainly there is evidence of convicts gaining places on convict transports while unhealthy. There may or may not have been dishonesty which led to such circumstances (Foxhall 2011).

The admiralty took direct control over convict transportation only in 1832. Prior to this, the vessels were chartered from private ship-owners (Brooke & Brandon 2005, 166). Shortly after they imposed the rule of deferred payments, where contractors received part of their fee once the convicts were delivered healthy at their destination (Brooke & Brandon 2005, 168). As such, conditions improved over the period of convict transportation. After improvements the average death rate per voyage improved from one in eighty five in the early days of transportation, to one in one eighty by the end of transportation (Brooke & Brandon 2005, 168). When taken in context, the transportation of convicts was not exceptionally hazardous. The Royal Navy estimated during the Napoleonic wars that one sailor in thirty would die of disease or accident. Moreover, the free emigrant ships to the United States in the mid-nineteenth century saw the same odds. Convicts are different because they were transported against their will and if they had not been sent the death rate would have been more favourable: male civilians aged between twenty and forty saw a death rate of one in eighty in Britain (Brooke & Brandon 2005, 165). The death rate of juveniles during transport for males was one in fifty, which compares unfavourably with transportation at any point. It would imply that juveniles were less likely to survive the voyage, or at least juveniles from London were. Martin Gavan survived until he reached the colony but he was one of the juveniles who died early in his sentence.

Case Study No.23: Martin Gavan

It is unclear how Martin died, but he only survived for two months in the colony before dying at Point Puer in the Port Arthur hospital. Aged only thirteen, he was the youngest juvenile to die. Born in 1829 he was eleven when he was convicted of pickpocketing a handkerchief. In his defence at the Old Bailey he stated that 'Another boy took it and chucked it down ... I could not do it with one hand ... I have one bad hand'. While we cannot know whether he did steal the handkerchief or not, it is possible to confirm that he did indeed have an injured arm. His arm was amputated while on the hulk awaiting transportation, but it is unclear why. He was given ten years' transportation and had already received fourteen days' imprisonment for 'Tossing'. His mother was living, named Mary, but he also had criminal connections in the family which would not have presented him in a favourable light. His brother-in-law, William Mill, was on the *Fortitude* and he had one sister, Ellen, already in Hobart Town. Ellen had arrived four years prior to Martin, but it is unclear if she was a convict or free immigrant. Martin arrived on the *Elphinstone* in 1842, leaving his native place of Bloomsbury. He was a Roman Catholic and could both read and write when he arrived. He committed no offences in the colony but then he had little opportunity too. Yet, he was described as a stone cutter in the colony. It is possible that his early hand injury may have been related to his work as a stone cutter.

Charles Henson died young like Martin Gavan, yet he managed to accumulate a number of offences first. This case reveals the dangerous work carried out by juveniles.

Case Study No.24: Charles Henson

Of those who did die under twenty, it is possible to explore how their lives were tragically cut short. One of these nine juveniles was Charles Henson, who died aged sixteen. Despite being recommended to mercy he was transported for seven years for housebreaking. The fact that he had previously been flogged for robbery likely weighed in on this decision. He arrived on the *Royal Sovereign* (a juvenile-only ship) in 1838. The Conduct Records state he was in Port Arthur when he died and make no mention of him being in Point Puer. However, it clearly states in the Wesleyan Church Death Register that his 'abode' was Point Puer. Given his age on arrival and the period he was sent, it is likely that he was stationed at Point Puer and the record keeper viewed Point Puer as a part of Port Arthur and felt no need to specify. Charles was ill on the voyage over according to the *Superintendent Surgeon Journals*. He suffered from ophthalmia, but was cured within four days. Despite dying only a matter of eighteen months after he arrived in the colony, he managed to accumulate twenty-three different offences. These were mainly regulatory offences; the more serious offences being 'intent to steal' and 'secreting items away', along with absconding. An inquest ruled his death an accident. Charles was rolled over by a runaway cart on a hill while working in the quarry. Charles was not the only juvenile to die after being run over by a cart. At the much later date of 1872, the then forty-five-year-old Michael Hodges was run over when in a state of intoxication in Ballarat. Charles's case points to the dangerous work these juveniles carried out.

A high percentage of these juveniles died young. Yet there is no discernible pattern demonstrating that their deaths were related to the number of offences committed, as previous researchers have found (Maxwell-Stewart 2016, 427). In fact, all age ranges when grouped in twenty-year intervals had a similar average number of offences. Juveniles who died under sentence were not more likely to have committed more offences than those who survived until freedom. But was it the punishments that these convicts endured which contributed to this shorter life-span? These punishments broadly include confinement, flogging and hard labour (see Chapter 4). Or instead was the large number of offences, within a short space of time, which led to juveniles being differently placed in the colony. For example, it was because of the number of offences committed by Charles Henson (*Case Study No.24*) that he was put to labour in the quarry. This highlights the need to explore the cause of death. Evidently those who were executed died directly due to their offences. Three convicts died as a result of accidents under sentence which was due to the work they were forced to carry out. The remaining convicts whose death causes are known, who died under sentence, died as a result of disease (the cause of death for seven remains unknown). The work juveniles were 'moved down' may have contributed to the deaths of some convicts. For others, added insults to the body caused by their working conditions may have contributed to their deaths through disease – for example Anthony Barkwith (*Case Study No.19*).

The juveniles all had relatively high numbers of offences and they were all sentenced at London. Kippen and McCalman (2015) found that the experience under sentence was related to the visibility after sentence. Specifically, for those with more conduct offences, reactive behaviour and insults were less likely to be found. This suggests that the convicts whose deaths were not found resemble those whose mortality was higher than that of the full male convict population. That is, if the deaths for these men had been included, male convict life-expectancy would be lower than indicated (Kippen & McCalman 2015, 355). It would follow that the juveniles would have had a higher rate of mortality than other convicts – because they offended more than other convicts – which is indeed the case. However, Kippen and McCalman's (2015, 360) mortality data shows that having fewer conduct offences under sentence was associated with lower overall mortality. This was not necessarily the case for juveniles, unless they died under sentence. Kippen and McCalman argue that the prudent convict who kept out of trouble and was compliant could be rewarded with a ticket of leave or pardon, the angry and recalcitrant convict would be sucked into a 'vortex of savage cruelty' (2015, 353). Therefore, the punishments received and their effects on mortality are important but there is no discernible pattern between the punishments juveniles endured and the length of their life-span. There is no correlation between lower life-spans and increased punishments including: number of hard labour days, number of lashes, number of solitary confinement days, or extra days of sentence. As in the case of juveniles, Kippen and McCalman (2015, 355) found that the number of lashes was not significantly associated with mortality after emancipation. However, they found that solitary confinement and accumulated insults were positively correlated with death under sentence. This was not the case for juveniles. Specifically, Kippen and McCalman found that every extra ten days in solitary confinement was associated with 3 per cent higher mortality (2015, 353). The period under study for Kippen and McCalman (2015, 361) was the probationary period, and in this period almost all prisoners spent time in chain gangs in line with the changing management of convicts in VDL. However, beyond those 'shared privations and insults' they found the most significant impact on mortality was solitary confinement. The same cannot be said of juveniles because the sample is too small to draw such conclusions. It may also be that for those juveniles who spent time in Point Puer and were sentenced to solitary confinement, they were not completely isolated due to the insufficient solitary cells at Point Puer, meaning that they were not undergoing true solitary confinement. This demonstrates the difficulties in finding the effects of a punishment, such as solitary confinement, when its practice varies between establishments (see Chapter 4).

Disease was also common; it would seem that juveniles were less able to cope with the work and conditions, for example the voyage over, than their adult counterparts. Kippen and McCalman's (2015, 355) study found that those who died under sentence were more likely to be older on arrival and born in industrial districts or London. Certainly juveniles were not old on arrival but they were all from London. It is possible that it was arriving in the colony and lacking skills useful to the colony which led to them being placed in unfavourable conditions. Just as employers may have seen older convicts with the less useful skills as being unable to adjust their skill base, juveniles with a similar lack of useful skills may also have been viewed in the same light. In turn, this could have led to them being placed in 'risky' or less favourable conditions. A combination of having more offences and lacking useful skills may have contributed to the early deaths of these juveniles who disproportionately died under twenty. Conversely, females had a far more favourable life-expectancy.

Female juveniles

The average age-of-death for all female juveniles is 53.1. Given survival to twenty and to freedom, the average age-of-death was 59.5. This excludes Eliza White who was the only female to die under twenty, the rest of the females lived until at least forty-three. What disease Eliza died of is unknown, but she fell ill on the voyage over and died within months of arrival.

Case Study No.25: Eliza White

Eliza White was born in 1832 and was convicted in 1845 of Simple Larceny. Eliza stole two dust-pans worth two shillings from a Lambeth dwelling house. Despite being recommended to the penitentiary she was transported under a seven-year sentence. In a previous trial that year, Eliza had been convicted of theft and confined for fourteen days. A petition was made by her parents, Mary and James White, who asked for mitigation on the grounds of her youth (she was fifteen) and they promised that she would not offend again. There were no other signatures on their petition and they were unsuccessful. In 1846, aboard the *Sea Queen*, Eliza was transported from Woolwich to Hobart. The surgeon-superintendent described her as 'Bad, Idle and dirty – sent to hospital' and unfortunately all other records are left blank. It was a relatively short journey for the convicts on this transport but Eliza died soon after arrival aboard the *Anson* hulk and was buried at the Prisoners Burial Ground at Trinity Cemetery. Records state she was fifteen when she died but if her trial record is to be relied on she would have been between sixteen and seventeen. The only information given in Eliza's Description List is that she was sick – so we do not know what she died of.

In their study of female convicts transported aboard the *Tasmania*, to VDL in 1845, Kavanagh and Snowden (2015) traced the lives of 138 females. Of these convicts, deaths were found for approximately 39 per cent, compared with 28 per cent of the female juveniles traced in this research. The juveniles were younger on arrival and therefore more likely to marry and migrate in the colony, making them more difficult to trace. It must also be noted that the female juveniles were evidently all juveniles and the ages of those on the *Tasmania* ranged from sixteen to sixty-four, and 5 per cent were aged over fifty. However, the majority, 51 per cent, were under twenty-nine. It cannot be ignored that the *Tasmania* female convicts were transported from Ireland and therefore the group may have differed from the London juveniles for a number of reasons. While these women were transported at the beginning of the great famine (1845–52), Ireland had suffered from economic issues since the Napoleonic wars and a rapid population growth which was at its height in 1845, leading the Irish working classes to struggle. However, while the Irish convicts would have had a poor nutritional intake, so too would the female juveniles from London. Female juveniles' average age-of-death (given survival to freedom and/or twenty years of age) was 4.8 years longer than those females transported aboard the *Tasmania*. Seven of the *Tasmania* female convicts died under sentence, the average age-of-death being 41.5. When *all* deaths are included the female juveniles still lived on average longer (0.9 years longer). Of those female juveniles who lived until freedom, they all lived until at least forty-three. Given survival until freedom, six of the *Tasmania* female convicts died under forty-three. Unlike 20 per cent of male juveniles, no female died of external causes; they died of either disease (3) or old age (2). We are dealing with *very* low numbers and so case studies take on greater importance.

Death in old age

Case Study No.26: Elizabeth Jones (aka Walford)

Elizabeth lived the longest of all the female juveniles. She was convicted in 1842 for stealing from her master: one shawl worth two shillings and two pence, one bonnet worth six pence and three pence in change. In her Old Bailey trial, she stated to the prosecutor: 'You gave me the bonnet to wear, and lent me the shawl you took me into your service at 1s. a week and my victuals you never gave me a farthing of money, and scarcely any victuals.' Nevertheless, she was sentenced to seven years' transportation. There was another indictment against her at the trial for stealing one gown and other articles, to the value of fifteen shillings – also the property of her master. She left aboard the *Garland Grove* in 1842, arriving in Hobart three months later. She was from St. Pancras and was fifteen years old, a member of the Church of England, she worked as a 'nurse girl', could read and was described as having a 'pock-pitted' face. Her father John was living in Edgeware road and she had two siblings.

Elizabeth only committed three offences which were all status offences while under assignment, including: being absent without leave, misconduct and disobeying orders. For these offences she generally received solitary confinement but the last offence resulted in six months' hard labour at the wash tub. Elizabeth received her ticket of leave in 1847 and received her conditional pardon in 1848 and in 1849 she was awarded her certificate of freedom.

Four years after becoming free, Elizabeth married Henry Rowbottom who was also a former convict who had arrived on the *Ostler and Carter*. Henry was a tradesman transported from London for seven years in 1844. In total they had four children between 1851 and 1858. The first was born before they married. Elizabeth died in an invalid depot in Launceston aged seventy-four and was buried in 1905 at Charles Street General Cemetery. Her husband Charles also died at the invalid depot, aged seventy-seven.

Eliza White, Eliza Jones and Sarah Hodge (below) all died of disease, their life-paths and deaths were very different. It cannot be known whether it was the conditions on the voyage which caused Eliza White's death, but she certainly died young. Sarah, on the hand, died of cancer at a relatively old age and had many children, two husbands, migrated and economically bettered herself. In short, she lived a full life before she died. Only superficial comparisons can be made between the female juveniles and the *Tasmania* female convicts with regard to causes of death. This is because causes of death for the female juveniles and *Tasmania*[2] female convicts are known for only 39 per cent and 25 per cent, respectively. We are dealing with very small numbers but what does become clear is that in both groups the most common cause of death was disease.

Case Study No.27: Sarah Hodge

Born in 1812, Sarah was aged thirteen when she was convicted of Grand Larceny in 1825. Sarah stole three shirts worth thirty shillings from her master, an army captain named Robert Budden, and was sentenced to seven years' transportation. There were two indictments against Sarah in the same session. That December Sarah was transported on the *Providence*. She was supposed to be thirteen according to her proceeding, her Description List records her age as eighteen. This discrepancy is probably due Sarah lying to the courts in the hope of a lenient sentence just as many other juveniles did. The gaol report described Sarah as having 'depraved habits', but the surgeon-superintendent described her as 'good'. When she arrived in the colony Sarah went on to commit five offences, this is less than average for female juveniles. None of the offences were serious and while two of the offences were committed while under assignment to a master, the last three offences were committed while under assignment to her husband.

Sarah received her free certificate in 1832 after eighty-nine days in the colony. Like Elizabeth Jones, Sarah was a nurse maid prior to transportation. Sarah married twice, first to John Wiggins at St. John Parish in Launceston in 1827 (after a year in the colony). John Wiggins arrived in the colony free and worked as a carpenter from 1830 to 1835, but by 1837 he was working as a publican. It is unclear whether her second husband was an emancipist or not, his name was James Holman and she married him in 1847 after making her way to Portland, Victoria. In total Sarah had eleven children. Nine of these children she had with her first husband, then she went on to have two daughters with her second husband. The *Argus*, in 1848, reported that her and her second husband had purchased land in a government auction at Warrnambool. All of her children died in Victoria and most of them in Portland – it would therefore appear that she took all of her children with her when she migrated. Sarah died of cancer of the head in 1859 aged fifty-two.

While no female juveniles died of external causes three *Tasmania* female convicts did. However, none of these were related to dangerous work unlike the male convicts. The *Tasmania* female convicts who died of external causes, died during their freedom and specifically due to manslaughter committed by her husband, falling timber at a relatively old age at home and drowning which was ruled an accident (Kavanagh & Snowden 2015, 300). While these deaths are not due to dangerous work, they do point to the unhappy circumstances that these females lived in. The same is not evidenced in the female juvenile group. The female juveniles who died of disease, whose details are known, died of different forms of cancer. On the other hand, Kavanagh and Snowden found that the most common cause of death was respiratory illness (2015, 248). Again, the female juveniles were relatively old when dying of these diseases. While the number of female juveniles whose age-of-deaths are known is admittedly small, all apart from one died *after* reaching freedom. The female juveniles were not sampled (all fitting the criteria were traced) and all deaths under sentence were recorded. Therefore, 94 per cent of female juveniles survived into freedom. Just as one female juvenile died as a result of disease on transport, one female died aboard the *Tasmania* of dysentery; this female was only twenty and had the responsibility of feeding her baby, which would have weakened her further. Numerically, 1 in 18 female juveniles died due to disease during the voyage, compared to 1 in 138 of female convicts from the *Tasmania* (Kavanagh & Snowden 2015, 127–128). Five per cent of the *Tasmania* female convicts died under sentence (Kavanagh & Snowden 2015, 241). Two of these deaths were aboard the *Anson* hulk, none of the female juveniles were found to have spent time aboard this hulk except for Eliza White who died aboard (*Case Study No.25*). Indeed, Kavanagh and Snowden (2015, 241) state that the deaths under sentence were 'usually in one of the colonial institutions' including the *Anson* hulk and Cascades Female Factory. Only one other female juvenile died in a colonial institution and this was in the Launceston Invalid Depot during old age. Excepting Eliza White, none of the female juveniles died under sentence while in a colonial institution. Importantly, of the *Tasmania* female convicts who died under sentence four were under thirty-three but one was forty-six and another was seventy-six. Therefore, the latter (at least) was expected to die under sentence. Female juveniles did not have a higher mortality rate under sentence but they did live, on average, longer than this comparison group. As with male juveniles, the offending of the females and their punishments were explored to assess their impact on mortality. However, while those female juveniles who died between the ages of forty-one and sixty had on average four more offences than those who died between the ages of sixty-one and eight, the numbers are too small to draw definitive conclusions. The same problem exists when looking at the punishments they endured.

Conclusion

Life-expectancy rates for male juveniles were comparable with the wider convict population both for those who died under sentence and for those who survived until freedom. They did not live as long as colonial-born males or English males at home. However, a number of male juveniles died under sentence and under twenty. This was not consistent with juvenile convicts sent to Point Puer. While acknowledging that there is an over-representation of male juvenile deaths, the common characteristics which may have contributed to these deaths were determined. There was no evidence to show that male juvenile life-expectancy was affected directly by punishment or by the number of offences. Moreover, the number of deaths attributable to external causes was higher for juveniles when compared with other male convicts. Since the juveniles had a higher rate of offending, it is possible that as a result of this offending they were moved to tasks or employment which exposed them to greater danger or worsened living conditions. This combined with their youth and inexperience may have led to the increased number of young deaths. Certainly, if deaths from external causes are removed, the average age-of-death of male juveniles (not given survival to any age and whose causes of death are known) is increased to sixty-two. This brings them in line with the more favourable life-expectancy of free Tasmanian males. Female juveniles lived longer than males generally and longer than the female convicts transported from Ireland on the *Tasmania*. In distinction from male juveniles the females did not die of external causes, only one female is known to have died under sentence and she was also the only female to die under twenty. This difference may be due to the different work in which females were employed. While it is not always clear what hard labour female juveniles were directed to after offending under sentence, it was generally hard labour at the wash tub which was not dangerous (though I am sure it was not pleasant). The different work carried out, and environments, these different groups were placed in had an impact on their life-outcomes.

8

Conclusion

This book has built on work which has explored the lives of juvenile convicts before and during punishment (Shore 1999a; Nunn 2015, 2017), by looking beyond the criminal justice records. Going beyond the institution and focusing directly on female and male juveniles was important in understanding the lives of this unique group. Juveniles were often treated differently from adult convicts. Therefore, their experience of punishment was inevitably different. Moreover, it has shown that convict transportation affected their life-outcomes in terms of experience, economic attainment, familial life and mortality. It is by no means argued here that being transported as a convict in adulthood was not life altering or arduous. However, it is stressed that the transportation of juveniles away from family and familiarity was a *different* experience because of their youth. It does not follow that their lives would have been better or worse if they had not been transported. What this research has explored is what these juveniles managed to achieve in spite of/due to their experience of transportation. This concluding chapter will now bring together the fragmented lives of these juveniles. By going beyond the convict records, this work has built on the historical life-course analysis work pioneered by Godfrey and colleagues (2007, 2010, 2017). The juvenile convicts' crimes, punishments, education, training, employment, relationships and mortality have all been explored.

While it is true that all female juveniles and the majority of males eventually stopped offending, it would be wrong to suggest that transportation broke the cycle of their offending. Conversely, Maxwell-Stewart (2016, 427) found that transportation did break the cycle of female offending when looking at the whole population. Yet, both female and male juveniles offended repeatedly, and in quick succession, for much of their servitude. Indeed, they accelerated in their offending after arrival. Importantly, despite this, after freedom most turned away from crime. It is likely that the high number of non-serious offences in both male and female juveniles, while under sentence, was affected by the assignment masters decision making and the increased time spent in institutionalized settings. Both situations led to reporting of relatively non-serious offending in juveniles more likely. This increased tendency to report juveniles is likely to be due to a mixture of increased surveillance of the group, and a decreased willingness to overlook the offences observed. This was partially due to the normalization of reprimanding children for poor behaviour and performance (as pointed out by Rowbotham 2017), as well as the decreased likelihood that these juveniles would possess the skills, experience and competencies in demand. The less skill a convict had, the greater the likelihood that a convict would be reported for offending. In this way a master would not be concerned about the time-consuming punishment their assignee might be subject to and the interruption of work that would result. This is suggested by Maxwell-Stewart (2016, 426) with reference to the general convict population, and this research has found that the juvenile convicts should not only be included in this but were particularly susceptible to it. It is likely that free settler masters, wanted a more skilled, experienced or simply stronger work force. Therefore, not only would masters be willing to lose their service for the duration of the punishment, their aim may have been to have them replaced. Similarly, in institutional settings there was always another convict to take over their work. Additionally, surveillance and punishment would have been more refined in the institutional settings. This reasoning is further enforced by the finding that most juveniles did not go on to offend outside of their Conduct Record and, even those who did, most desisted from crime before death.

The experience of punishments varied per convict, and because of these variations in practices and institutions, and the relatively small sample size, trends are difficult to uncover. This reflects the variation in practice in British prisons back home found by Johnston (2008). However, generally juvenile convicts were punished more than adult convicts, and punishments were gendered. What punishments juveniles received was related to the ad hoc management system in place for their age and sex (and not necessarily the broader management systems adults were subjected to, i.e. the assignment and probation systems). Not only was life different for a juvenile convict from an adult convict, it was also different for male and female juvenile convicts, and directly related to both their worth as workers and the ability and inclination to punish them.

Whether these juveniles were able to survive and settle in the colonies was assessed in relation to their education, skills and employment. As employment of juveniles demonstrates, the males arrived in the colony with few skills compared with adult convicts and free emigrants. As Nunn (2015) has suggested, they arrived with potential human capital to be exploited, rather than being a ready workforce. It was due to a *combination* of their pre-transportation skills, trade training and varied assignment tasks they were able to be flexible in their employment allowing them to survive in the colony. It is also likely that the lack of familial ties led to their willingness to migrate in search of work, adding to their increased work–life fluidity – in the male sample especially. Few of the juveniles managed to break through prevailing class barriers into the professional class but many sustained themselves in respectable employment. This is similar to the findings of Godfrey and colleagues (2017) in their study of youth offenders in England. However, it would appear more movement and fluidity was required of the juveniles, and largely thanks to their lack of familial ties they were willing and able to migrate to both different types of employment and different locations for that employment. The majority remained among the working classes but many went onto work in respectable trades. Male juveniles suffered from initial disadvantage due to a lack of skills, experience and small physiques which worked against them; but 'special' management aimed at training and educating them worked for them even if those juveniles did not remain in the trades they were taught. This finding builds on the work of Nicholas (1988) and Oxley (1996), who explored the pre-transportation employment of convicts. Here, with a particular focus on juveniles, it has been possible (given the digital advances of recent years and the increasing availability of records) to explore their post-transportation trades too. This not only tells us their economic status, but also gives us a measure of how they settled into the colony. Unfortunately, due to contemporary disinterest in female skills and trades, there is limited knowledge of adult employment of the female juveniles. This is largely due to the fact that most females married very early in their colonial lives. This is not to say they did not supplement their husband's income, only that there is no written record. As with the work of Oxley (1996), it has been largely only through their criminal records that any knowledge of the female working lives have been uncovered. When leaving the convict system, their economic lives unfortunately become invisible. However, many of the women did go on to quickly marry husbands with respectable trades and form families – setting down their own colonial roots.

Many of the males did not marry. This, and their lack of extended family networks, may be a factor in why the juveniles are over-represented among the pauper population. With their extended family and their resources back in Britain, more than expected ended their days in pauper establishments. Essentially, it would seem they lacked a family structure to support them in old age. However, excepting the work of Piper (2010), little work has focused on pauper-emancipists. Further research is needed to draw attention towards those who struggled in old age, instead of an unconscious focus on the contribution of 'successful' and resilient convicts (Nicholas 1988; Oxley 1996; Smith 2008b). These juveniles were certainly resilient, if not all 'successful'. Indeed, while most did not live extraordinary working lives post-transportation, male juveniles lived average working-class lives in a variety of different trades *despite* their early-life upheaval. For females it is clear that on the assignment market their limited skills did not prevent their ready assignment, and the relative freedoms in assignment likely enabled them to meet their husbands early on. The female juveniles were both more likely to go on to marry and have children, and to do so sooner in their colonial lives, and at younger ages, than the males. Indeed, these male juvenile convicts married at a considerably lower rate than males leaving the reformatory system back home in Britain (Godfrey et al. 2017). While increasing number of offences would certainly have delayed marriage for both female and male juveniles, the main factor in whether they married was their sex. There is evidence in both male and female samples of varying degrees of familial 'outcomes' and the struggle of some of the females to maintain their households. Nevertheless, most of the families formed continued to live quietly out of the sight of the colonial authorities.

While many of the male juveniles lived full and long lives and died due to disease and natural causes, a number of males died under sentence and under twenty, and this brought down the average life expectancy of the group. Those sent to Point Puer had a lower mortality rate than those at Port Arthur, and both Vandemonian males and free English men at home. The high proportion of young male deaths from the sample is, therefore, a significant finding of this research. It is acknowledged that there is an over-representation of young male juvenile deaths, and so more research is needed in this area using the whole sample of juvenile Vandemonian convicts. Since juveniles had a higher rate of offending, it is possible that as a result of this offending they were moved to tasks or employment which exposed them to greater danger. This combined with their youth and inexperience led to the increased number of young deaths. Certainly, if deaths from external causes are removed, the life-expectancy of male juveniles increased in line with free Tasmanian males generally, and gives them a longer life-expectancy than both English convicts and free English males at home. Therefore, it may have been the dangerousness of their work that affected their mortality, and they were more likely to be removed to more dangerous work if they had a greater number of offences and lower skill base. On the other hand, the female juveniles lived long lives. In distinction from the males, they did not die of external causes and only one female is known to have died under sentence and she was also the only female to die under twenty. This difference may be related to the different work the female juveniles were employed in which, though arduous, was less dangerous. Female juveniles died under sentence at a similar, although slightly higher, rate than their female convict comparison group (Kavanagh & Snowden 2015) but were less likely to die under sentence as compared with their male counterparts. This may be due to a number of reasons not least their lack of extended sentences which were handed out to this group compared to the males, and due to the different work carried out by, and environments of, these differing groups.

The fact that the majority of juveniles turned away from crime reflects the findings of Godfrey and colleagues (2017) and, therefore, is likely to point to a pattern in youth offending more broadly and *not* reflect the reformative 'success' of this particular punishment system. These juveniles were thrust into a colony in which they had no ties, either social or economic, while this pushed the female juveniles into marriage, the males (who were competing with older more skilled and more established males in a colony with a scarcity of females) were often unable to form companionship and instead moved through the colony in search of work or tried their luck in the gold mines of Victoria, and less often New Zealand and California. This research has explored the shared experiences of juveniles but also the lack of standardization of their punishment experience and their resultant 'divergent pathways' and outcomes. As pointed out by Sampson and Laub's key findings (1993, 1998, 2005) and more recently supported by Godfrey and colleagues (2017), 'shared beginnings' led to 'divergent lives'. There were those who continued in crime and struggled to survive and settle in the colony. Yet, this research shows that despite such early-life upheaval, above average crime rates and corresponding punishments, despite arriving with little skills and education in a colony without social ties or support – the *majority* of male and female juveniles were able to live normal working-class lives.

Despite their extraordinary beginnings, in terms of their social and geographical dislocation, they did not lead extraordinary lives post-transportation but they did settle in terms of what could reasonably be expected of them. This research has uncovered the brutal punishments that these young offenders endured, including hard labour, solitary confinement and flogging. Such punishments for this population were not rare. Such harsh treatment, combined with feelings of subjugation and heteronomy, led a minority to resist the colonial authorities through, often petty, offences (through insolence and impertinence). They demonstrated that even as juveniles and prisoners they had agency. Others, who became caught up in the punishment system never managed to leave the convict system and died under sentence (like Michael Connor who died under sentence aged thirty of consumption after being convicted aged thirteen in London). A minority of male juveniles went on to commit serious offences including murder. Yet, the majority endured and survived their sentence of transportation, and the repeated punishments that resulted from it and settled into colonial life. We can never know the subjective experience of punishment felt by these particular individuals. However, this does not mean they did not suffer, and their 'survival' should not disguise the brutality of the system that they went through. Certainly contemporary studies of individuals punished in Britain today conceptualized their punishment as 'deprivation of liberty' and as 'hard treatment' (van Ginneken & Hayes 2017). We can only guess at how these particular young offenders would have described their experiences in old age (for those of them who reached old age that is).

It seems now fitting to return to the life of Mary Ann Oseman, the life of whom this book opened with. Her life-outcome may seem very ordinary – she married and had children, then remarried when her first husband passed away and lived a very quiet life. Yet, the 2015 headstone erected by her descendants and her recognition as an early pioneer of Wallaroo in the 2015 Kernowek Lowender were devised to highlight the significance of her life (Watkins 2015b). However, while her descendants may disagree, it is argued here that the importance of her life is *not* that its outcome was extraordinary; instead, it is that her life was representative of many of the other juveniles arriving in the colonies – she blended into the population and remained free from crime.

Notes

Chapter 1

1. Of the 534 male juveniles transported, 100 were sampled. Only eighteen females fitting the criteria arrived in VDL; all were included.
2. The age that an individual was considered a juvenile varied widely in contemporary social discourse from fourteen to seventeen, and even to twenty. This is demonstrated in the 1819 Select Committee in which commentators referred to the upper age limits of seventeen and twenty (May 1981, 80). This is also pointed out by Magarey (1978, 16) who stated that in British prisons the distinction between juveniles and adults 'was drawn at a variety of different ages in different local prisons, but the maximum age of juvenile classes in prisons was seventeen'. Within VDL, Point Puer held 'juveniles' up to twenty years old but the majority were fourteen. As such, juveniles under fourteen were sampled in this study based on nineteenth-century law: juveniles aged between seven and fourteen could be prosecuted 'only' if the child knew they were committing a crime (*doli capax*), rather than being 'naughty' (*doli incapax*). Those over fourteen were considered adults in the eyes of the law during trial. While the juveniles were under fourteen upon conviction, many waited years for a transport ship. By the time they arrived in VDL the majority (88 per cent) were sixteen and under (the oldest female was nineteen; the oldest males were eighteen; the youngest female was twelve; the youngest male was ten).
3. In order to fully understand the lives of these transported juveniles, one penal colony was focused on. VDL was chosen because only one male was sent to Western Australia (WA) and only thirteen males arrived in Victoria as exiles, and no female in the sample arrived in WA or Victoria. VDL was chosen largely due to the records available, both digitized and archival, and the larger number of juveniles arriving as compared with New South Wales (NSW). See bibliography for digital and physical archival information and for a full discussion of sources, method and methodology: Watkins and Godfrey (2018); Watkins (2018, 75–90).

Chapter 2

1. This work was based on property offenders aged under seventeen.
2. 1821 Bill for the Punishment, Correction and Reform of Young Persons Charged with Privately Stealing from Houses, or the Person in Certain Cases.

3. 1821 Bill for The Punishment, Correction and Reform of Young Persons Charged with Privately Stealing from Houses, or the Person in Certain Cases.

Chapter 3

1. Criminal Petitions for Clemency 1819–1839 (HO17 and HO18) are a detailed source but are only available for 17 per cent of those traced. Yet, when they are available they provide information on the family unit, economy and background of the offender. These records provide details of 16,309 people for the period 1817–1858. Convicted criminals, or their family and friends, made a petition when they wanted to mitigate the sentence.
2. Conduct Records were initiated by Lieutenant Governor Arthur in 1803. They include: details of pre-transportation and colonial offences; punishments (including locations and dates); and the offenders' status, meaning whether they were assigned, confined at a penal station or on the public works.
3. A 1-in-25 sample was systematically chosen from all male convicts arriving in VDL whose Police Number ended 06, 33, 56 and 83. In total there were 2405 convicts. This 1-in-25 sample was transcribed by Maxwell-Stewart and the *Founders & Survivors* team but coded by the author. The records used were: Con31, Con32 and Con33. For the purposes of this analysis the sample was looked at as a whole and then broken into the following groups for further analysis: the assignment period convicts who arrived between 1816 and 1840 (total 1281); the probation period convicts who arrived between 1840 and 1853 (total 1124); and those male convicts who are known to be nineteen and under. Offences from all groups were categorized into the same levels of severity as described for the male juveniles in Table 1. By taking all known juvenile convicts from the 1-in-25 sample it was possible to compare them with the male juveniles in this research. Unfortunately, the ages of convicts in the 1-in-25 sample are only provided for those arriving in the probation period. Consequently, these juveniles arrived from 1840 onwards (this gave 177 male juvenile convicts). This is problematic because the male juveniles in this research arrived between 1817 and 1848, and therefore many arrived in the assignment period. The treatment of adult convicts under these two different systems, the assignment and the probation period, was very different. However, while it was not always the case, juvenile convicts were largely treated differently from adult convicts. Therefore, the changing system of treatment for convicts affected juveniles less than adults. This was not only because of their placement at Point Puer. It was also practice, when juveniles could not be assigned, to keep them in the prisoners' barracks. They were kept in the barracks for practicality and not as an additional punishment.

4   Selection Criteria: All females fourteen and under sentenced to transportation at the Old Bailey, between 1816 and 1850.
5   This report names George Pickering's wife as 'Ann', since his only known wife is 'Jane' this may be a misprint or he may have remarried and no record has been found.
6   It has been suggested that 'oystermen' is a euphemism for working as a 'pimp' or having a connection with a brothel but it is not confirmed George had such a connection.

Chapter 4

1   On the whole, 17 per cent of the juveniles underwent punishments not recorded in their Conduct Records. These were mainly fines or imprisonment.
2   There were other punishments pronounced on female convicts, including fines. This was relatively rare. Only two juveniles were fined and this was after their ticket of leave was earned.

Chapter 5

1   At least 50 per cent of these male transportees could already read and write pre-transportation and a further 17 per cent could read. Only two (11 per cent) could neither read nor write, and for a further four (22 per cent) the information is unavailable.
2   These juvenile transportees worked as a labourer, a bookbinder, a tailor, a tailor who also worked in another trade post-transportation, there were two shoemakers who also worked in another trade, and a labourer who also worked in another trade post-transportation.

Chapter 7

1   It must also be pointed out that of those who died under sentence, 31 per cent (all male) were under either a second punishment or an extended punishment, and two of these were executed.
2   Total known causes-of-death for female convicts transported on the *Tasmania* = 34 (25 per cent of total 138). Specifically, disease (67 per cent), external cause (9 per cent), old age/natural causes (24 per cent) and child birth (3 per cent) (Kavanagh & Snowden 2015, 300).

Bibliography

Anderson, C. (2016) 'Transnational Histories of Penal Transportation: Punishment, Labour and Governance in the British Imperial World, 1788–1939', *Australian Historical Studies*, 47(3), pp. 381–397.

Aries, P. (1962) *Centuries of Childhood* (New York: Vintage).

Atkinson, A. (1985) 'Convicts and Courtship'. In *Families in Colonial Australia* (eds) Grimshaw, P., McConville, C. & McEwen, E. (London: George Allen & Unwin), pp. 19–31.

Bailey, V. (1987) *Delinquency and Citizenship: Reclaiming the Young Offender, 1914–1948* (Oxford: Clarendon Press).

Beck, W. (2003) 'The Prosopographia Imperii Rani and Prosopographical Method'. In *Fifty Years of Prosopography – The Later Roman Empire, Byzantium and Beyond* (ed.) Cameron, A. (Oxford: OUP/British Academy), pp. 11–23.

Becker, G S. (1981) *A Treatise on the Family* (Cambridge, MA: Harvard University Press).

Beddoe, D. (1979) *Welsh Convict Women: A Study of Women Transported from Wales to Australia 1787–1852* (Bridgend: S. Williams).

Ben-amos, I K. (2005) 'Book Review, Becoming Delinquent: British and European Youth, 1650–1950 (Aldershot: Ashgate Publishing, 2002)'. In *Continuity and Change*, 20(1), pp. 143–145.

Berlanstein, L R. (2001) 'Vagrants, Beggars and Thieves: Delinquent Boys in Mid-Nineteenth Century Paris', *Journal of Social History*, 12(4), pp. 531–552.

Bernard, J. (1876). Statistics of Van Diemen's land'. *Compiled from the Official Records in the Colonial Secretary's Office* (Hobart Town: Government Printer).

Bernard, J. (1849) 'Statistics of Van Diemen's Land for 1848'. *Compiled from the Official Records in the Colonial Secretary's Office* (Hobart Town: Government Printer).

Booth, C O' H (July 1837) 'Commandant Charles O'Hara Booth to Colonial Secretary John Montagu' (24 July 1837), *Archives Office of Tasmania Document*: CSO 5/35/728.

Bradley, K. (2009) 'Inside the Inner London Juvenile Court, c. 1909–1953', *SOLON Crimes and Misdemeanours: Deviance and the Law in Historical Perspective*, 3(2), pp. 37–59.

Bradley, K. (2007) 'Juvenile Delinquency, the Juvenile Courts and the Settlement Movement 1908–1950: Basil Henriques and Toynbee Hall', *Twentieth-Century British History*, 19(2), pp. 133–155.

Bradley, J. & Short, H. (2005) 'Texts into Databases: The Evolving Field of New-Style Prosopography', *Language and Linguistic Computing*, 20, pp. 3–24.

Brand, I. (1990) *The Convict Probation System – Van Diemen's Land 1839–1854* (Hobart: Blubber Head Press).

Brooke, A. & Brandon, D. (2005) *Bound for Botany Bay* (Surry: The National Archives).

Brown, A. (2013) *Inter-War Penal Policy and Crime in England: The Dartmoor Convict Prison Riot, 1932* (Basingstoke: Palgrave Macmillan).

Burn, D. (1842) 'An Excursion to Port Arthur in 1842', *Tasmanian Journal of Natural Science*, 1, pp. 1–3.

Burton, F. (1986) *The Moral Lever: Education and Teachers of Convicts and Free Children at Port Arthur and Point Puer Juvenile Prison, Tasman Peninsula 1830–1877* (Sandy Bay: National Parks and Wildlife Service of Tasmania).

Cale, M. (1993) 'Girls and the Perception of Sexual Danger in the Victorian Reformatory System', *History*, 78(253), pp. 201–217.

Carlen, P. (1983) *Women's Imprisonment – A Study of Social Control* (London: Routledge).

Carmichael, G. A. (1996). From floating brothels to suburban semi-respectability: Two centuries of non-marital pregnancy in Australia. Journal of Family History, 21, 281–315.

Causer, T. (2011) '"The Worst Types of Sub-Human Beings"? The Myth and Reality of the Convicts of the Norfolk Island Penal Settlement, 1825–1855'. In *Islands of History* (ed.) Australia, A B. (Sydney: Anchor Books), pp. 8–31 (Open Access [Online] Available at: http://discovery.ucl.ac.uk/1331354/1/Worst_Types_Norfolk_Island_%282010%29.pdf, pp. 1–35), accessed October 2016.

Chesney, K. (1970) *The Victorian Underworld* (London: Maurice Temple Smith Ltd).

Christiaens, J. (1999) 'A History of Belgium's Child Protection Act of 1912: The Redefinition of the Juvenile Offender and His Punishment', *European Journal of Crime, Criminal Law and Criminal Justice*, 7(1), pp. 5–21.

Clark, M. (1987) *History of Australia* (Melbourne: Melbourne University Press).

Clark, M (1956) 'The origins of the convicts transported to Eastern Australia, 1787–1852' *Historical Studies: Australia and New Zealand*, Vol 7, Issue 27, pp.314–327.

Cohen, M L. (2006) 'Researching Legal History in the Digital Age', *Law Library Journals*, 99(2), pp. 377–393.

Conley, C A. (1991) *The Unwritten Law: Criminal Justice in Kent* (Oxford: Oxford University Press).

Cowley, T. (2008) 'Female Factories of Van Diemen's Land'. In *Women Transported: Life in Australia's Convict Female Factories*, [Online] Available at: http://tradecoastcentralheritagepark.com.au/_dbase_upl/women_transported.pdf, accessed October 2016, pp. 53–69.

Cox, P. (2003) *Bad Girls in Britain: Gender, Justice and Welfare, 1900–1950* (Basingstoke: Palgrave Macmillan).

Cox, P. & Shore, H. (2003) (eds) *Becoming Delinquent: European Youth, 1650–1950* (Farnham: Ashgate).

Crone, R. (2015) 'Education in the Working-Class Home: Modes of Learning as Revealed by Nineteenth-Century Criminal Records', *Oxford Review of Education*, 41(4), pp. 482–500.

Crone, R. (2012a) 'The Great "Reading" Experiment: An Examination of the Role of Education in the Nineteenth-Century Gaol', *Crime, History & Societies*, 16(1) [Online] Available at: http://chs.revues.org/1322, accessed October 2016.

Crone, R. (2012b) *Violent Victorians: Popular Entertainment in Nineteenth-Century London* (Manchester: Manchester University Press).

Crone, R. (2010) 'Reappraising Victorian Literacy through Prison Records', *Journal of Victorian Culture*, 15(1), pp. 3–37.

Cunningham, H. (2005) *Children and Childhood in Western Society since 1500*. Second Edition (Harlow: Pearson Longman).

Damousi, J. (1997) *Depraved and Disorderly: Female Convicts, Sexuality and Gender in Colonial Australia* (Cambridge: Cambridge University Press).

Davies, A. (2008) *The Gangs of Manchester: The Story of the Scuttlers, Britain's First Youth Cult* (Preston: Milo Books).

D'Cruze, S. (2000) 'Introduction – Unguarded Passions: Violence, History and the Everyday'. In *Everyday Violence in Britain, 1850–1950: Gender and Class* (ed.) D'Cruze, S. (Essex: Routledge), pp. 1–26.

Dekker, J H J. (2005) 'The Will to Change the Children at Risk: The Transformation of Philanthropy into Social Policy in 19th-Century Western Europe'. In *Agency and Institutions in Social Regulation: Towards Historical Understanding of Their Interaction* (eds) Fecteau, J-M. & Harvey, J. (Saint Foy: Les Presses de l'Universite du Quebec), pp. 420–434.

Dickens, C. (1838) *Oliver Twist* (London: Penguin UK).

Dixon, M. (1975) *The Real Matilda: Women and Identity in Australia 1788 to 1975* (Ringwood, Victoria: Penguin Books Australia, – A Pelican original).

Doust, J. L. (2008). Two English immigrant families in Australia in the 19th century. The History of the Family, 13(1), 2–25.

Duckworth, J. (2002) *Fagin's Children – Criminal Children in Victorian England* (London: Hambledon and London).

Elder, G H., Jr. (1974) *Children of the Great Depression: Social Change in Life Experience* (Chicago, IL: University of Chicago Press).

Ellis, H. (2014) (ed.) *Juvenile Delinquency and the Limits of Western Influence, 1850–2000* (Basingstoke: Palgrave Macmillan).

Emsley, C. (2010) *Crime and Society in England, 1750–1900*. Fourth Edition (London: Routledge).

Evans, L. & Nicholls, P. (1984) *Convicts and Colonial Society 1788–1868*. Second Edition (Melbourne: Macmillan).

Ewing, T J. (1843) *Statistics of Van Diemen's Land from 1838 to 1841* (Hobart Town: Government Printer).

Fleming, C. (2012) *The Transportation of Women from Kildare to Van Diemen's Land in 1849* (Dublin: Four Courts Press).

Foucault, M. (1975) *Discipline and Punish: The Birth of the Prison* (New York: Penguin).

Foxhall, K. (2011) 'From Convicts to Colonists: The Health of Prisoners and the Voyage to Australia, 1823-53', *The Journal of Imperial and Commonwealth History*, 39(1), pp. 1–19.

Franklin, J. (1843) *A Confidential Despatch from Sir John Franklin on Female Convicts, Van Diemen's Land* (Adelaide: Sullivan's Cove).

Frost, G S. (2008) *Living in Sin* (Manchester: Manchester University Press).

Frost, L. (2011) 'The Politics of Writing Convict Lives: Academic Research, State Archives and Family History', *Life Writing*, 8(1), pp. 19–33.

Frost, L. & Maxwell-Stewart, H. (2001) *Chain Letters: Narrating Convict Lives* (Melbourne: Melbourne University Press).

Gandevia, B. (1977) 'A Comparison of the Height of Boys Transported to Australia from England, Scotland and Ireland, c. 1840 with Later British and Australian Development', *Australian Paediatric Journal*, 13, pp. 91–96.

Gard, R L. (2009) *The End of the Road: A History of the Abolition of Corporal Punishment in the Courts of England and Wales* (Boca Raton: Brown Walker Press).

Garland, D. (1985) *Punishment and Welfare: A History of Penal Strategies* (Aldershot: Ashgate Publishing Limited).

Gatrell, V A C. (1996) *The Hanging Tree: Execution and the English People: 1770–1868* (Oxford: Oxford University Press).

Giele, J Z. & Elder, G H., Jr. (1998) 'The Life Course and the Development of the Field'. In *Methods of Life Course Research: Qualitative and Quantitative Approaches* (eds) Giele J Z. & Elder Jr. J H. (London: Sage), pp. 5–27.

Ginneken, E F J C van. & Hayes, D. (2017) '"Just" Punishment? Offenders' Views on the Meaning and Severity of Punishment', *Criminology and Criminal Justice*, 17(1), pp. 62–78.

Godfrey, B. (2014) *Crime in England, 1880–1945 – The Rough and the Criminal, the Policed and the Incarcerated* (Cornwall: Routledge).

Godfrey, B. & Maxwell-Stewart, H. (2016) 'Artful Dodgers Down Under?' Unpublished.

Godfrey, B S., Cox, D J. & Farrall, S D. (2010) *Serious Offenders: A Historical Study of Habitual Criminals* (Oxford: Oxford University Press).

Godfrey, B S., Cox, D J. & Farrall, S D. (2007) *Criminal Lives: Family, Employment and Offending* (Oxford: Oxford University Press).

Godfrey, B., Cox, P., Shore, H. & Alker, Z. (2017) *Young Criminal Lives* (Oxford: Oxford University Press).

Goldscheider, F K. & Waite, L J. (1986) 'Sex Differences in the Entry to Marriage', *American Journal of Sociology*, 92, pp. 91–109.

Goffman, E. (1963) *Stigma: Notes on the Management of Spoiled Identity* (London: Penguin).

Goldson, B. (2008) *Dictionary of Youth Justice* (Cullompton: Willan).

Goldson, B. & Muncie, J. (2006) (eds) *Youth Crime and Justice* (London: Sage).

Gordon, A C. (1996) 'From Floating Brothels to Suburban Semi-Respectability: Two Centuries of Non-Marital Pregnancy in Australia', *Journal of Family History*, 21(3), pp. 281–315.

Gorton, K. & Ramsland, J. (2002) 'Prison Playground? Child Convict Labour and Vocational Training in New South Wales, 1788–1840', *Journal of Educational Administration and History*, 34(1), pp. 51–62.

Gorovitz, S. (1969) 'Aspects of the Pragmatics of Explanation', *Nous*, 3, pp. 61–72.

Gorovitz, S. (1965) 'Causal Judgements and Causal Explanations', *Journal of Philosophy*, 62(23), pp. 695–711.

Gray, D D. (2010) *London's Shadows: The Dark Side of the Victorian City* (London: Bloomsbury).

Hampton, J. (August 1846) BPP. 'Transportation', vol. 7, 1843–47, Comptroller General to Lieutenant Governor, 1 August 1846.

Hartwell, R M. (1954) *The Economic Development of Van Diemen's Land 1820–1850* (Melbourne: Melbourne University Press).

Hay, D. (1975) 'Property, Authority and the Criminal Law'. In *Albion's Fatal Tree: Crime and Society in Eighteenth-Century England* (eds) Hay, D., Linebaugh, P., Rule, J G., Thompson, E P. & Winslow, C. (London: Allen Lane), pp. 17–63.

Hendrick, H. (2006) 'Histories of Youth Crime and Justice'. In *Youth Crime and Justice* (eds) Goldson, B. & Muncie, J. (London: Sage), pp. 3–17.

Hendriksen, G. (2009) 'Women Transported: Myth and Reality', Paper presented at Parramatta Heritage Centre, National Archives of Australia [14 June 2009]. Available at: http://tradecoastcentralheritagepark.com.au/_dbase_upl/women_transported.pdf

Hooper, F C. (1967) *Prison Boys of Port Arthur: A Study of the Point Puer Boy's Establishment, Van Diemen's Land, 1834–1850* (Melbourne: University of Melbourne).

Hooper, F C. (1954) 'The Point Puer Experiment: A Study of the Penal and Educational Treatment of Juvenile Transportees in VDL 1830–1850' (MEd thesis, University of Melbourne).

Horne, B. (1843) 'Benjamin Horne's report on Point Puer Boys' Prison, to His Excellency Sir John Franklin K.C.H. and K.R. Lieut. Governor of Van Diemen's Land, Point Puer, March 7 1843', Edited extracts from *Archives Office of Tasmania document*: C0280/157/520.

House of Lords (1863) 'Report from the Select Committee of the House of Lords on the Present state of Discipline in Gaols and Houses of Correction Together with the Proceedings of the Committee, Minutes of Evidence', Ordered by the House of Commons, 24 July 1863, 499.

Hughes, R. (2003) *The Fatal Shore* (London: Vintage).

Humphrey, K. (2008) 'Objects of Compassion: Young Male Convicts in Van Diemen's Land, 1834–1850', *Australian Historical Studies*, 25(98), pp. 13–33.

Humphrey, K. (1997) 'Point Puer Images and Practices of Juvenile Imprisonment in Convict Australia', *Unpublished Report to the Port Arthur Historic Site Management Authority, Tasmania*.

Ignatieff, M. (1978) *A Just Measure of Pain: The Penitentiary in the Industrial Revolution 1750–1850* (New York: Pantheon Books).

Inwood, K., Maxwell-Stewart, H., Oxley, D. & Stankovich, J. (2015) 'Growing Incomes, Growing People in Nineteenth-Century Tasmania', *Australian Economic History Review*, 55(2), pp. 187–211.

Jackman, G. (2009) 'From Stain to Saint: Ancestry, Archaeology, and Agendas in Tasmania's Convict Heritage – A View from Port Arthur', *Historical Archaeology*, 43(3), pp. 101–112.

Jackman, G. (2001) 'Get Thee to Church: Hard Work, Godliness and Tourism at Australia's First Rural Reformatory', *Australasian Historical Archaeology, Special Issue: Archaeology of Confinement*, 19, pp. 6–13.

Jackson, L. & Bartie, A. (2014) *Policing Youth: Britain, 1945–70* (Manchester: Manchester University Press).

Jefferies, J. (2005) 'The UK Population: Past, Present and Future'. In *Focus on People and Migration* (London: United Kingdom Office for National Statistics), pp.1–17.

Johnston, H. (2015) *Crime in England 1815–1880: Experiencing the Criminal Justice System* (Oxon: Routledge).

Johnston, H. (2008) 'Moral Guardians? Prison Officers, Prison Practice and Ambiguity in the Nineteenth Century'. In *Punishment and Control in Historical Perspective* (ed.) Johnston, H. (Basingstoke: Palgrave), pp. 77–95.

Johnson, P. & Nicholas, S. (1995) 'Male and Female Living Standards in England and Wales, 1812–1857: Evidence from Criminal Height Records', *Economic History Review*, 48(3), pp. 470–481.

Jordan, T E. (1985) 'Transported to Van Diemen's Land: The Boys of the *Francis Charlotte* (1832) and *Lord Goderich* (1841)', *Child Development*, 56(4), pp. 1092–1099.

Kalmijn, M. (1998) 'Intermarriage and Homogamy: Causes, Patterns, Trends', *Annual Review of Sociology*, 24, pp. 395–421.

Kavanagh, J. & Snowden, D. (2015) *Van Diemen's Women: A History of Transportation to Tasmania* (Dublin: The History Press).

King, P. (2006) *Crime and the Law in England, 1750–1840: Remaking Justice from the Margins* (Cambridge: Cambridge University Press).

King, P. (1998) 'The Rise of Juvenile Delinquency in England, 1780–1840', *Past and Present*, 160(1), pp. 116–166.

Kippen, R. (2002). An indisputable duty of government: Civil Registration in nineteenth-century Tasmania. Tasmanian Historical Studies, 8(1), 42–58.

Kippen, R. & McCalman, J. (2015) 'Mortality under and after Sentence of Male Convicts Transported to Van Diemen's Land (Tasmania), 1840–1852', *The History of the Family*, 20(3), pp. 345–365.

Kippen, R. & Gunn, P A. (2011) 'Convict Bastards, Common-Law Unions, and Shotgun Weddings: Premarital Conceptions and Ex-Nuptial Births in Nineteenth-Century Tasmania', *Journal of Family History*, 36(4), pp. 387–403.

Kirby, P. (2003) *Child Labour in Britain, 1750–1870* (Basingstoke: Palgrave Macmillan).

Kociumbas, J. (1997) *Australian Childhood: A History* (St. Leonards: Allen & Unwin).

Lake, M. (2003) *Convict Women as Objects of Male Vision: An Historiographical Review* (Hampshire: Aldershot).

Lamont, R. (September 2014) *'Let Every Man Have His Own Wife?': Convict Marriage in Early-Colonial Australia* (Liverpool: Paper presented at the British Crime Historians Symposium).

Laney, A S. & Weissman, D N. (2015) 'Respiratory Diseases Caused by Coal Mine Dust', *Journal Occupational Environment Medicine*, 56(10), pp. 18–22.

Lempriere, T J. (1954 [1839]) *The Penal Settlements of Van Diemen's Land, Macquarie Harbour, Maria Island and Tasman's Peninsula*, Royal Society of Tasmania (Hobart), p. 96. Available at: http://search.slv.vic.gov.au/primo-explore/fulldisplay?vid=MAIN&docid=SLV_VOYAGER739385&context=L, accessed October 2016.

Macfarlane, A. (1986) *Marriage and Love in England 1300–1840* (Oxford: Basil Blackwell).

Magarey, S. (1978) 'The Invention of Juvenile Delinquency in Early Nineteenth-Century England', *Australian Society for the Study of Labour History*, 34, pp. 11–27.

Maruna, S. (2001) *Making Good: How Ex-Convicts Reform and Rebuild Their Lives* (Washington, DC: American Psychological Association).

Mause, L. (1874) *The History of Childhood* (New York: Vintage).

Maxwell-Stewart, H. (2016) 'The State, Convicts and Longitudinal Analysis', *Australian Historical Studies*, 47(3), pp. 414–429.

Maxwell-Stewart, H. (2010) 'Convict Transportation from Britain and Ireland 1615–1870', *History Compass*, 8(11), pp. 1221–1242.

Maxwell-Stewart, H. (2008) *Closing Hell's Gate: The Death of a Convict Station* (NSW: Allen Unwin).

Maxwell-Stewart, H. & Kippen, R. (2015) '"What Is a Man That Is a Bolter to Do? I Would Steal the Governor's Axe Rather than Starve": Old Lags and Recidivism in the Tasmanian Penal Colony'. In *Transnational Penal Cultures: New Perspectives on Discipline, Punishment and Desistance* (eds) Miller, V. & Campbell, J. (London: Routledge), pp. 165–183.

Maxwell-Stewart, H., Inwood, K. & Stankovich, J. (2015) 'Prison and the Colonial Family', *The History of the Family*, 20(2), pp. 231–448.

May, M. (1981) 'A Child's Punishment for a Child's Crime: The Reformatory and Industrial School Movement in Britain c. 1780–1880' (PhD thesis, University of London).

May, M. (1973) 'Innocence and Experience: The Evolution of the Concept of Juvenile Delinquency in the Mid-Nineteenth Century', *Victorian Studies*, 17(1), pp. 7–23

McAra, L. & McVie, S. (2007) 'Youth Justice? The Impact of System Contact on Patterns of Desistance from Offending', *European Journal of Criminology*, 4(3), pp. 315–345.

Meredith, D. (1988) 'Full Circle? Contemporary Views on Transportation'. In *Convict Workers: Reinterpreting Australia's Past* (ed.) Nicholas, S. (Cambridge: Cambridge University Press), pp. 14–27.

Meredith, D. & Oxley, D. (2005) 'Contracting Convicts: The Convict Labour Market in Van Diemen's Land 1840–1857', *Australian Economic History Review*, 45(1), pp. 45–72.

Montagu, J. (June 1843) *Colonial Secretary to Commandant*, 5 June 1843, AOT. CSO 22/76/1658.

Muncie, J. (2009) *Youth and Crime*. Third Edition (London: Sage).

Newman, T. (Unk) 'Becoming Tasmania: Convicts after 1853', *Parliament of Tasmania*, [Online] Available at: http://www.parliament.tas.gov.au/php/BecomingTasmania/Convicts1853.pdf, accessed October 2016, pp. 1-4.

Nicholas, S. (1988) 'The Care of Convicts and Feeding of Convicts'. In *Convict Workers: Reinterpreting Australia's Past* (ed.) Nicholas, S. (Cambridge: Cambridge University Press), pp. 180-198.

Nicholas, S. & Shergold, P R. (1988) 'Unshackling the Past'. In *Convict Workers – Reinterpreting Australia's Past* (ed.) Nicholas, S. (Cambridge: Cambridge University Press), pp. 3-13.

Nicholas, S. & Shergold, P. (1982) 'The Heights of British Male Convict Children Transported to Australia, 1825-1840. Part II', *Australian Paediatrician Journal*, 18, pp. 80-83.

Nicholas, S. & Oxley, D. (1993) 'The Living Standards of Women during the Industrial Revolution 1795-1820', *Economic History Review*, 46(4), pp. 723-749.

Nolan, B. (2013) 'Up Close and Personal: Lesbian Sub-Culture in the Female Factories of Van Diemen's Land', *Journal of Lesbian Studies*, 17(3-4), pp. 291-304.

Nunn, C. (2017) 'Becoming Men: Masculinities and the Juvenile Convict Institutions of Carters' Barracks and Point Puer in Nineteenth-Century Australia', *Gender & History*, 29(1), pp. 158-175.

Nunn, C. (2015) 'Juveniles as Human Capital: Re-Evaluating the Economic Value of Juvenile Male Convict Labour', *Labour History*, 108, pp. 53-69.

Old Bailey Online 'Punishments at the Old Bailey', [Online] Available at: https://www.oldbaileyonline.org/static/Punishment.jsp#corporal, accessed October 2017.

Oppenheimer, V K. (1988) 'A Theory of Marriage Timing: Assortative Mating under Varying Degrees of Uncertainty', *American Journal of Sociology*, 94, pp. 563-591.

Oxley, D. (1996) *Convict Maids: The Forced Migration of Women to Australia* (Cambridge: Cambridge University Press).

Payne, H S. (1961) 'A Statistical Study of Female Convicts in Tasmania, 1843-53', *Tasmanian Historical Research Association Papers and Proceedings*, 9, pp. 56-71.

Pearson, G. (1983) *Hooligan: A History of Respectable Fears* (Basingstoke: Palgrave).

Perrott, M. (1983) *A Tolerable Good Success: Economic Opportunities for Women in New South Wales 1788-1830* (Sydney: Hale & Iremonger).

Philips, D. (1977) *Crime and Authority in Victorian England: The Black Country, 1835-1860* (London: Croom Helm).

Pinchbeck, I. & Hewitt, M. (1973) *Children in English Society Volume II: From the Eighteenth Century to the Children Act 1984* (London: Routledge & Kegan Paul).

Pinchbeck, I. & Hewitt, M. (1969) *Children in English Society – Volume 1: From Tudor Times to the Eighteenth Century* (London: Routledge & Kegan Paul).

Piper, A. (2010) '"Mind-Forged Manacles": The Mechanics of Control Inside Late-Nineteenth Century Tasmanian Charitable Institutions', *Journal of Social History* (IV), pp. 1046-1063.

Pitts, J. (2005) 'So What Does Work?' *Community Safety Journal*, 4(2), pp. 24-36.

Platt, A M. (1969) *The Child Savers – The Invention of Delinquency* (Chicago, IL: University of Chicago Press).

Pollock, L. (1983) *Forgotten Children: Parent-Child Relations from 1500–1900* (Cambridge: Cambridge University Press).

Porter, J. (2003) *The Travails of Jimmy Porter: A Memoir 1802–1842*, Prepared by Davey, R I. & Maxwell-Stewart, H. (Strahan: Round Earth Company).

Quinlan, M. (2014) 'Australia, 1788–1902: A Workingman's Paradise'. In *Masters Servants and Magistrates in Britain and the Empire 1562–1955* (eds) Hay, D. & Craven, P. (Durham: The University of North Carolina Press), pp. 221–230.

Radzinowicz, L. & Hood, R. (1990) *The Emergence of Penal Policy in Victorian and Edwardian England* (Oxford: Clarendon Press).

Radzinowicz, L. & Hood, R. (1986) *A History of English Law and Its Administration from 1750 – Volume 5: The Emergence of the Penal System* (London: Sweet & Maxwell).

Reid, K. (2007) *Gender, Crime and Empire* (Manchester: University of Manchester Press).

Reid, K. (2003) 'Setting Women to Work: The Assignment System and Female Convict Labour in Van Diemen's Land, 1820–1839', *Australian Historical Studies*, 121(34), pp. 1–26.

'Return of Crown Prisoners at Port Arthur Showing the Number of Each Trade for the Month Ending 30th September 1833' (30 September 1833), Archives Office of Tasmania Document: CSO 1/511/11180.

'Return of Prisoners Employed in the Public Works at Port Arthur for the Preceding Two Months' (1 March 1831), Archives Office of Tasmania Document: CSO 1/511/11180.

Rigby, S H. (1995) 'Historical Causation: Is One Thing More Important than Another?' *History*, 80(259) (June), pp. 227–242.

Robinson, P. (1988) *The Women of Botany Bay: A Reinterpretation of the Role of Women in the Origins of Australian Society* (Sydney: The Macquarie Library).

Robinson, P. (1985) *The Hatch and Hood of Time: A Study of the First Generation of Native-Born White Australians 1788–1828* (Oxford: Oxford University Press).

Robson, L L. (1976) *The Convict Settlers of Australia: An Enquiry into the Origin & Character of the Convicts Transported to New South Wales & Van Diemen's Land 1787–1852* (Melbourne: Melbourne University Press).

Ross, J. (1831) *The Hobart Town Almanac for the Year 1831* (Hobart Town: The Government Press).

Rowbotham, J. (2017) 'When to Spare the Rod? Legal Reactions and Popular Attitudes towards the (In)appropriate Chastisement of Children, 1850–1910', *Law, Crime and History, Special Issue: The Child at Risk in Modern Britain*, 1, pp. 98–125.

Rush, P. (1992) 'The Government of a Generation: The Subject of Juvenile Delinquency', *The Liverpool Law Review*, 14(1), pp. 3–43.

Salt, A. (1984) *These Outcast Women: The Parramatta Factory 1821–1848* (Sydney: Hale & Iremonger).

Sampson, R. J., Laub, J. H., & Wimer, C. (2006). 'Does marriage reduce crime? A counterfactual approach to within-individual causal effects Criminology, 44.

Sampson, R J. & Laub, J H. (2005) 'A Life-Course View of the Development of Crime'. In *Developmental Criminology and Its Discontents: Trajectories of Crime from Childhood to Old Age* (eds) Sampson, R J. & Laub, J H. (London: Sage), pp. 12–45.

Sampson, R J. & Laub, J H. (1998) 'Integrating Quantitative and Qualitative Data'. In *Methods of Life Course Research – Qualitative and Quantitative Approaches* (eds) Giele J Z. & Elder Jr. G H. (London: Sage), pp. 213–230.

Sampson, R J. & Laub, J H. (1997) 'A Life-Course Theory of Cumulative Disadvantage and the Stability of Delinquency'. In *Developmental Theories of Crime and Deviance. Advances in Criminological Theory 7* (ed.) Thornberry, T. (New Brunswick, NJ: Transaction Publishers), pp. 133–162.

Sampson, R J. & Laub, J H. (1993) *Crime in The Making: Pathways and Turning Points Through Life* (Boston, MA: Harvard University Press).

Shaw, A G L. (1966) *Convicts and the Colonies: A Study of Penal Transportation from Great Britain and Ireland to Australia and Other Parts of the British Empire* (London: Faber).

Shergold, P R. (1988) 'Unshackling the Past'. In *Convict Workers: Reinterpreting Australia's Past* (ed.) Stephen N. (Cambridge: Cambridge University Press), pp. 3–13.

Shore, H. (2015) *London's Criminal Underworlds, c.1750–c. 1930: A Social and Cultural History* (Basingstoke: Palgrave Macmillan).

Shore, H. (2011) 'Inventing and Reinventing Juvenile Delinquency', *Memoria Y Civilizacion*, 14, pp. 1–31.

Shore, H. (2003) '"Inventing" the Juvenile Delinquent in Nineteenth Century Europe'. In *Comparative Histories of Crime* (eds) Godfrey, B., Emsley, C. & Dunstall G. (Oxon: Willan), pp.110–124.

Shore, H. (2002) 'Transportation, Penal Ideology and the Experience of Juvenile Offenders in England and Australia in the Early Nineteenth Century', *Crime, History and Societies*, 6(2), pp. 81–102.

Shore, H. (1999a) *Artful Dodgers: Youth and Crime in Early Nineteenth-Century London* (Suffolk: Boydell Press).

Shore, H. (1999b) 'Cross Coves, Buzzers and General Sorts of Prigs – Juvenile Crime and the "Underworld" in the Early Nineteenth Century', *British Journal of Criminology*, 39(1), pp. 10–24

Shore, H. & Johnston, H. (2015) 'Introduction: Thinking about the Future of Our Criminal Past', *Law, Crime and History, Special Edition: Our Criminal Past – Caring for the Future*, 1, pp. 1–11.

Shorter, E. (1976) *The Making of the Modern Family* (New York: Basic Books).

Sidney, J. (1847) *A Voice from the Far Interior of Australia* (London: Smith, Elder and Co., Cornhill).

Slee, J. (2003) *Point Puer Unpublished Report for Port Arthur Historic Site Management Authority* (Unpublished: Available at Port Arthur Library, Tasmania), pp. 1–40.

Slee, J. & Tuffin, R. (June 2003) 'Point Puer' (Paper presented at the Strahan 'Escapes' Conference).

Smith, B. (2008a) *Australian's Birthstain – The Startling Legacy of the Convict Era* (NSW: Allen Unwin).

Smith, B. (2008b) *A Cargo of Women: Susannah Watson and the Convicts of the Princess Royal*. Second Edition (NSW: Allen Unwin).

Springhall, J. (1986) *Coming of Age: Adolescence in Britain, 1860-1960* (London: Gill and Macmillan).

Stack, J A. (1992) 'Children, Urbanization and the Chances of Imprisonment in Mid-Victorian England', *Criminal Justice History*, 13, pp. 113–139.

Statistical Returns of VDL from 1824–1835 during the Administration of Colonel Arthur Compiled from the Official Records with an Explanatory Letter to His Excellency from the Colonial Secretary (1836), (Hobart Town: James Ross).

Stone, L. (1977) *The Family, Sex and Marriage in England 1500-1800* (New York: Harper and Row).

Strutt, W T. (1887) *Statistics of the Colony of Tasmania for the Year 1886* (Hobart Town: Government Press).

Sturma, M. (1978) 'Eye of the Beholder: The Stereotype of Women Convicts, 1788–1852', *Labour History* (34), pp. 3–10.

Summers, A. (1975) *Damned Whores and God's Police: The Colonization of Women in Australia* (Ringwood, Victoria: Penguin Australia).

Thomas, D. (1998) *The Victorian Underworld* (London: John Murray).

Thompson, E P. (1975) *Whigs and Hunters: The Origin of the Black Act* (London: Breviary Stuff Publications).

Tikoff, V K. (2002) 'Before the Reformatory: A Correctional Orphanage in Old Regime Seville'. In *Becoming Delinquent: British and European Youth, 1650-1950* (eds) Cox, P. & Shore, H. (Ashgate: Dartmouth Publishing Co Ltd), pp.59–76.

Tobias, J J. (1967) *Crime and Industrial Society in the Nineteenth Century* (London: B. T. Batsford).

Trepanier, J. (1999) 'Juvenile Courts after 100 Years: Past and Present Orientations', *European Journal on Criminal Policy and Research*, 7(3), pp. 303–327.

Turner, J. (2009) 'Offending Women in Stafford, 1880-1905: Punishment, Reform and Re-Integration' (PhD thesis, Keele University).

Tuffin, R. (2007) 'Point Puer: Overview History', *Unpublished*, pp. 1–27.

van Schellen, M., Poortman, A. & Nieuwbeerta, P. (2012) 'Partners in Crime? Criminal Offending, Marriage Formation and Partner Selection', *Journal of Research in Crime and Delinquency*, 49(4), pp. 545–571.

Vikstrom, L. (2011) 'Before and after Crime: Life-Course Analyses of Young Offenders Arrested in Nineteenth-Century Northern Sweden', *Journal of Social History*, 44(3), pp. 861–888.

Watkins, E D. (2018) 'Transported beyond the Seas: Criminal Juveniles'. In *Nineteenth Century Childhoods in Interdisciplinary and International Perspectives, Series: Childhood in the Past (6)* (eds) Baxter J E. & Ellis, M. (Oxford: Oxbow), pp. 75–90.

Watkins, E D. (2015a) 'The Case of George Fenby', [Online] Available at: https://emmadwatkins.wordpress.com/2015/06/, accessed October 2016.

Watkins, E D. (2015b) 'The Case of Mary Ann Oseman', [Online] Available at: https://emmadwatkins.wordpress.com/2015/08/19/the-case-of-mary-ann-oseman/, accessed October 2016.

Watkins, E D. & Godfrey, B. (2018) *Criminal Children: Researching Juvenile Offenders 1820-1920* (Yorkshire: Pen & Sword).

Weatherburn, H. (1979) 'The Female Factory'. In *Pursuit of Justice* (eds) Mackinolty, J. & Radi, H. (Sydney: Hale and Iremonger).

Weijers, I. (1999) 'The Debate on Juvenile Justice in the Netherlands, 1891-1901', *European Journal of Crime, Criminal Law and Criminal Justice*, 7(1), pp. 63-78.

Wiener, M J. (1990) *Reconstructing the Criminal – Culture, Law, and Policy in England 1830-1914* (Cambridge: Cambridge University Press).

Williams, L. (2014) *'At Large': Women's Lives and Offending in Victorian Liverpool and London* (PhD thesis, University of Liverpool).

Williams, L. & Godfrey, B. (2015) 'Intergenerational Offending in Liverpool and the North-West of England, 1850-1914', *The History of the Family*, 20(2), pp. 189-203.

Wolter, R M. (2014) *Sound and Fury in Colonial Australia: The Search for the Convict Voice, 1800-1840* (PhD thesis, University of Sydney).

Wood, A G. (1922) *The Discovery of Australia* (London: Macmillan).

Wrightson, K. (1982) *English Society 1580-1680* (London: Rutgers University Press)

Primary sources used to trace convicts and build case studies

Archives

The National Archives Kew, Richmond: Surrey, TW9 4DU, United Kingdom
Port Arthur Historic Site Resource Centre: Arthur Hwy, Port Arthur TAS 7182, Australia
National Archives of Australia, Tasmania: 91 Murray St, Hobart TAS 7000, Australia

Digital Repositories

Ancestry, *Family History*[1], Found at: www.ancestry.co.uk
Australian Newspapers Online, *Trove*[2], Found at: http://trove.nla.gov.au/newspaper
British Newspaper Archive, *19th Century British Library Newspaper Collection*, Found at: http://www.britishnewspaperarchive.ac.uk
Find My Past, *Family Tree*, Found at: www.findmypast.co.uk
Tasmanian Government, *Tasmanian Names Index*, Found at: http://linctas.ent.sirsidynix.net.au/client/en_AU/names/

The Proceedings of the Old Bailey, London's Central Criminal Court, 1764–1913, Found at: http://www.oldbaileyonline.org//

State Library of Queensland, Convict transportation registers database, Found at: http://www.slq.qld.gov.au/resources/family-history/convicts/

Databases Consulted

Female Convicts Research Centre Inc., *Female Convicts in VDL Database*, available at: https://www.femaleconvicts.org.au/index.php/database/database-research

Founders and Survivors, '1-in-25 Sample of Male & Female Convicts Arriving in VDL' transcribed from *Con 31 and 32 – Male Convicts Arriving in the Assignment Period 1807–1840; Con 33 – Male Convicts Arriving in the Probation Period 1840–1853; Con 37 – Male Convicts Locally Convicted or Arriving on Minor Ships; Con 40 – Female Convicts Arriving in the Assignment Period 1812–1843; Con 41 – Female Convicts Arriving in the Probation Period 1844–1853* (Also available at: http://linctas.ent.sirsidynix.net.au/client/en_AU/names/).

1 **Sources used include:** HO13 Home Office – Criminal Entry Books 1782–1871; HO17 Home Office – Criminal Petitions, Series I; HO18 Home Office: Criminal Petitions, Series II; HO19 Home Office – Registers of Criminal Petitions; HO8 Home Office – Convict Hulks, Convict Prisons and Criminal Lunatic Asylums: Quarterly Returns of Prisoners; HO9 Letter book for the convict hulk establishment; HO10 Home Office – Settlers and Convicts, New South Wales and Tasmania: Records; HO11 Home Office – Australian Convict Transportation Registers; HO24 Home Office – Prison Registers and Statistical Returns 1838–1875; HO26 Home Office: Criminal Registers, Middlesex; HO77 Home Office – Newgate Prison Calendar 1782–1853; United Kingdom Census 1841.

2 **Newspapers used include:** *Colonial Times, Hobarton Guardian, or, True Friend of Tasmania, Launceston Examiner, The Age, The Argus, The Cornwall Chronicle, The Courier, The Mercury, The Tasmanian* and *Taunton Courier and Western Advertiser*.

Index

Acts
    Criminal Justice Act (1848) 53
    Gaol Acts (1823) 19, 84
    Gaol Act (1824) 19
    Habeas Corpus Act (1679) 23
    Juvenile Offenders Act (1847) 19
    Malicious Trespass Act (1827) 13
    Masters and Servants Act 105
    Metropolitan Police Act (1829) 13
    Registering Births, Deaths and Marriages in VDL and its Dependencies (1838) 127–8
    Transportation Act (1824) 25
    Transportation Act (1718) 23
    Transportation Act (1717) 24
    Vagrancy Act (1824) 13
Aftercare Institution 19–21, 28
Assignment 24–6, 77
Association 15, 18–19, 22, 25, 83

Booth, Charles O'Hara 52, 82–3, 89, 95–7

Childhood 11–12
    Children (having of) 138–44
    Illegitimate 140–1
Civil Records 2, 4, 81, 85, 90–1, 102, 111, 127–8, 130, 141, 147, 150–1, 155
Colonial Secretary
    Burnett, John 74
    Pakington, John 28
    Stanley, Edward 27, 109
Conduct Records 4, 23, 36–8, 42–4, 51, 54–5, 57, 67, 75, 84–6, 98, 110, 115, 178
Crime
    Absconding 35, 45, 63, 97
    Bushranging 38
    Domestic Violence 38–41
    Drunk 33, 35
    Horse theft 87, 143
    Larceny (theft) 19
    Murder 38, 151–3
    Pickpocketing 17, 31–2
    Piracy 38, 60–1
    Shop theft 30
    Sodomy / Unnatural Crime 65–6, 137
    Robbery 29, 62
    Uttering 71–2
Criminal Class 9–11, 17, 23, 31
Criminal Petitions 31, 38–9, 58, 99, 125, 155, 159, 165, 178

Death 147–70
    Female 164–70
        Disease 164–8
        Old Age 166–8
    Male 147–64
        Cause 151–64
        Disease 153–6, 158–60
        Execution 151–3
        External Cause 158
Desistance (from crime) 45–6

Education 84–93
    Colonial 92
    Female 90–1
    Male 85–90
    Point Puer 88–90
Employment 98–121
    Female 110–18
    Male 98–107
    Prostitution 111–15
    Unemployment 120–1
    Wages 118–20

Female Factory 28, 74–6
    Cascades 72, 74–5, 114–5, 126, 139–40, 168
    George Town 74–5, 126
    Hobart Town 74–5
    Launceston 72, 74–5, 77, 115, 126
    Ross 74–5, 114–5
Fry, Elizabeth 4, 21, 90

Gold Mine/Rush 120, 134–5, 150, 175

Hill, Matthew Davenport 21, 55
Hulk 18, 23–4, 32, 74–5, 160

Invalid 64, 154, 166, 169

Juvenile Delinquency 11–18, 83

Lieutenant Governors
   Arthur, George (VDL) 26, 45, 49, 63, 74, 85, 116–7, 124
   Denison, William (VDL) 28
   Eardley-Wilmot, John (VDL) 27, 75, 109
   Franklin, John (VDL) 27, 83, 88, 127
   Macquarie, Lachlan (NSW) 63
   Sorell, William (VDL) 63, 137
Life-Course Method 5–7
London 17–8, 34–5, 45, 88, 102, 149–50, 164

Marriage 123–38
   Common Law/Cohabitation 137–8
   Female 128–32
   Male 132–4
   Permission-to-Marry 123–7
      Female 125–7, 137
      Male 127
Migration 27, 37, 42, 96, 109, 117–8, 134–5, 149–51
Molesworth Committee 20, 26

New South Wales (NSW) 23–4, 27–8, 46, 83, 91–3, 101, 107, 111, 134–6
New Town Pauper Establishment 64, 66

Paupers 91, 120–2, 173–4
Prison (British)
   Millbank 90
   Parkhurst 20–1
Penal Settlements 63–70
   Macquarie Harbour 63–4
   Norfolk Island 66–7
   Point Puer 82–3, 88–90, 93–8, 150, 164
   Port Arthur 64
Probation 24, 26–7, 34, 70, 77, 178
Punishment 49–79
   Extended Sentence 58–61
   Execution 58–63
   Female 70–8
   Flogging 52–5, 63
   Hard Labour 50–1, 57, 71, 73
   Male 52–70
   Solitary confinement 50–1, 55–7
   Treadmill 50, 57–8

Reformatory Schools 14, 21–2
   Beerem 21
   Mettray 21
   Nederlandsch Mettray 21
   Parisian La Petite-Roquette 21
   Rauhes Haus 21–2
   Red Hill 21
   Ruysselede 21
   Saint-Hubert 21

South Australia 109

Ticket of Leave 25, 27
Trade Training 93–8
Turner, (Rev) Sydney 21

Van Diemen's Land 24
   Economy 108–10
   Population 134–7
Victoria 24, 134–5, 175

www.ingramcontent.com/pod-product-compliance
Lightning Source LLC
Chambersburg PA
CBHW052044300426
44117CB00012B/1968